Take Stage!
How to Direct and Produce a Lesbian Play

CAROLYN GAGE

Scarecrow Press
1997

SCARECROW PRESS, INC.

Published in the United States of America
by Scarecrow Press, Inc.
4720 Boston Way
Lanham, Maryland 20706

4 Pleydell Gardens, Folkestone
Kent CT20 2DN, England

Copyright © 1997 by Carolyn Gage

All rights reserved. No part of this publication may be reproduced, stored in a retrieval system, or transmitted in any form or by any means, electronic, mechanical, photocopying, recording, or otherwise, without the prior permission of the publisher.

British Cataloguing in Publication Information Available

Library of Congress Cataloging-in-Publication Data
Gage, Carolyn.
    Take stage! : how to direct and produce a lesbian play / Carolyn Gage.
       p.   cm.
    Includes index.
    ISBN 0-8108-3208-9 (pbk. : alk. paper)
    1. Lesbian theater. 2. Theater—Production and direction.
I. Title.
PN2270.L47G34   1997
792′.023′086643—dc21   96-44777
                                                              CIP

ISBN 0-8108-3208-9 (pbk. : alk. paper)

∞ ™ The paper used in this publication meets the minimum requirements of American National Standard for Information Sciences—Permanence of Paper for Printed Library Materials, ANSI Z39.48—1984. Manufactured in the United States of America.

The greatest danger is not being radical enough.

—Mary Daly

Plays by Carolyn Gage

The Amazon All-Stars (music by Sue Carney)
The Anastasia Trials in the Court of Women
Artemisia and Hildegarde
The Boundary Trial of John Proctor
Calamity Jane Sends a Message to her Daughter
Cookin' with Typhoid Mary
The Evil That Men Do: The Story of Thalidomide
Harriet Tubman Visits a Therapist
Heterosexuals Anonymous
A Labor Play
The Last Reading of Charlotte Cushman
Radicals
The Roar of Silence Trilogy
Sappho in Love
The Second Coming of Joan of Arc
Sleeping Beauty: A Fable of Child Sexual Abuse
The Teachers' Lounge
Ugly Ducklings
Women on the Land (music by Sue Carney)

Contents

Acknowledgments — vii

Preface — ix

Introduction — xi

Part I: Getting Started

1. The Bottom Line — 3
2. Co-Producing with Another Lesbian Organization — 5
3. Co-Producing with Non-Lesbians — 7
4. Growing Your Own Organization — 9
5. Accountability and Sisterhood — 11

Part II: Laying the Foundation

6. Two Heads Are Better Than One — 17
7. Learning to Lead — 20
8. Victims and Victimizers — 24
9. Volunteering, Recruiting, and Boundaries — 28
10. The Deadly "Isms" — 31

Part III: Setting up Shop

11. Selecting the Script — 36
12. The Space — 39
13. The Money — 42

14. The Schedule — 45
15. The Tickets — 48

Part IV: The Folks behind the Scenes

16. The Designers — 55
17. The Assistant Director and the Stage Manager — 60
18. The Techies — 64
19. The House Staff — 69
20. Everyone Else — 72

Part V: Putting out the Word

21. The Press Kit — 79
22. Publicizing Auditions — 84
23. Publicizing the Show — 87
24. Troubleshooting — 92
25. The Program — 94

Part VI: On with the Show

26. Approaching Sacred Ground — 99
27. Auditioning Lesbians — 103
28. Production Meetings — 110
29. The First Rehearsal — 112
30. Blocking the Show — 116

Part VII: Into the Vortex

31. Some Notes on Acting — 123
32. Advice to the Director — 127
33. After the Third Week — 129
34. Time Out! — 132
35. Tech Week and Dress Rehearsal — 135

Part VIII: Opening and Beyond

36. Opening — 143
37. Pickup, Strike, and Postproduction — 144
38. Touring — 146
39. For Women Only — 148
40. The Future — 151

Appendixes — 153

Index — 201

About the Author — 207

Acknowledgments

The author and the publisher would like to thank the following for permission to reproduce material used in this book:

Excerpt from *Pure Lust: Elemental Feminist Philosophy* by Mary Daly (Boston: Beacon Press, 1984).

Photographs of Debra Wright and Carolyn Gage by Pamela Newman.

The flyer for *One Fool* by Terry Baum, with photo by Cammie Tolovi and poster design by Marty Selim.

Ticket layout sheet, flyer, program, and press release for *The Last Reading of Charlotte Cushman*, produced by Catherine Onellion of River Moon Productions.

Sample light plot by Krystal Locke.

Sample audition flyer by Jan Marks.

Information on wheelchair accessibility and sample ticket seller's contract from *Note by Note: A Guide to Concert Production*, used with permission. Copyright - 1996 Community Music, Inc. Available from Community Music, Inc., PO Box 5778, Takoma Park, MD 20913, 1-800-669-3942.

Accessibility Survey by Catherine Odette, Sara Karon, Kathy Younger, and Melinda Burns. It originally appeared in *Dykes, Disability & Stuff Quarterly* (PO Box 8773, Madison, WI 53708- 8773), vol. 4, number 1, issue 13. This survey has been updated and modified since its development in 1992, and has been in use by The United, one of Madison's Lesbian and Gay core organizations. For more detailed information on creating access, including specific or detailed ADA (Americans with Disabilities Act) codes, or for development of accessible media for your community, write *DD&S* at the above address.

Preface

Lesbian theatre is as diverse as are Lesbians, and this book makes no claim to being definitive on the subject. In fact, this is a highly subjective book about one woman's perspective: mine. It is axiomatic in theatre that universal truths can be communicated only through the specific—and the more specific, the better. Don't just be the woman waiting for the bus. Be the forty-eight-year-old woman, who is late for the dental appointment for a root canal, who is waiting in the rain at the stop on Salmon and Fifth with no umbrella for the 4:10 bus that is now fifteen minutes late.

So with that advice to the players in mind: I am not a generic expert writing about "Lesbian theatre." I am the forty-four-year-old, Anglo-European Lesbian living in the United States, who has lost teaching jobs and mainstream theatre jobs on the basis of her politics, who has had a very rough time working with Lesbian theatre collectives, who had to leave her home state because of the controversy generated by her radical Lesbian theatre company, and who is writing as much for her own edification as for anyone else's. I am a playwright frustrated by lack of opportunity, an ex–touring performer, a director all dressed up with nowhere to go, and an ex-producer.

I write to demystify the process of putting on a play, to encourage Lesbians to start our own theatres, and to break the silence about our process in organizations. I write to hear myself into being, because my work as a Lesbian, as a feminist, and as an artist is continually erased by the dominant culture, and sometimes even by Lesbians.

I want to thank Rosemary Curb for her helpful comments on an early draft of the manuscript, and I want to thank her for believing in Lesbian theatre enough to edit an anthology of Lesbian plays. I also want to acknowledge my debt to Sarah Hoagland, to Barbara Smith, to Fox, to Julia Penelope, to Mary Daly, and to Marilyn Frye for their pioneering work in exploring the dynamics among Lesbians. To borrow a phrase from Julia Penelope and apply it to this book: "All errors of commission and omission are mine alone."

Most of all, I want to thank the Lesbians who are working in Lesbian theatre. I owe a special debt of gratitude to the women who have allowed me to work with them: the Portland Women's Theatre Company, Portland, Oregon; No to Men, Ashland, Oregon; Tribad Productions, Petaluma, California; the League of Lesbian Actors (LOLA), Santa Rosa, California; Catherine Onellion of River Moon Productions, Santa Rosa, California; and Debra Wright, who has performed and toured in my work.

Introduction

Lesbian theatres, like Lesbians, are not supposed to exist. The men occupy center stage in patriarchy. The women who are their wives, their mothers, their daughters are allowed to enter and exit, to say a few lines, and to take a graceful bow when it's all over. Lesbians have no place in this theatre.

It is time for us to take stage.

The way we will do that is with a theatre of our own. We will take stage in our living rooms, at the women's festivals, in rented halls. We will tell our stories. We will speak the lines we write, with ourselves at center stage. We will tell a Lesbian-centered story in a Lesbian-centered language. We will rage, we will howl, we will laugh, we will embrace with a Lesbian passion.

We will reflect our lives back to one another, so that we can never forget the significance of our woman-touching acts: the breaking of our silence about what the fathers have done to us, the dangerous labyrinths we have braved to rescue one another from the dungeons of patriarchy, the ecstatic reconnection to our pure girl spirits, the Re-membering of our mothers, the beauty—the Out-rageous beauty of our bodies when we take them to ourselves—and the terrible battles we have fought, and sometimes lost, to an enemy as subtle as an idea left over from childhood.

Lesbian theatre, like Lesbian anything, cannot be done the way anything else has ever been done. Lesbian theatre, like Lesbian anything, must be built from the ground up, from the inside out, on the foundation of honest interactions.

This book is about how to produce a Lesbian play. It tells how to schedule publicity, draw up a budget, audition the actors. It tells how to plan the rehearsals, how to work with designers, how to coordinate the technical aspects of production. But this book is also about how to be honest—about power, about money, about talent, and about priorities. Because this book is by, for, and about Lesbians.

Part I

Getting Started

Chapter 1

The Bottom Line

So you want to produce a Lesbian play? Great!

I'll tell you right up front, I have a vested interest in seeing you succeed, because I'm a Lesbian playwright, and the more Lesbians that are out there producing Lesbian theatre, the better my chances of selling my scripts.

That's what's in it for me. Now, the next question is, What's in it for you?

Why do you want to produce a Lesbian play? For fun? For profit? For experience? Because you wrote the thing and nobody else will put it up? For your resume? So your lover can act out somewhere else?

Seriously, what is your reason? "Reason," singular. Because even though you want to create great art, make lots of money, show off for your friends, foment a revolution against patriarchy, have a good time, and get dates, one of these is going to be more important than the others. One, and only one, of your reasons will be the famous "bottom line" we've all heard so much about. And a woman who doesn't know her bottom line is going to end up at the mercy of a lot of "tops."

So, *know your bottom line*. And here, women, especially Lesbians, are at a tremendous disadvantage.

Boys are taught early not to be ashamed of their bottom line. They want something—they go for it. They want money, they want sex, they want a promotion—they go for it. They don't have to be ashamed of ambition, competition, aggression. They don't have to worry if their bottom line is hanging out. In fact, they flaunt it.

But women, especially Lesbians, have grown up with a very mixed message. Little girls are taught early that their bottom line is an extension of someone else's bottom line. We are taught that we don't really have one of our own, that we want what Daddy wants us to want. This is nonsense. Every woman has a bottom line, all her own, not anybody else's. It's just that with all the terror and all the brainwashing, it's hard for us to remember where we hid it.

So you want to produce a play as a gift to your community? You want to showcase your friends' talent? You believe in the message of the play? You love art for art's sake? You want to raise money for the women's shelter?

Be very careful. If you say these things, I'm sure you mean them. And I'm sure there's a lot of truth in them. A lot of truth, but probably not a bottom line. What's in it for you?

Live theatre is a high-pressure, dangerous, demanding, precise, and tremendously powerful undertaking. It has its own imperatives. It gives no quarter to the self-deceived. You had better know your bottom line.

If you're genuinely confused about your motivation, here's a trick that might help you cut through the myths of altruism: Make a list of all your possible reasons for producing a play, and then, one at a time, imagine failing to meet each goal. There should be one failure that stands out in your mind as more significant than the others. There should be one failure that would make you wish you'd never produced the play in the first place. A rotten review? A cast that won't speak to you? A financial disaster? Four weeks of empty houses? Find the one failure that would render the project meaningless for you, and you've probably got your bottom line.

Once you know your bottom line, you will have a standard from which to make responsible decisions; you will have a position from which you will be able to negotiate honestly with your cast and crew members, who will each have their own bottom lines (be sure to find out what they are!); and you will be able to take credit for your success and learn from your mistakes.

So, before you read any further, What's in it for you?

Chapter 2

Co-Producing with Another Lesbian Organization

Structure—oh, no!

Oh, yes. Everything has a structure. Remember high school biology with the "endoskeleton" and the "exoskeleton"? It either shows or it doesn't. The structures that show are overt, like a board of directors, like a collective, like a boss. The structures that don't show are covert, like the Lesbian whose opinion weighs more than anyone else's, like the group that seemed to have made up its mind before the official meeting.

No one chooses a covert structure. It evolves when there is either no structure at all, or one that is not working. In theatre, covert power structures are deadly—not that they're ever particularly jolly to work with anywhere else; but in live theatre, frankly, the stakes are too high and the time is too precious to waste trying to figure out who's got the power and how you need to approach them. Also, in covert structures the real decision-makers are hidden, and so they are rarely accountable for the results of their decisions. This is grotesquely unfair to the actors, who have no choice but to put themselves on the line night after night.

Choose an overt structure and try to work within its framework.

So what's your structure going to be? If you produce a play, you can do it all by yourself. You can be a DBA ("doing business as"), in which case you are the big cheese, and that means you get the whole enchilada: You get to make all the rules, you get to keep all the money—or lose it, as the case may be. You get to have all the responsibility, unless you can delegate well. The DBA approach is not a bad way to go for a first production, but it will probably not hold up structurally for more than two or three shows. By that time, your staff—if they have any kind of self-esteem—should be agitating for inclusion in the decision-making. (In that case, see Chapter 4.)

Another option is that you can produce through an already-existing Lesbian organization. If you take this route, don't count on universal sisterhood to see you through. Now that you know your bottom line, be sure to find out the organization's!

If you are fresh out of graduate school and in the active phase of resume building, the local women's theatre collective whose raison d'être is politics or recreation may not be the way to go—unless all parties are very clear about the bottom line. You may be able to negotiate a degree of professionalism that is a cut above their standards of production in exchange for a script the politics of which are just left of your personal comfort zone. The thing to watch out for is that sneaky, internalized voice that assures us, "Once we get going, I know I can make them see things [do things, want things] my way." This is disrespectful, unethical, and—more to the point—generally ineffectual.

On the other hand, you may be the one with the radical political agenda, but the Lesbian organization underwriting your endeavor may count on broad-based community support for its survival. *Don't* try to put one over on them. They just may decide to pull the rug out from under you midproduction, causing a division in community loyalties that may extend even to the members of your company.

As a Lesbian producer, it's possible to match up with a Lesbian organization that is exactly on your wavelength, and then you won't have to face these kinds of challenges. Possible, but not probable. Expect to negotiate. You don't need to fear compromise if you know your bottom line. Negotiations become scary when the negotiators have agendas that are hidden from even themselves. That's when Lesbians either give away the farm or become so rigid that dialogue becomes pointless.

Learn to distinguish the myths (altruism, art for art's sake, universal sisterhood, changing the world, etc.) from the business aspect of your theatre—unless you plan to meet all your needs through your congregation or your cadre. In this case, prepare yourself for total dictatorship, because that's how churches and revolutions are led.

But we were talking about structure. What about working with mainstream theatres or gay-and-Lesbian organizations?

Chapter 3

Co-Producing with Non-Lesbians

The same rule that applies to Lesbian theatre applies to non-Lesbian theatre: Find out what's in it for them. Is the mainstream theatre trying to reach a segment of the population that doesn't usually patronize its season of heterosexual bedroom romps? In this case, you could expect cooperation with publicity, but you might have to fight for artistic control. Or is it trying to impress its corporate donors with the diversity of its season? In this case, expect a token budget.

Even if a mainstream theatre is working with you as a token cultural minority, you can still meet your bottom line. Be sure to negotiate for full artistic control (including hiring/approval of staff), a say in how the publicity is handled, and a budget that will do justice to your vision. And get it all on paper. Get them to spell out the limits of your responsibility and the limits of your authority.

Never allow feelings of gratitude to take the edge off your negotiating skills. Women with African roots have been allowed to live free of the threat of overt slavery in the United States for only a little more than a hundred years. Women with Asian roots have been allowed to live free of the crippling practice of foot-binding for only a hundred years. Women with European roots have been allowed to live without the fear of organized witch-hunts only in the last two hundred years. Latina women who live in the United States must still contend with ongoing harassment by the government, and First Nations women are still fighting for the rights to their own land. Women working outside the home in this country have been allowed to earn a living and keep our wages only in the last hundred years. Women artists in Western society have been allowed to take charge of our own culture only in the last twenty years. Lesbians have been allowed public recognition that we exist only in the last five years. Don't let knee-jerk feelings of gratitude sap your Lesbian energy when a little historical perspective can keep you charged up with radical indignation. Remember, the grateful prisoner may get extra rations, but the indignant one gets over the wall.

Approach your co-producing organization with confidence and pride. You are about to do something that very few women in the history of the world have ever done before. You are about to do something on the cutting edge of world consciousness. You are about to break the cultural sound barrier. You are going to shift the context of patriarchy, ever so slightly, but ever so absolutely. You are going to produce a Lesbian play. You obviously have one hell of a nerve to start with, and from that everything else should follow.

What about working with a gay-and-Lesbian theatre? Be careful! Just because it's called "gay and Lesbian" is no guarantee you won't still receive token status. Gay men are still men, and the bottom line for some of these theatres is often, "Keep the men happy." Too frequently, these theatres are top-heavy with gay male administrators or Lesbians identified with gay male interests, and their seasons and budgets reflect the bias. Again, go for final say on artistic decisions, a budget that reflects the amount of money spent on a comparable gay male play in their season, and control of publicity.

Let's face it: Women have been trained to defer to men, and when our deference is so second-nature that we aren't even aware of it, and when the men have automatically assumed responsibility for the "dirty work" of theatre—the fund-raising, the leasing contracts, the technical logistics—it can seem like a free lunch to get hired to work in one of these organizations.

It is a lovely notion that someone else can give us power, or that we can be granted equality by the dominant culture. But the fact of the matter is this: We must *take* our power, and we must *assert* our equality. Otherwise, they can be recalled just as readily as they were granted. A certain lack of responsibility may be tempting, but it is always accompanied by a lack of authority that is devastating.

One final caution: Gay men don't sleep with women. Some of us Lesbians find more feminist affinity with straight men than with our gay "brothers," because we share issues that arise from attempting primary intimacy with women. Men partnering with women may be much more aware of the impact of violence against women, of how incest conditions women for patriarchy, and so forth. Gay male culture, however, excludes women altogether, caricaturing us in drag shows. Also, there are some aspects of gay culture that have traditionally tolerated child sexual abuse. *Watch your bottom line!*

Chapter 4

Growing Your Own Organization

In the last two chapters, we talked about working with organizations that already exist. What about growing your own?

For a first production, this is an ambitious goal. Most theatres evolve over time, as the interest in the community becomes established. Sometimes the women involved in a production become a collective, or they develop a board of directors, or they form a limited partnership. These structures all have legal ramifications. For instance, if your theatre becomes a nonprofit corporation with federal tax-exempt status (the coveted "501[c]3"), your patrons' donations can be tax-exempt and the theatre can qualify for grants. On the other hand, nonprofits are public corporations subject to the regulations of the state. You must have a board of directors, and the size of this will be determined by the particular state in which you register your corporation. Boards of directors have their own liabilities, particularly with regard to institutions as volatile as theatres.

One of the principal jobs of a good board of directors is raising money. Although artistic decisions are theoretically the bailiwick of the artistic director, there is a law of human nature that dictates that the ones who provide the money will be very concerned with how it is spent.

A board of directors who have aggressively talked their friends in the corporate world into donating generous chunks of money may be feeling a certain social pressure to see that the season will reflect at least some of the interests of these benefactors. And because their bottom line is a financial one, they may choose to focus on the economics and not the politics of sliding-scale ticket prices.

Frequently, there are class conflicts between a company of artists and a board of community businesswomen. A written mission statement for the theatre can defuse a number of tensions by providing impersonal boundaries and guidelines. For example, if the goal is to produce high-quality feminist theatre for as broad a base of audience as possible, then a radical agitprop play is not consistent with this mission, and the economic liabilities need never even enter the discussion. Likewise, if the mission is to produce censored and subversive work, then it is understood by all that box office receipts must take a backseat to content. Again, there is no need for a board and an artistic director to lock horns.

But collective structures have their liabilities, too.

Although covert power structures do occur on boards, they seem positively indigenous to collectives. The reason for this is that true equality is hard to come by. In the collective, where responsibility is supposed to be shared equally, it rarely is. Often there is one member with more time, more experience, more motivation, or all of the above, who evolves into a kind of de facto artistic director.

In the beginning, many members of the collective are probably secretly relieved to have someone else take on the dirty work. But over time, this busy bee begins to take on aspects of a queen bee, assuming the authority that she (justifiably) feels is warranted by her additional responsibilities. And then there is trouble.

At this point, the collective will need to take back the power they were all too happy to let slip away. The woman who has been minding the store for them may not be so happy to turn over her files, explain her system, or train the other members. In fact, she may have evolved her own little "kitchen cabinet" within the collective, and this group may split off to start a new theatre. The moral of the story is: If you want to have your cake and eat it, don't be surprised when you end up eating it.

True collective process requires a high degree of personal accountability from every member. When one member begins to do more than her share, the collective needs to check in again with its bottom line: Is retaining the integrity of collective structure a priority, or, if the theatre has begun to outgrow the collective process, is it more important to go with whatever fosters commercial success? It is important to remember there is no right or wrong here, only bottom lines.

Every structure has its advantages and its disadvantages—and its stereotypes. Collectives, for instance, have a reputation for not being accountable. Boards, on the other hand, get a bad rap for being authoritarian and out of touch. But stereotypes are only useful for bolstering preexisting prejudices anyway. Plenty of board members lack accountability, and plenty of collectives are sadly out of touch.

If your collective is large and open to all on an equal basis, expect factionalizing and the development of a covert power structure, probably composed of the members with the most longevity in the organization. This might be avoided if membership in the collective is contingent on being involved in previous productions.

If you go with a board of directors structure, and your board is made up of Lesbians who are not involved in the actual production of the plays, expect a gap between what the board thinks you should be doing and what you think the board should be doing. Ideally, this type of board should raise money, so that the artistic directors can realize their artistic visions; but round pegs and square holes aside, the reality is that the ones who provide the money generally want a say in how it's spent. Again, *know your bottom line.*

This is all I intend to say about organizing a group to sponsor your production. Libraries have shelves of books on the subject of nonprofits, arts organizations, and corporations. For your first production, I would advise using a more informal structure—and then wait. If you continue to produce, your audience continues to grow, and your group begins to have ambitious plans, then move toward a more formal structure. At that time, you will have a better idea of who's going to be there for the theatre in the long run and what kind of organization is going to best fit your needs.

If there are more than one of you who want to put on a play, or if you are able to recruit some co-producers, consider involving them on the production staff. That's plenty of organization for a first production.

Chapter 5

Accountability and Sisterhood

Accountability and sisterhood are sometimes strange bedfellows in Lesbian community.

After all, we are the leaders in humanizing the workplace, aren't we? We understand all about child care, about PMS, about when one loses a lover, don't we? Well, yes. On the other hand, if you have ever been stuck onstage, improvising business to kill time until the actor who missed her cue gets it together to make the entrance, you will probably be feeling something stronger than sisterly empathy by the time she finally arrives. If you are the producer of the event, and you find that your press release did not make it into the monthly gay-and-Lesbian paper because the publicist had a family crisis, you may find you care more about your lost audience and revenue than you do about the publicist's personal problem. If you are a director who shows up at the theatre for dress rehearsal to discover that another show is in progress, you may not give a damn that the woman responsible for the scheduling checked into a hospital for gallbladder surgery on Friday and forgot to follow through on her job.

Sisterhood aside, such are the exigencies of live theatre. That it is a volunteer effort, that it is considered recreational or amateur, that it is supposed to be fun—none of these factors weigh in when you get down to the crunch. Accountability is a bottom-line issue in theatre.

Men learn accountability in team sports and the military, which are both far more institutionalized in male culture than in Lesbian community. Many boys and young men have early experience with the "no excuses" ethic, the one that women have found so brutalizing in the workplace. On the other hand, the "any excuse" ethic can also be pretty brutalizing.

Accountability comes with power. Most women have not been allowed to experience ourselves as powerful, and so the idea of accountability can be somewhat foreign to us. I placed this chapter here in the section about getting started, because even though every member of a theatre company needs to be accountable, the producer is the Lesbian with ultimate accountability. Be sure you understand what that means and accept the responsibility that goes with the position.

So what does it mean? It means that if the director skips town halfway through rehearsals, you are accountable, because you hired her. It means that if the show loses money because of an earthquake, you are accountable for the loss. It means that in the world of organizational buck-passing, the buck stops with you. Shit happens, yes, but ultimately, you will be the one accountable for seeing that it gets cleaned up, even if it's not your shit. You may *delegate* to the cleanup crew, or you may appoint the shitter to clean up after herself, but you are still the one who ultimately owns the problem—especially if others are not willing or able to be accountable.

It's very important for the producer to understand accountability, because she sets the tone for the theatre. The members of the company will, for the most part, follow her lead. If the producer does not keep her agreements, neither will the staff. If the producer changes the rules, most likely so will the director. You will not get accountability unless you are accountable.

It's important to remember that *organizations are not accountable, people are*. You are that person, and the responsibilities are going to be sobering.

Know yourself! If you tend to avoid conflict, to let your answering machine field unpleasant calls, to break down physically when the going gets tough, to hide behind a lover, boss, or landlord when called to account for your actions, then do everyone a favor and *don't* direct or produce. Pull the curtain, hand out programs, or sell tickets, but *do not* direct or produce.

And *never* work for a producer or a director that you know to be unaccountable. It simply won't be worth it, because you will, if you are conscientious, have to take up the slack for her.

What causes so many Lesbians in leadership positions to resort to unavailability? Usually it is fear about competency. And this is a shame.

When we are afraid to work with women who have more knowledge, skill, talent, or experience than we do, we keep ourselves and our culture from growing. Fears about our competency are almost always coupled with self-deception and projection. How often will a woman say, "I really don't want you in my organization, because you know so much more than me, and I'm afraid I'll look bad by comparison"? I have never yet heard it said, but I have seen the dynamic dozens and dozens of times. The woman who is perceived as a threat is trashed and scapegoated. This is usually very easy, because often the woman with superior skills or knowledge has some degree of privilege that will lay her open to charges of elitism, classism, or patriarchal poisoning. Of all the therapy words that have infiltrated our Lesbian lexicon, I have yet to hear the word "jealousy" used in analyzing community dynamics. It is conspicuous in its absence.

We are jealous, and we have good reason to be. We have been unjustly robbed of our identities, denied access to resources, and our work has been appropriated and distorted by the dominant culture. It hurts to see a woman with more patriarchal privilege be better at something. It can feel damaging to ourselves to support that woman, when the injustice done to us has not been addressed, when our own struggle has not been validated. How do we deal with this? The answers are not easy, but there is one thing I have learned from much painful experience: When we try to arrange our environment to protect ourselves from our fears of incompetency, we burn the word "failure" more deeply into our psyches than any external circumstance could ever do. We may fool others around us, but I suspect we don't fool many, and we don't fool them for long.

When we try to punish the woman whose skills are "making us feel bad," we are working for the enemy. Just because we feel threatened around certain women does not mean that they are necessarily doing something to us. Sometimes in our rush to reclaim feelings, we make bad connections between cause and effect. If we feel ashamed of our journal writings in the presence of a brilliant novelist, it's important to remember she probably did not "intimidate" us. Most likely, we projected onto her and then were triggered by our own projection. It's a knee-jerk response to say, "I feel better when she isn't around, therefore she must be doing something to me, and therefore I am within my rights to get rid of her." If we continue to act out this primitive reflex, our culture will stay mired in the swamps of low self-esteem.

And here I am talking about situations that involve Lesbians working with other Lesbians in community. In the academic world or other mainstream venues, we are often victims of deliberate intimidation, elitism, or sabotage, and a certain degree of "healthy paranoia" can be a very handy survival skill in such contexts. It's just that too often we carry this attitude into our own community, without considering how it might be masking a self-esteem issue.

So, you are the producer. How can you be accountable? Know your bottom line, know your limits and be honest about them, be accessible, be open to input, have a clear structure, use contracts and job descriptions, communicate expectations and consequences clearly, and follow up on your communications. Most important, *know yourself*. Remember, if you are self-deceived about your bottom line or your boundaries, or if you have hidden agendas (fears about your competency, a need for approval), you will not be able to be accountable, and neither will anyone else.

Enough about you. What about the director?

Part II

Laying the Foundation

Chapter 6

Two Heads Are Better Than One

So you have the fire in your belly to produce. Does this mean you should also direct? Just what is the difference between the producer and the director?

To make a long story short, the producer is the person responsible for everything. The producer must have or come up with the theatre or performance space, the money, the budget, the publicity, and the staff. Probably, but not necessarily, the producer is you, since this was all your idea.

The director is usually responsible for the choice of the play—although not always. Sometimes she is hired to direct a play that has already been chosen. It's a better practice to allow the director some input in the choice, because if she is not excited about the material, it will probably not be an inspired production.

The director is also in charge of the physical production. She approves all the design elements (set, lighting, sound, costumes, props), and she casts the show. She should also have a say in the publicity that is circulated. Although the producer gives her the budget, it is usually the director, working with her designers, who divides this into individual budgets for the set, costumes, props, and so forth. The director is responsible for what happens onstage. How she does this is up to her. She may serve as a dictator, guide, or selector; but whatever her personal style, she is in charge of the production.

The producer and director should be two separate women! In smaller theatres or first productions, the same woman will often take on both roles. This is not a good idea, even if you are Superwoman. The functions of a producer and a director are very different, requiring entirely different sets of priorities and temperaments. Unless a Lesbian is interested in cultivating schizophrenia, she will have a very difficult time wearing both hats equally well, and generally one aspect of production will go begging. Imagine having to shift your focus from something two miles away to something two inches away, and having to perform this shift rapidly and constantly for, say, six weeks. You've got a pretty good picture of the stress level for the Lesbian who tries to produce and direct at the same time. Mostly likely, she will end up cross-eyed and burned out, with everyone angry at her.

The director can become so caught up in realizing the vision, money becomes no object; and the producer can get so nervous about money, she starts performing radical surgery when the patient is doing fine.

If the director and producer are separate Lesbians, they can provide checks and balances for their respective artistic and financial obsessions. Also, the producer can generally commit herself to full-time support for the show if she is not required to agonize over the details of production. This support is critical to the director, who will be dealing with the usual skirmishes with the cast and sleepless nights over artistic decisions.

The producer should give the director complete cooperation and authority for as long as she is director. The producer should stay out of the rehearsal process and the artistic decisions. It is not her job or her business.

And watch the gossip! A producer who takes the side of the cast on the issue of artistic decisions is way out of line, and the director, her credibility and authority seriously compromised by her producer's weakness, is within her rights to quit. If the director is guilty of overt abuse or ethical violations, the producer will need to confront her, but casting choices, rehearsal methods, time lines and scheduling, and artistic decisions are the director's business.

The producer may have made a disastrous choice, but interfering with a director's methods, expressing concerns about the quality of her work, or, especially, talking behind her back to the actors will only intimidate or antagonize her. A bad director can become exponentially worse if she feels her producer is losing faith in her and cutting her loose—or, worse, throwing her to the shark pool of insecure actors.

In a case like this where a hiring mistake has been made and the show is in production, the producer can try to get out of her contract, but most likely her best alternative is to promise herself never, ever, ever to hire the woman again—and then put on a good front for the duration.

And just as the producer must accept responsibility for her relationship to the director, so the director must take responsibility for her relationship to the producer. Part of this responsibility is to make sure she isn't set up by a "tag team."

Often the producing body will be more than one person—a collective, a board, or a partnership. The director should *never* have to do business with more than one representative at any given time. Ideally, it should be the same representative for the run of the show.

Lesbians seem to have difficulty with this concept. Maybe it's because we have such an aversion to speaking for someone else. Or maybe it's because the tag-team dynamic, unfair as it is, does give us the edge in negotiations. The director who is required to do business with six different members of a collective—who may or may not be speaking to one another—is at a distinct disadvantage. And when discrepancies in policy and commitments turn up, the director, who is an outsider, gets my vote for Most Likely Scapegoat.

Sometimes the head of a theatre will try to hide behind her board of directors in order to keep her options open. She will negotiate a contract with the director and then come back to her with something like, "I'm really sorry, but my board won't approve your salary." This is unprofessional and manipulative, and don't put up with it. The head of the company has just admitted that she lacked the authority to negotiate the contract, and you are well within your rights to request that you deal directly with the chairman of the board for the remainder of your business. If this causes a shake-up in "business as usual" for the company, so much the better. It's their problem, and it's high time someone held them accountable for it.

If all of the producers insist on meeting with you as director, fine; but stick to your guns about only one of them being the representative for negotiations. Then, if a conflict arises among members of the producing body, they will need to excuse themselves and hammer it out among themselves, instead of hammering on you in a tag-team move. Where producers disagree, it is not your job to intercede.

And a special word of warning: If you are hired by a collective to direct a show and the collective's members are also going to be in the cast, you are in for a world of woe! In a nutshell, your workers will also be your boss. In a situation like this, there are no boundaries to enforce, and you are all likely to fall back on family politics, mythologies about sisterhood, or sex appeal to see you through. It may be possible at the outset to negotiate a compromise where actors in the show will temporarily relinquish their roles as producers, but it's best to just avoid this whole setup.

In the excitement and glamour of putting on a show, both producer and director will often start with the assumption that whatever isn't spelled out will be worked out. This is a nice theory, but in practice, it's a disaster. The director needs to have a guarantee of what her budget will be, a guarantee about her rehearsal and performance space and dates, a clear understanding about what kind of staff she will have and who is responsible for recruiting them, and her salary (fee, wages, stipend, percentage?) spelled out. She should also have editorial approval of all publicity, including the program (more on this later).

The contract should specify who will be her liaison to the organization producing the play, and it should specify that this liaison be accountable to her for decisions made about the production. It's not a bad idea to spell out the time and place for the meetings with the producer and that phone calls be returned within twenty-four hours. Many women who get in over their heads in business situations practice a form of "management via inaccessibility," and once this dynamic gets under way, the director—if she's conscientious—will be compelled to take up the slack for the sake of the actors.

From the producer's point of view, the director's contract should specify how many hours the director will rehearse with the cast, whether or not she will be required to attend all performances, and what her responsibilities will entail. This includes which staff members she will supervise. (See Appendix 1 for a sample director's contract and Appendix 11 for a supervisory flowchart.)

All of this may seem terribly formal for a "little" community theatre, but I have worked in all kinds of Lesbian productions, and I have yet to see a "little" piece of theatre. Even if the financial resources are slim and the professional ones are nonexistent, the emotional investment is *always* tremendous, and that is why it is important to have all the issues that will bear on that emotional investment spelled out in advance.

Firm boundaries between the director and the producer make for strong and responsible leadership and will set a tone that will be reflected in the way that you organize the rest of your staff. But first, let's look at some of the basics of leadership.

Chapter 7

Learning to Lead

What would you think of a farmer who takes up the study of cow psychology to deal with the cows who keep going through the hole in the pasture fence? This is an obvious case of someone who is looking for the solution to her problem in the wrong area. But what about the Lesbian who watches in despair as yet another organizational meeting heads down the path of family dysfunctional behaviors? What about the Lesbian who gives up on working with other Lesbians because she is so disgusted with "the way Lesbians do business"? Are these valid critiques of our culture or not?

Yes and no. Yes, we have had a history of incredibly unproductive—and occasionally destructive—processes at conferences and meetings. No, we don't do business this way because we are Lesbians. We do business this way because we are human, and because we have not had good leadership or good role models for doing business.

Lesbian organizations in the early days of the women's movement tended to follow a model of collective anarchy or charismatic dictatorship, or some combination of the two. This was because we seldom had women with management skills in these early grassroots organizations, or, when we did, there was such an investment in the myths of Lesbian spontaneous sisterhood and collective will that these women were not encouraged to share or implement practices that would have made for more productive meetings. Also, the possession of management skills was seen as a class marker, and instead of encouraging a Lesbian to use these as tools for subversion, she was frequently shamed for possessing them and shunned for suggestions that reflected her access to this privileged knowledge. Fortunately, people and movements grow.

Any organization of people that tried to run itself without leadership, without an agenda, without a budget, without some kind of process, without realistic goals—both long-term and short-range—would find itself having meetings just like the ones for which Lesbians have gotten a bad rap. The problem is human nature, not Lesbians.

The problems of human nature may be amplified in Lesbian organizations by the fact that we have been deliberately shut out of leadership positions, that we have very limited resources, that we are terribly suspicious of anyone exercising any kind of power, and that we have endured centuries of conditioning that fostered competition and sabotage among ourselves. Also, for many people who have been disenfranchised and oppressed, the first impulse upon gaining a voice or a vote is to use it to vent some of the pent-up rage from so many years of silence and helplessness.

In addition, our core identity as Lesbians exists in resistance to the dominant culture's regime of compulsory heterosexuality. We have learned certain skills and attitudes that have enabled us to survive years and years of going against the grain. Unfortunately, these skills (disruption, sabotage, subversion) and attitudes (defiance, hypervigilance, distrust) do not help us when we try to work with one another.

So, yes and no: Lesbian organizations do face special challenges, but let's focus on the holes in the fence rather than the psychology of the cows. Let us accept that people and cows will transgress poorly defined boundaries. They always have, they always will.

So . . . on to the holes. Bottom lines and boundaries again. I remember participating in a drumming workshop at a Lesbian festival. The woman leading it was very insistent that we all get on the same downbeat before we went off on our separate rhythms. She would beat her drum and listen to see if we were all with her. And then she would stop and tell us to try again. We spent a full half hour just trying to achieve what she called "consensus on the downbeat."

Time spent gaining consensus on the downbeat is time well spent. The first consensus on the downbeat for an organization is its mission statement. The statement of purpose, or bottom line, for an organization. Some sample mission statements for Lesbian theatres might be: "to allow Lesbians in our city the opportunity to take part in amateur theatricals that reflect our culture" (emphasis here on the experience of the participants); or how about: "to bring quality Lesbian entertainment to our community, breaking down stereotypes about Lesbians and increasing awareness of our issues" (emphasis on the audience). The next consensus on the downbeat is the organizational structure, with clear lines of accountability for each position. Who does what, when, and where, and for how long?

At the practical level, the consensus on the downbeat for the meetings is the agenda. Everyone should have a copy. Everyone should know what's going to be going on and what they will be expected to contribute.

And on a personal level, every member of a meeting needs to know what her responsibilities at that meeting will be: to be on time, to know what she wants added to the agenda, to be prepared with materials to help the group with her agenda item or items, to avoid unnecessary communications that disrupt, and so forth.

Few people are born with leadership skills. Some of us are naturally gifted as communicators, but we haven't a clue how to organize anything. Others of us are tremendous at logistics, but we are at a complete loss when it comes to motivating others. Most women need to learn leadership skills, either from observation, apprenticeship situations, or through formal courses of study or books.

Now, here is another area where women are at a disadvantage. Many of us grew up in patriarchal families, where the females did not have direct access to power in the family. We watched our mothers second-guess the patriarch, employ methods of psychological manipulation, and sometimes resort to deceit. Many of us later found ourselves in jobs where it was necessary to use similar subversive tactics to get around a boss who was threatened by honest communication. In other words, many of us grew up studying cow psychology instead of basic fence construction.

One of the most inefficient and ineffective ways to operate in an organization is to attempt to manipulate the members psychologically. Good leadership is not charismatic leadership. Good leadership is good management.

As women, we have been actively kept in the dark about management principles. We have been taught to believe in unrealistic models that have very little to do with human nature. Until very recently, the battered woman was brainwashed by society to believe that patience, prayer, and her martyrdom would bring about a change of heart in the batterer. We have also been taught that we will be discovered or rescued if we just keep our motives pure and do our work well. Ha. How many women have been passed over time and time again for promotion because of that myth? We have been led to believe that those who are our friends will automatically respond to our needs given only the subtlest of clues. How many otherwise productive workplace relationships have been sacrificed on that altar of co-dependence? We have learned that a position of authority is a guarantee of respect. How many women have been unable to implement their ideas for lack of the most basic management skills? And worst of all, we have learned that when our models don't work, it's the fault of other people. The cows, not the fence.

Conversely, sometimes women from tyrannical families learn to model themselves after the tyrant. These women frequently rise to the top of graduate programs and patriarchal organizations (what a surprise!). These woman are in for a shock, however, when they bring this orientation into Lesbian communities. We haven't gone through all the trouble of coming out just so we can create our own little mini-patriarchies within our own communities!

But let's not throw the baby of leadership out with the bathwater of patriarchal process. Leadership is not to be confused with dictatorship. Leadership is a fine quality, and one that all of us should learn to cultivate.

Leadership is about problem-solving. One of the biggest challenges you will encounter in Lesbian theatre is women who try to make their problems your problem: the woman whose schedule changes because she had to get a new job; the woman who can't afford to pay for child care anymore; the woman who hasn't learned her lines on time; the woman whose car broke down. Good leadership empowers women by helping us learn to solve our own problems. This does not occur if you take on the task of changing a person. Why? Because the bottom line is that you have then accepted the problem as yours: to change the person. She's off the hook.

Well, good communication, problem-solving, and leadership skills are the subjects of many books, but not this one. Suffice it to say that a six-week rehearsal period is woefully inadequate for learning by trial and error. Take some classes, read a book, or find a mentor in management somewhere. But do take it seriously that these are important skills and that you will need them as a director or producer. In patriarchal theatre, the producer gains respect by being successful. Anything else is irrelevant. Likewise, the director can be inconsiderate, dictatorial, violent, abusive, sexist, and the like, and these traits are accepted as necessary concomitants to genius. But in Lesbian theatre? Don't count on it!

There are several good books about communication and management. My favorite is *Leadership Effectiveness Training* by Thomas Gordon (New York: Bantam, 1977). This book starts with the basics of communication (including assertiveness), outlines practical models for determining who owns the problem (anti-codependency training) and steps for conflict resolution, and spends a great deal of time on the subject of how to run productive meetings. Gordon makes the point that ineffectual use of meeting time is the single greatest factor in the failure of most businesses and organizations. Most people are very creative and resourceful when it comes to solving problems if their capacity for problem-solving is tapped effectively and collectively at meetings.

Another book that I found very useful is *Dinosaur Brains: Dealing with All Those Impossible People at Work*, by Albert J. Bernstein and Sydney Craft Rozen (New York: Ballantine, 1989). Often Lesbian leadership skills are hampered by our expectations of one another. Just because a woman is a Lesbian doesn't mean she's not going to be territorial, use her job for cruising, or practice manipulation to get her way. And Lesbians can lie, cheat, and steal. Denying that these things are happening will gut your effectiveness as a leader. To model your management style after some utopian idea of what people should be is as silly as the idealistic farmer who removes her fences because she needs to believe that the cows in her pasture will respect her boundaries. As an individual, it may be your prerogative to practice denial in your personal affairs, but when you are in a leadership situation, denial is downright unethical, because other women will be stuck cleaning up your mess.

The Need to Thrive by Judy Remington (St. Paul, MN: Minnesota Women's Press, Inc., 1991) is a book about women's organizations in the Minneapolis—St. Paul area. Remington has researched the history of several organizations from 1965 to 1990, and she outlines the causes behind the rise and fall of each. She pays special attention to the victim mentality that sets "survival" as an organizational goal. Remington makes the point that, in order to succeed, our organizations need to set their sights on *thriving*.

Lesbian Ethics by Sarah Hoagland (Palo Alto, CA: Institute of Lesbian Studies, 1989) is another excellent book about the ways in which Lesbians interact. She draws attention to the destructive practice of shunning used as a covert method of social control, because our culture has not yet evolved the dynamics and institutions of a true community.

We need more books about Lesbian organizing and Lesbian organizations. I wrote this one because there was a need. If your theatre takes care to document and archive its history, who knows? You may be responsible for the next book on the subject of Lesbian theatre. We need to stop keeping Lesbian family secrets and start sharing experiences. Otherwise, we will not be able to take advantage of the experience of successive generations of Lesbians, and we will be reinventing individual and isolated wheels over and over again, instead of figuring out a way to link them together so we can get our culture in gear.

Chapter 8

Victims and Victimizers

Patriarchy is divided and subdivided into those with the power and those without. A man may have little power at work, but in his home he may be an absolute tyrant. A woman may be battered in her marriage, but she may be a terrorist toward her children. Lesbians who are treated like dirt in many areas of our lives may clone the worst behaviors of our oppressors when we hold positions of authority in our own community. These are patterns learned in childhood, values taught in the culture, and nobody is immune. It's work to unlearn them.

What makes a Lesbian vulnerable to acting abusively? First and foremost, her denial about her victimization. The Lesbian who has never allowed herself to feel the grief and rage about her oppression can transfer that same denial right over to her victims the first time she finds herself in a position of power. She can adopt the myth that this is part of "paying one's dues" or "building character." In a self-perpetuating myth, the abuse does tend to harden successive generations into being abusers.

The woman who stays stuck in victim behaviors is also practicing a form of abuse. The skills of victims are subversive ones: We lobby other groups of victims in secret, we sabotage the authority figure, we perform minimally under pressure. When we go into a Lesbian organization, these patterns often follow us.

If we have learned that our place in the script of life is that of the victim, we will walk into any new situation and automatically orient ourselves that way. We will create a constellation of abusers and potential allies (co-victims) wherever we go. The woman with the most power will always be the most likely candidate for the title Official Abuser. A woman socialized all her life to be a victim cannot always determine when these situations are created by her. This is how she has learned to sort her perceptions, and it takes powerful counterconditioning to undo a lifelong orientation.

It is helpful for women in organizations to be aware of situations where we have been victimized in the past and to be able to talk about these, especially when we feel that a dynamic or process is replicating an earlier pattern that resulted in our abuse.

Another thing that women have learned to do in patriarchy is to betray one another. Theatre has a long and bloody history of women betraying women. The target of the betrayal tends to take the situation personally, and often it will bring up devastating issues from the victim's family of birth, especially abandonment or betrayal by a mother. This personalizing is unfortunate, because it prevents the potential victim from gaining the perspective she needs to protect herself. Often, she will be so overwhelmed by pain left over from childhood trauma that she will act inappropriately—resorting to "overkill" against the betrayer, or quitting the organization in a crisis situation.

These drastic responses to betrayals by a "sister" are often more destructive than the consequences of the betrayal. Designed in part to draw attention to the victim's pain, they often backfire, because the betrayal is rarely personal—and most women outside the relationship can see that very clearly. Often, it's evolutionary: The mentoree has simply outgrown her mentor, and she is feeling a need to stretch her wings. That was the whole point of the mentorship, wasn't it? If the woman who is feeling betrayed can step back and see the situation as one wherein another woman is experiencing limited opportunities and frustration at her inability to expand, maybe then the woman with the position of authority can create opportunities that will allow the woman with ambition to meet her needs without having to resort to betrayal.

In patriarchy, ambitious women are simply neutralized, by terrorism, humiliation, demotion, incarceration, crazy-making, slander, or a sentimental appeal for her to consider the good of the family. We should not adopt these methods to deal with ambitious Lesbians. We should expand our organizations and provide more opportunities for talented individuals. We should be happy to recruit the women who know more than we do. We should make room for dissent; we should allow enough space in our organizations for the rebels to try out their ideas. We should not force defections and takeovers by our own territoriality.

There is an excellent book on the subject of women betraying women, *Sisterhood Betrayed* by Jill Barber and Rita E. Watson (New York: St. Martin's Press, 1991). Using the prototypes from the movie *All About Eve*, the authors point out how leading lady Margo Channing contributed to her own downfall by allowing her out-of-control emotions to play into the hands of her would-be rival, Eve Harrington. As the authors point out, Eve was not out to get Margo. She was simply out to get power. If Margo had not been so overwhelmed by her own jealousy and fear of ageing, she could have appealed to Eve's ambitions by creating opportunities for her away from her own personal sphere.

As it was, Margo became frozen by her own fatalism. The film does not provide us with the history of this fatalism, but we can make some educated guesses: Did Margo need to play out some ancient family drama in which she was perpetually the odd girl out? Did she need to test her lover's loyalty? Had she herself risen to fame by betraying a mentor, and did she feel this was her karma? Whatever her reasons, Margo forfeited an opportunity to become Eve's ally, retreated to a victim stance, and focused her considerable energy on turning people against Eve. Those who stood outside the drama could not believe that the great Margo Channing was being menaced by her understudy, and Margo's efforts backfired. One by one her support people felt compelled to abandon her for what they saw as petty and paranoid behaviors.

Eve Harrington and Margo Channing represent two of the worst models for women we have inherited from patriarchal theatre. Unfortunately, Eve and Margo continue to reincarnate generation after generation, even in our Lesbian theatres. Our same-sex liaisons only raise the stakes for the betrayal.

There is another factor that complicates the dynamics among Lesbians in theatre: the phenomenon called "dissociative disorders." All of us are dissociative from time to time. Daydreaming is a mild form of dissociation. Focusing on your boss's chin while he is yelling at you is another form of dissociation. Losing track of time and space during a creative endeavor is another. On the far end of the spectrum, changing into an alter personality and checking into a hotel for three days under another name is a symptom of an extreme form of dissociation called Multiple Personality Disorder.

This is not a book on psychology, and the field of literature on dissociative disorders is rapidly growing and changing. I just want to say that dissociation is normal. And some of us have learned to dissociate more frequently and more readily than others. Some forms of dissociation are helpful to us (meditation, self-hypnosis, daydreaming, immersion in the character's reality during performance), and some forms are not helpful. When a dissociative behavior is not under our conscious control and results in actions that are inappropriate to the situation, it can be very confusing and destructive.

Some dissociative behaviors were developed in response to trauma, often trauma during childhood.

These behaviors can become triggered by situations that appear to replicate a dynamic from the earlier trauma. When a situation begins to resemble family-of-birth dynamics, with scapegoating as the paradigm, a Lesbian may find that all of her professionalism as a director, all of her analysis of patriarchy as a feminist, all of her ethics as a Lesbian, all of her integrity as an artist, and all of her dignity as an adult are at risk of flying out the window.

The older, deeper conditioning from what has been a life-threatening situation in the past can override the more recent adult programming in her brain. She begins to "act out" from this primitive mode of thinking, mixing up the past with the present, projecting motives onto people based on a past experience, confusing co-workers with an abusive parent, and reacting in the present to something that happened to her as a child. In other words, she dissociates.

What makes it even trickier is that the woman who is dissociating rarely realizes that she is doing anything wrong. In fact, she probably sees herself acting heroically under fire. A person in a dissociated state is not capable of analyzing that state. It's like asking a person who is completely underwater if they feel wet. When the perception of a situation is all-encompassing, there is no outside point of reference from which to stand back and critique what's going on.

Women dissociate in all kinds of situations. Some of us dissociate if people raise their voice at us. Some of us dissociate under deadline pressures. Some of us dissociate at the first hint of criticism, even when it's impersonal and well intended. Some of us dissociate in the presence of someone under the influence of drugs or alcohol. Some of us dissociate in bed. The dissociative state can last a few seconds, or it can persist for weeks. It can become an all-encompassing reality, or it can pertain to just a small part of one's life. In Lesbian theatre, it's very important to understand the phenomenon of dissociation, because we will be working with a population that has self-selected for a high incidence of dissociation.

Actors are experts at dissociation. We do it every time we create a role. We are able to put ourselves into a controlled altered state to become someone else for the purposes of the play. This is a healthy way to exercise our dissociative powers. Just because we have this talent for creative dissociation doesn't necessarily mean that we also have out-of-control behaviors, but it can.

This is where the stereotype of the "drama queen" came from. That is a derogatory term for someone who seems to enjoy turning every situation into a crisis. In fact, the drama queen is most likely an unwitting victim of dissociative disorders. She doesn't know that the director was preoccupied when she ignored her. She is sure that she is once again being singled out and persecuted by a powerful authority figure. She doesn't know that she's experiencing a garden-variety backstage crush on the leading lady. She is sure that this must be the great love of her life for whom she has waited so long.

Dissociative disorders are confusing. How many times have we been at a meeting—especially when the issue of money is brought up—and seen women "go off," becoming verbally abusive and irrational? How many times have we seen lovers deliver speeches and ultimatums, and then exit with a grand slam? How often have we gotten that uncomfortable feeling that we are suddenly trapped in someone else's movie that has nothing to do with us? And how often have we been confused by the fact that we really like and trust a woman, but her behaviors are compelling us to distance ourselves from her? When good women do destructive things that defy logic, what we're probably seeing is dissociation.

So, Lesbians dissociate, and theatre is all about the art of dissociation, and Lesbian organizations often resemble miniature families. What can we do? Knowledge is power. The ability to name something is power. If you can identify dissociation when it's going on, you are automatically armed with an analysis that will allow you to make better choices about how to protect yourself. Engaging with a person who is "going off" is usually fruitless, because it pulls you into the movie, validates her behavior (because you engage with it), and causes you to lose your sane vantage point. Whatever else may be the shortcomings of the Al-Anon program, its principle of detachment for dealing with alcoholism applies nicely to dissociative disorders.

Don't trash the woman. Don't punish the woman. Don't hate the woman. But don't allow her to use you, don't allow yourself to suffer because of her choices, don't do things for her if she should do them for herself. Don't cover for her. Don't create or prevent a crisis. *Do* protect yourself and your organization, cast, and crew from the effects of her dissociation. If you were raised in a crazy family and find yourself protecting and enabling a woman who is dissociating, get help and support for yourself. Don't believe that you can control the person, because you can't.

And while we're on the subject of dissociation, let's look at lies, secrets, and silencing, which are controlling tactics used in dysfunctional families. Lies, secrets, and silencing will, unfortunately, "work" to control children. Children will respond with fear, guilt, and internalized shame. Children can be recruited to keep family secrets—even ones about their own abuse—because they perceive their loyalty to the family as critical to their survival.

In positions of power, dysfunctional adults, or adults with dissociative disorders, will often revert to tactics that they saw modeled by their parents: lies, secrets, and silencing. But healthy adults are not children, and we will not respond to abusive tactics as if we were powerless. We will not act against our own interests to protect the person in power, or even the organization. Our highest loyalty is to ourselves, and that's why the bottom line is so important. We need to make sure up front that our needs and the organization's needs are compatible.

This has been a long and painful chapter. In summing up, I would say that it's essential for Lesbians to understand what has been done to all of us, individually and collectively, and we have to have tremendous compassion for ourselves when we slip into the old victimized ways of thinking and acting—compassion, but also detachment. As we undergo the transition from victims to leaders, we can help one another only as much as we can help ourselves.

With that in mind, let's take a look at some of the issues involved in recruiting volunteers.

Chapter 9

Volunteering, Recruiting, and Boundaries

Like countries that have been invaded too many times, many women have a poor sense of their boundaries. Not knowing where the boundaries are is as fatal to Lesbian organizations as not knowing one's bottom line.

The expression "Lesbian burnout" is frequently used to describe the state of a Lesbian who suddenly finds herself physically exhausted and psychically depleted from some endeavor. The burnout usually manifests as a sudden and complete withdrawal from the project or organization. Frequently, no one knew it was coming, least of all the Lesbian with the so-called burnout.

Because Lesbian causes are usually so right-on and so badly understaffed, the Lesbian who is committed to working for them often feels guilty about scaling back her involvement or taking a sabbatical. Nothing short of a mental or physical breakdown, or a major and irresolvable conflict with the other members, will excuse her from abandoning her post.

"Burnout" is a handy term to describe a highly noticeable phenomenon. But in terms of doing triage in Lesbian culture, it might be more useful to use the term "Lesbian overcommitment." That is the real problem.

Lesbian organizations and projects seem to follow a model based on dysfunctional relationships. There is a love-at-first-sight stage, which is based on the fact that the idea behind the project or the goals of the organization are absolutely wonderful. Being Lesbian, they usually are. This is followed by some kind of ritualized bonding behaviors—the enthusiastic volunteering for positions within the organization. The next stage is the moving in together. After a brief honeymoon, the partners begin the phase known as "working on our shit." This is the least productive, but frequently the most drawn out, phase of the relationship. And then, finally, neither side wanting to take responsibility for calling it quits, some kind of violent episode is manufactured so that there is a final split, after which each party recruits her friends to take her side of things.

We can either move on to the next love-at-first-sight organization, or we can stop and figure out what went wrong with the last one. Two things went wrong: Ignorance of the bottom line and bad boundaries. These often are related, but it is possible for a Lesbian to know what her bottom line is and still be unable to draw the proper boundaries to protect her interests.

In an organization, there are many boundaries for

members to consider. What are our limits in terms of time commitments? What kinds of tasks will we absolutely not do? With which committees or individuals is it unproductive for us to work? How much of our own money are we expected to spend for things like transportation? And what kind of treatment will we not tolerate?

Because of the training received by most females in the world—the point of which is to allow males unlimited access to our resources—women often have neither the skills nor the self-esteem to acknowledge our boundaries. That doesn't mean they don't exist. It just means the boundaries have been so chronically violated that it became adaptive for us to ignore the incursions, pretending we gave permission or denying that the boundary exists. If a girl has not been allowed to protect her boundaries, fire warning shots, or prosecute trespassers, she may have a difficult time as an adult realizing that she has any recourse other than acquiescence.

Many violated women will present themselves as if they have no boundaries. They wait until the number of transgressions have built up to a critical mass, and then they will either explode or burn out. For women who have healthy skills in defining and defending our boundaries, these explosions are quite a mystery. Maybe our co-worker is experiencing PMS, or projecting her anger, or perhaps there is something in the current situation that is triggering a flashback for her. All of these may be true, but the bottom line is that the exploding co-worker is defending her boundaries the only way she knows how.

A woman with poor boundaries may seem like the Goddess's gift to a struggling Lesbian organization. She is often willing to do anything anybody asks of her at any time, for no money. She may even use her own money to pay for things. She's always willing to step in at the eleventh hour and take over for someone else. Great, right? Wrong, on several counts.

First, the organization, in exploiting this woman's weakness, may actually become dependent on her. Her excessive volunteerism can create a false picture of the resources of the company. When she burns out—and she will—it may be impossible to replace her without substantial reorganization. And, like the woman discussed in an earlier example about collective theatre, she may be the only one who really knows what's going on.

Second, the Lesbian organization that takes advantage of a woman who can't say no is really violating its own principles. Just because the storm troopers of patriarchy have broken down the door and stomped through her house so many times that she has learned to consider herself a public resource is no excuse for Lesbians to take advantage of the situation.

Lesbian organizations and institutions lead the world in the critique of oppression. We need to apply that analysis to the ways in which women have been hurt by patriarchy. We need to help one another recognize our bottom lines. We need to help one another define and defend our boundaries. We should never exploit the women who are not in touch with their limits.

And, no, it's not co-dependent behavior to help a woman deprogram herself. In fact, it is co-dependent to exploit her in the areas where she is damaged.

Recruiting and training volunteers is a big part of community theatre. Determining the bottom line and the boundaries of the workers is essential in building a stable company. The bottom line is that there is always a bottom line. The commitment of a worker will rise no higher than the degree to which her bottom line is being met. If you know her bottom line, you can help the worker meet it. The woman who is involved because she is in love with theatre is someone you won't mind asking to show up during Tech Week to help gel the lights. The woman who is involved because she wants to gain some experience with publicity and fund-raising is perfect to recruit for selling theatre nights to women's organizations. The woman who wants to meet other women might be interested in getting a committee together to put out the mailing.

On the other hand, if you don't know the bottom line of a worker, you will probably make a number of wrong assumptions, the worker may find herself in positions that do not satisfy her, and, eventually, she will leave—possibly with an act of sabotage.

Always take the time to ask, "What's in it for you?"

The same goes for boundaries. Ask, "What are the limits to your commitment?" A volunteer may say, "I'll do whatever needs to be done." Watch out! Sounds like she has a potential problem with her boundaries; and since your property is going to border hers, it's only neighborly to take a little time to ride fences with her.

Ask her about her time commitment. Ask her about her skills. Ask her about her previous experience. Ask her what she enjoys most. Ask her what she feels she does best. Ask her what she'd like to learn. Ask her what kind of people she likes to work with. Ask her what kind of supervision works best for her on a job. Give her information about the kinds of jobs that need to be done, so that she can make an informed choice about her preferences. Help her determine the limits of her commitment.

Another poor boundary can be created when a volunteer envisions her task taking place under ideal conditions. Yes, she'll be responsible for the publicity, but does she understand that the graphic artist might hang her out to dry on the flyer design? That she might have to locate another one at the last minute, and hand-deliver all the information? Can she envision a mailing party where only two women show up? What about the news editor who just keeps misplacing those darn Lesbian press releases? And what if the prints from the first photo shoot come back out of focus? If she takes on publicity, she needs to understand that she will be responsible for dealing with all of these errors, whether or not they were her fault.

Few tasks related to theatre follow a best-case scenario. There are problems with human nature, problems with materials, problems with design, and sometimes just plain problems with the universe. A volunteer whose services are offered on the condition that everything go according to how she envisions the job might need a little reality check in terms of what she can expect as obstacles. If she takes the job, she should understand that she takes it for better or for worse, for richer or for poorer (unless she has a budget in her contract), in sickness or in health, 'til closing night do us part.

Trust me, the limits—like the bottom line—always exist. You would do well to discover them before you are in the middle of production. Better to get a minimal, but firm commitment from a worker than a seemingly open-ended one that will result in burnout.

Chapter 10

The Deadly "Isms"

Racism, sexism, anti-Semitism, looksism, sizeism, ageism, ableism, classism, adultism—not necessarily in that order: Patriarchy is rife with "isms," and it behooves us to understand that traditional theatre has not only been a bastion of these isms, but that the very function of this theatre is the propagation of ism-oriented values:

The female character in love must be attractive according to the rigid standards of the white, able-bodied, middle-class, Anglo-Eurocentric hetero-patriarchy or else how can the audience be expected to identify with her? (Odd concept, since so few women conform to those standards.) Fat women must be funny. Old women must be bitchy or ridiculous. Physically challenged women need to be in special plays where the subject is disability. Women of color will not be considered for the majority of roles. And what about the Christian-based assumptions, references, and rituals that pervade the culture?

Then there's classism—where to begin? All of the isms constitute class hierarchies. In addition, there is a special hierarchy based on income, background, and/or education. What is the class to which your theatre is catering? Does your theatre's structure or pay scale reflect traditional class prejudice where the ones who already have get more, and the ones who never had in the first place still get nothing? And what about the inhouse class structure that ranks the actors as more valuable people than the technicians and the technicians as more valuable people than the ushers?

Lesbian organizations and institutions have traditionally led the world in the critique of oppression. We challenge ourselves to be rigorously honest and accountable about our prejudices. And we challenge ourselves to eliminate both the subtle and the blatant forms these prejudices take.

Ideally, all Lesbian theatres would be multicultural in makeup. At this point in time, however, many of the Lesbian theatres are made up of mostly white Anglo-European Lesbians. Open casting, where the race or ethnic background of an actor is not a factor in the casting, is a step in the right direction, but only a step. How nonracist is it to tell the woman of color that she is free to read for a play about white Anglo-European women, written by a white Anglo-European woman, directed by a white Anglo-European woman, performed by a company of 99 percent white Anglo-European women, for an audience which is 95% white Anglo-European women? Even if the roles in a play are purportedly not specific for race or ethnicity, this frequently means they will read as white.

A stronger approach would be for a white Anglo-European Lesbian theatre to make a commitment to attract and offer resources to directors and actors who have been discriminated against because of their race or ethnic background. One predominantly white gay-and-Lesbian theatre wrote a grant proposal specifically for a project that would help them locate and offer resources to African American Lesbian playwrights. This was in a large city, but white Lesbian theatres in smaller towns can still implement affirmative-action policies.

A multiculturally unbalanced theatre can make a commitment to include in every season a play written and directed by a woman of color. If there are no women of color directors currently in the company, or if no one can locate an appropriate script, the theatre should advertise for both. Money should be set aside for this production. If the theatre is in a small community and there are no takers and/or no scripts for one season, the money should be left in the account and added to the following year's budget. The theatre should continue to let women know that the opportunity exists. Commitment of resources provides incentive. Sitting around waiting for women of color to show up and want to join a white women's theatre is racist.

Ableism, ageism, looksism, sizeism . . . these are isms deeply entrenched in the performing arts. Even Lesbian theatres tend to favor casting the woman who most conforms to mainstream theatre's standards for the lead role. Theatres need to have guidelines about these prejudices, and the women in the theatre need to continue to challenge and critique the casting practices for the shows.

Unfortunately, live theatre has gotten caught up in imitating the film industry, when the two are entirely different genres. Film emphasizs moving image. Live theatre has traditionally emphasized the spoken word. Obviously, where the emphasis is on the image, verisimilitude becomes a priority. In other words, if the heroine is supposed to be a skinny, rebellious seventeen-year-old, the filmmaker will look for an actor who is skinny and around seventeen. Her image will have to bear close scrutiny, in close-up, on a 20-foot screen. There's only so much that makeup can do with a situation like that.

Live theatre, however, is the art of illusion. A forty-year-old woman can easily play that seventeen-year-old. All she needs to do is put across the *thinking* of that woman, which is done with action (including speech), not image. In fact, a woman who can look back on her teenage years from a certain distance of safety is in a better position to commit to the honesty and pain of that period. In the heyday of live theatre, before the age of electronic media, it was not unusual for actors in their forties and fifties to play youthful women. Mrs. Patrick Campbell was in her fifties when Shaw wrote the part of Eliza Doolittle for her in *Pygmalion*. At the age of seventy, Eleanora Duse was still playing the role of Portia in *The Merchant of Venice*.

The same is true for height, weight, physical challenges, and looks that defy the traditional notions of beauty. Beauty onstage is portrayed by attractiveness. And attractiveness is purely and simply the qualities of a person that attract. The audience is not compelled to focus on blown-up images of facial features. The audience is called upon to endow the actors, the stage, and the situation with the qualities that will make the play live for them, much as radio drama makes similar demands on the imagination. Why is it that audiences are expected to take one cardboard pillar to represent an entire ballroom, but that same audience is considered incapable of assimilating a wheelchair—unless of course the whole scene is about the chair. One of the reasons why is that too few directors have made the demand.

This is not to say that a director should go out of her way to cast a woman just because her appearance does *not* conform to traditional audience expectations. Auditions are always competitive, and they should be. Not every actor can play every role. Some parts will just have a certain actor's name on them. Other parts may be a reach for that actor. And some, frankly, may be outside the range of what she sees herself capable of playing—or wanting to play.

If an actor feels deep down that she is making a fool of herself trying to read a butch role, or trying to play thirty years younger than her real age, it's her job to work through those prejudices in her own mind before the auditions. And if she thinks she's cool about it but is still worried that the director or the audience will reject her, she needs to work on projected fears. This is not to say that the director or audience may not have a prejudice, but it is to say that if the actor wants to win the audition, she needs to project absolute confidence; and if she is nurturing projected fears—however grounded in experience of mainstream culture—she will not be convincing.

These are painful realities about the nature of an art form where the body is the instrument. But, as the reader must know by now, I do not subscribe to soothing mythologies. The director who casts an actor who does not believe in herself is suffering delusions of grandeur or acting out of a false altruism—and neither of these motivations will do our art or our community any good.

So what about classism? This is one of the most subtle and most difficult isms to tackle. Class is often the culprit behind many interpersonal differences. Women of different class backgrounds focus on different priorities, approach problems in different ways, process information differently, and frequently communicate in different styles. Without an understanding of how class impacts a Lesbian's perception of and orientation to the world, these differences can escalate into conflicts that become personalized; and once they are personalized, they are almost impossible to resolve, because the root of the conflict is not located in personalities.

Frequently, the concerns of the low-income Lesbian are perceived as petty and obsessive by middle-class Lesbians. For example, if a theatre company expects the actors to buy their own costumes, the Lesbian for whom this is a hardship may be treated as if she were being uncooperative. On the other hand, the theatre company may patronize her by making a special allowance for her situation, or even by having the other actors chip in to cover "her expenses." Low-income Lesbians on the technical crew may not be in the position to pay for materials out of their own pockets and then turn in their receipts for later reimbursement. Any policy that is insensitive to the needs of Lesbians on restrictive budgets needs to be revised. The low-income woman should not be required to disclose her financial situation or pass as having higher income in order to be part of the company.

And what about the way the isms relate to the audiences? Is your audience all white? All middle-class? Are you appealing to a younger cross section of Lesbians? How can a theatre reach out to segments of the population that are staying away? Are the ticket prices too high for seniors on fixed incomes? What allowances do you make for women of poverty-class income? Are the plays irrelevant to women of color? Are they classist?

And what about the performance spaces? Of course, they should always be wheelchair accessible. And that doesn't just mean ramps instead of stairs. That means accessible water fountains, bathrooms, theatre seating. Do you have folding chairs for friends of people in wheelchairs? Are your concessions marked for folks with food allergies? Have you made provisions for seating people of all sizes? Theatre seats are too narrow for many people.

And what about sign-language interpretation of the performances? Some women's organizations have a commitment to sign every event, regardless of whether or not any hearing-impaired women are present. Some organizations never sign their events at all. Some hire signers if they know in advance there will be a contingent of hearing-impaired women. If so, for how many performances, and which ones? Again, this is an issue for every theatre to take up with the members.

One of the subtler ways that patriarchy controls our thinking is that it makes attention to the "isms" seem like an activity for the hyperconscientious politico—an obsession about mental housecleaning, or even a luxury. Lesbian culture is filled with jokes about being politically correct. But the term "politically correct" is meaningless jargon for the woman in the wheelchair who cannot get into the stall of the bathroom at a performance that was advertised as accessible. It becomes a sadistic taunt to the fat actor who has spent her life playing stereotyped roles in mainstream theatre, only to find herself passed over for the serious roles in Lesbian theatre on the basis of appearance.

Patriarchy makes it easy to feel sidetracked or derailed by constant attention to the isms, when in fact, we should feel sidetracked and derailed from our art any time we are not practicing it in an inclusive environment. White women's ignorance of other cultures diminishes the humanity of Lesbian theatre, and if women had not been raised in patriarchy to feel at home with numbing out and splitting off, we would, all of us, feel a personal urgency about recovering our fragmented sense of humanity.

The members of a theatre company who sit down to tackle the isms by drawing up affirmative-action, antidiscrimination policies should be honest about their attitudes toward this commitment. If the work seems burdensome, like some begrudging concession to the price of membership in Lesbian culture, if it feels like having to be "politically correct," then these very attitudes should be the first item on the agenda of consciousness-raising.

There are excellent workshops and materials on antiracism, anticlassism, and so on. It's beyond the scope of this book to give detailed information on how to identify and confront the isms within an organization, but there are some resources in Appendix 2 for your reference.

Real commitment to inclusive theatre *must* be a bottom-line issue for the Lesbians involved. And it *should* be a bottom-line issue. We can and must help one another get there. Otherwise, as Lesbian theatre workers, we are no more than a front for patriarchy, a Trojan horse transporting the armies of isms right into the heart of our own culture.

With this in mind, let's look at how to pick a script.

Part III

Setting up Shop

Chapter 11

Selecting the Script

Lesbian plays are finally in print!! Hurrah!

Appendix 3 is a select bibliography of play collections and other sources where you can find Lesbian plays. You might also want to ask around. Ask your friends if they have any recommendations. Contact some of the women's theatres or the gay-and-Lesbian theatres, and ask them if they have any suggestions for plays that might meet your production needs. Consider the work of local Lesbian writers.

One Lesbian theatre in northern California got tired of scouting for plays and advertised a Lesbian playwriting contest in national Lesbian newsletters, magazines, and women's presses. (Most of these publications will print submission calls free of charge.) The theatre offered a small cash prize and guaranteed production. Suddenly, the manuscripts came looking for them, instead of the other way around. The Dramatists Guild newsletter will run submission calls from theatres at no charge.

In addition, there are two excellent organizations with newsletters providing information about Lesbian plays: The Lesbian Exchange of New Drama (LEND) and The Purple Circuit. Dialogus is a press that publishes nothing but gay and Lesbian plays.

The Internet is an excellent place for play referrals as well. There are networks for women playwrights, for Lesbian writers, for Lesbian studies enthusiasts, and for women in theatre. Folks on the Net are more than willing to share information, locate plays, and offer suggestions tailored to your specific needs. Also, there is a site called Theatre Central, which is a clearinghouse for all kinds of information about playwrights, plays, and theatres. It's a brave new world for Lesbian playwrights!

The criteria for picking a script? The most important consideration is whether or not you like it. There should be something in the script that really pulls you. Maybe it's the story line about two camp counselors falling in love, because it reminds you so much of your own coming out. Maybe it's the wild and crazy Lesbian who's always getting into trouble, because she keeps telling everybody off. Maybe it's the fact that it's a musical with so many hot numbers. Maybe it's the way it breaks the silence about a serious social problem, like the effects of being trashed by one's own community. Or maybe it's the fact that the play grossed $15,000 in six weeks when it played a city of comparable size to your own.

In addition to your bottom line for producing, you should also have a bottom line for choosing a certain play. And the two bottom lines should work together. If your bottom line is making money, it might not be such a good idea to produce a new play by an amateur writer that depicts an onstage bulimic episode—even if eating disorders are one of your issues. If the bottom line for you is gaining a reputation as a serious artist, you might want to avoid *Lesbian Vampires from Hell*—even if it's tearing up the box office all over the country.

It's very helpful to know up front what it is about a play that made you choose it in the first place. Later, when you get into the craziness of hanging lights, baby-sitting distraught actors, giving press interviews, and worrying about that awkward transition in the second act, it's often impossible to see the woods for the trees. In fact, sometimes it's impossible to see the trees for the bark. At moments like this, when you might be considering cutting scenes or rearranging budget priorities, it's very good to have a clear memory of what you once—eons ago—considered the strong points of the script. If you loved it for the moxie of a certain character, be sure she hasn't gotten upstaged by the other actors. If you loved it for that one devastating confrontation, be sure you've adequately set the stage for it in the previous scenes. If you loved the numbers, don't skimp on the budget for those chorus costumes.

Many Lesbian hours are going to go into even the most modest production of a play. Be sure there is something strong enough in the script to justify that kind of investment. It's a good idea to do a reading of the play in front of a small audience before you make your final selection. Most terminal flaws will turn up in a reading, and a reading is a pretty painless way to find out if you've picked a loser.

There are practical considerations in selecting a play. I have not addressed these earlier, because it has been my experience that where there is a will, there is a way. Even if you think the set requirements or the costuming are beyond your budget, ask around. Lesbians never cease to amaze me with our resources and our connections—and our resourcefulness.

One director I know produced a play that required a bedroom, a locker room, and a bar. Besides her teeny-weeny budget, she had no storage space at all for furniture at the theatre. (She was producing in a dance hall.) The solution? She used the same two benches in the locker room to make the bar (stacked and draped with metallic fabric) and the bed (set side by side and covered with a piece of plywood and a quilt).

If the script looks impossible because you need a boathouse, a ballroom, and a chariot race, remember that Shakespeare's *Antony and Cleopatra* had something like twenty-three different scene changes, ranging from a palace to a street scene, from a battlefield to a galley ship—all of which were effected on a bare stage through the use of dialogue alone. A large part of the thrill of live theatre is that the audience has to play make-believe right along with the actors. Never feel that you need to compete with reality! In fact, audiences enjoy productions that make strong demands on their imagination. Remember *Our Town*? Never apologize for skimpy sets or somewhat less than accurate period costumes. Just don't expect your audience to fill in the gaps between dropped lines and late cues!

If you love the script but the technical problems seem insurmountable, don't give up until you have consulted with several different women about the situation—preferably, but not necessarily, ones with experience in theatre. There are very few plays that can't be adapted to minimal staging and small budgets.

Another feasibility question might concern the casting of the show. Can you get five great singers and a tap dancer from the talent pool of your Lesbian community? I give this an even lower priority than the technical considerations.

I not only believe that miracles do happen, but I believe they occur with regularity at auditions. There have been shows I was sure I couldn't cast, but I have gone ahead anyway and held the auditions and lo and behold, there she is!—the woman who can play harmonica, belt the blues, and do floor splits. I never saw her before in my life, and after the show I may never see her again, but there she is, right on time for the production. My advice then, is that if you love the show, go ahead and put the word out. You may think you know every Lesbian in the territory, but miracles do happen, and you never know until you try.

What if you want to write your own script as you go along, or write it collectively with the actors? Many Lesbian theatres have produced shows this way. Usually, these are shows composed of a series of monologues, or vignettes about a certain issue, such as incest or Lesbian dating mores. Shows written like this can have the advantage of being very specific to the community in which they are written, very topical, and occasionally very powerful, because the actors are often portraying incidents from their own experience.

Shows written collectively can also be of ragged quality, preachy or self-indulgent, and can suffer from a serious lack of perspective in terms of production values. This last is understandable, because it's difficult to make objective decisions about subjective material. What these shows gain in immediacy, they may lose in artistic value.

If this is the route you take, again, know your bottom line and know your collaborators' bottom lines. The theatre piece itself should have a bottom line. What is the idea for the show that should tie it all together and keep it coherent? Have some set (better yet, written) procedures for who gets to write what, deadlines for when you need it, the format or guidelines for the material, and selection criteria for the material to be included. And watch out for covert power structures.

Once you have chosen your script, contact the author or the author's agent for permission to produce. Speaking as a Lesbian playwright, *don't* produce without permission! This is just like copying cassette tapes or videos. It's a copyright infringement and, to put it bluntly, common theft. Just because a play has been published does not mean it's in the public domain. It still belongs to the author, and it is her option to lease the rights of production to others. And in case you're thinking she's sitting back and making money doing nothing, consider the years that went into researching, writing, editing, rewriting, workshopping, and marketing the play—all completely unpaid.

Most Lesbian playwrights will charge you royalty fees for producing their work. This is essentially a rental fee. Sometimes it is a flat fee, like $50 for every performance (musicals are usually higher, one-acts usually lower), or sometimes it is based on a percentage of the total box office receipts. The Dramatists Guild, which is the national organization of playwrights in the United States, has a standard contract for small theatres that recommends a royalty payment of 5–7 percent of the gross box office receipts. If you settle on a 6 percent royalty rate and your theatre grosses $5,000 for the whole run, you will owe the playwright $300 in royalties. The percentage royalty may protect you if your box office is skimpier than you anticipated, because the lower your gross, the lower your royalty.

Royalties are often negotiable, especially in Lesbian theatre. If you feel that the fee quoted to you is unreasonably high (and use the 6 percent equation as a standard), don't be afraid to talk about your budget and the conditions under which you are producing. Playwrights have a heart. But we also have a budget. Play fair and pay fair.

It's a good idea to negotiate royalties as soon as you pick the play. In rare cases, the fees may be so high you can't afford the show, and you need to know this before you get started on production. Also, you will need to figure the royalty into your budget, so the sooner you know it, the better.

The other reason for contacting the author or agent before you begin production is that there may be special clauses in the contract that might affect your production. Most licensing agreements will require the playwright's written permission for any changes to the script or for any videotaping. There may also be clauses about the playwright's billing in publicity and the length of the rehearsal period. Some may have special affirmative-action casting requirements. Remember, you haven't really selected your script until you have signed the licensing agreement that gives you permission to produce the show!

Chapter 12

The Space

Before you do anything else, book your performance space!

Why? Because the performance space will probably be the most expensive item in your budget. Another reason is that your designers will need to know the site in order to design the show. Yet another reason is that you may not be able to find what you need, on the dates you need it, for the price you can afford.

Remember, you will need to lease the space for Tech Week (the week before opening) as well as for the performance nights. If you are inclined to cut corners here, *don't*. Some directors have tried to save money by leasing a theatre three days before the opening. This is a terrible hardship on the actors and puts the technicians under tremendous pressure. The tech period is one long game of Beat the Clock, the actors see all their subtle work go out the window, and the crew develops a take-it-or-leave-it attitude. Your cast has been working for weeks. They deserve working conditions that demonstrate your respect for their efforts.

The producer should count on moving the show into the actual performance space seven days before production, five days at the very least. If this is impossible, find another theatre or cancel or postpone production plans.

The only exception I would make to this rule is for a show that is designed to tour. Touring shows must be simple and portable enough to go into a space—sight unseen—the same day as the performance. The technical requirements are minimal, and the lighting and sound cues must be designed to be run by total strangers who sometimes have only a half hour in the theatre to "tech" the cues with the actors. If you are opening a show that is designed to tour, *theoretically* you won't need a week of rehearsal in the actual space. It has been my experience, however, that a same-day tech for any opening is stressful and that even with a touring show, it's a good idea to book at least one rehearsal in the space before opening.

So, what kind of space to book?

You will need to be able to estimate your audience size. It's better to pack an 80-seat studio theatre than to lease a 350-seat house and have it look empty. On the other hand, Lesbian theatre at this point in history does not attract too many heterosexual women or men. Often, a Lesbian theatre will have a relatively fixed audience base regardless of whether the production is a musical or a one-woman show, whether it runs two weeks or four weeks, whether it receives great reviews or poor ones. In this case, you might do well to rent a larger theatre for a shorter run.

Make accessibility a forethought, not an afterthought. (See Appendix 4 for some assistance in this area.) If a building is not accessible in the first place, don't count on being able to fix that after the fact. Entrances to the building, to the performance space, and to the bathrooms need to be accessible to people using wheelchairs. This means ramps or elevators must be present, and the doorways need to be 34–36 inches wide and unobstructed. Bathrooms and tight corners need a 5-foot turning radius. Talk with the building manager or the person leasing the space to you. And be sure to check out the performance space in person. If you are looking at taking out chairs or unbolting sections of seats, consider that a wheelchair will take up twice the space of an average seat.

Here is a more specific list of criteria from *Note by Note: A Guide to Concert Production* (Takoma Park, MD: Community Music, Inc., 1996):

1. No stairs, inside or out (including to restrooms), unless an alternate path of travel via ramp or elevator is available. Ramps should be sturdy and shallow, not exceeding one inch in height for every 12 inches of length (if space is very tight, certainly no more than one inch in height for every 10 inches in length). Ramps should be 48 inches wide (if space is constrained, no less than 36 inches wide).

    Either short curbs (a couple of inches high) or handrails should be provided on each side of the ramp to ensure no one falls over the side. Handrails are helpful to semi-ambulatory people as well.

2. Seating available to people using wheelchairs which is as integrated as possible; that is, a choice of places for wheelchair users to sit, similar to the range of choices available to non-disabled people. This may mean removing some seats. Many halls are not physically equipped to allow for maximum integration. Other options are: reserve aisle seats for wheelchair users and have them transfer into those seats (their chairs should be kept close by); flat seating at the top or back of the hall; aisle seating that does not block exits. In all situations, non-wheelchair friends should be able to sit next to the wheelchair users, often in moveable or folding chairs. Pathways to all seating areas should be approximately four feet wide (if space is constrained, at least 36 inches wide).

3. Wheelchair-accessible restrooms with doorways at least 32 inches wide (including the doors to restroom stalls), corridors approximately four feet wide (especially if a turn is required), and sturdy grab bars mounted near the toilet. A clear area, five feet in diameter, is ideal and helps maneuverability in restrooms.

4. All other public areas such as food/drink concession areas, literature/record tables, public telephone, drinking fountain, etc., in wheelchair-accessible areas should be configured as described above.

Information about accessibility should be included on all of your promotional materials. (See the chapters on publicity in Part V.) If the building is completely wheelchair accessible, you can use the wheelchair accessibilty graphic alone without a text. If only part of the building is accessible, you will need to inform the publicist of the specifics. Your publicity may need to read, "Performance space is accessible, restrooms are not," or it may need to specify that there are two steps into the hall and that assistance will be provided.

And while we're on the subject of accessibility, take a look at the performance space. If you are going to have the show sign-language interpreted, where will you put the interpreter? Can you light her with the existing instruments, or will you need to bring in extra instruments?

If you are new at producing and confused about the spaces you're looking at, talk to people with experience in this area. Contact the producers of other women's events in your community, but also call around to the local theatre groups. A play is not a k.d. lang concert, and a four-week run of a play with three set changes is not a one-night stand. Before you lease a space, be confident that you have explored all your options.

Get the leasing agreement on paper. Know what it includes, especially in terms of lighting and sound equipment. If there are lights in the space when you look at it, that doesn't necessarily mean they come with it. They may belong to the current leaser, or they may cost extra. Some theatres insist that you also hire their technician to run shows in their space.

And *read the fine print*. This is especially important if you are leasing space in a performing arts complex.

Such complexes are notorious for hidden costs: platform rental, lighting rental, concession table rental. They may offer all of these amenities in a spirit of helpfulness, and it's a shock to find out that what you took to be gestures of courtesy were actually services for which you are going to pay through the nose. And another caveat: If the performance space has its own ticket outlet, be sure you understand how much it will charge for handling your ticket sales and when you can expect to see your money.

Try to sign a lease that requires only a deposit, with the balance to be paid after you open. This will cut down your need for advance capital enormously.

And, finally, a word about image. The space you lease will create the first and strongest impression on your potential audience. Your choice about where to produce makes a statement about your expectations of the show, the audience you are looking to attract, and your investment in the project.

Most Lesbian producers don't have many options about location because of our budgets, but keep in mind that "where" says a lot about "who" and "how." If you have a great deal of faith in the quality of your production or if you expect it to cross over to mainstream audiences, consider taking some risks with leasing a more expensive facility. Mainstream audiences will still travel to obscure storefront performance spaces to discover a jewel of a production, but this rarely happens without a rave review in the mainstream press.

Now that you have your space, how are you going to pay for it?

Chapter 13

The Money

Money. You were wondering when I was going to get around to it.

Well, money in Lesbian theatre isn't really that big of a deal. If you are producing on Broadway, it is. If you are producing at a Shakespeare festival, it is. If you are trying to establish a rep company that does the classics, it is. But with Lesbian theatre, the finances involved can be covered in this chapter.

Why isn't money a big deal? Because Lesbian theatre has what money can't buy. We have something to say that has never been said before, at least not from a public stage. Maybe two hundred years from now, the women's theatre that is doing revivals of Lesbian classics will need tons of money to dress up these old standards, to find gimmicks to make them contemporary. But right now, we don't need the frills. We've already got the goods.

But you will need some money. Not a lot, but some. There is the business of reserving the performance space and renting the rehearsal hall. And then there are sets, costumes, lights, and props. And, of course, publicity. And what about paying the actors and the staff?

Theatres have different policies regarding who gets paid and how. Some theatres pay the director, designers, the stage manager, and the tech director a fixed amount that is decided on in advance, but not the actors or crew. These theatres will either not pay actors or crew at all, pay them a percentage of the profits, or give them the door for an actor's benefit night. Other theatres don't pay anyone anything.

Another option is to use a unit system for distributing money. Every five or ten hours worked is one unit. Everyone who works on a production, including the director, keeps a log of her hours; at the end of the show, each turns in a record of these hours. A percentage of the profits is set aside to pay the workers, and these profits are divided by the total number of units worked. The workers are paid the same amount per unit, with those who worked more units receiving the most money.

This system acknowledges the differing investments of the workers. The actor who has been working on the show for eight weeks should receive more acknowledgment (and the money will always be a token amount anyway) than the lightboard operator who started work the week before opening. On the other hand, this system will certainly penalize the professional, whose years of experience are not taken into account.

Whatever system you decide to go with, never underestimate the symbolic significance of money. Just because the amount is token payment, don't think people will be casual about it. There is a law of inverse proportions in operation with Lesbian theatre: The smaller the monetary stakes, the larger the concern over the politics of distribution. And this is not a mark of pettiness.

Putting on a Lesbian play is a supreme act of self-esteem, and that same self-esteem that allows an actor to get up onstage and say what is patriarchally taboo will also demand to monitor the emblem of esteem in our culture, that is, the money. You bet. And a good Lesbian theatre should encourage this concern—even over token amounts. We Lesbians have been lied to about money all our lives. We have been forced to make choices between work that generates income and work that has relevance to us as Lesbians. Lesbian theatre should be working to heal this split.

But let's get back to the subject of how to get the money in the first place. The first step is to have a budget. There is a sample production budget in Appendix 5. If you have a production staff assembled, it's helpful to get their input. The publicist should be able to give you the figures on typesetting and printing, for example. And the technical director (or scene designer) can provide the cost of building the set. Sometimes the producer knows how much money she has to start with, and she allocates the budget accordingly. The staff must then work with what she gives them. On the other hand, a producer could start with the attitude that she can raise whatever she needs. In that case, she could ask her staff to submit proposed budgets. The producer might want to have two budgets: a best-case budget and a bare-bones budget.

So, now you have your proposed budget. How much of it will you need before you open? You will need the money to reserve the performance space. (Some theatres may even demand total payment as many as sixty days in advance. Ouch!) You will need the money to rent lights, sound equipment, and costumes. You will need the money for set, prop, or costume construction. And you will need the money for your publicity. You should be able to negotiate paying full rental for the space, royalties, and wages after the show has opened.

This book is written for those intrepid Lesbians undertaking a first production. After you have had a successful show, you should be able to salt away some of the profits for the up-front money you will need on your second show. Once you're really up and running, you can begin to sell season tickets in advance, which will also generate advance capital for you. And then, of course, after you have a track record, there is always the possibility of writing some grants.

But let's assume for now that you have no money. You have two options: (1) Borrow the money; (2) get the money donated.

Borrowing money means making a commitment to pay it back. Most people will be leery of loaning money to any new enterprise, but especially to a theatrical one. You might as well ask for a donation, because, frankly, that is how most pople are going to view their "loan."

So how do you go about getting the money? The same way you went about starting the theatre in the first place: looking for the bottom line. What is the bottom line for those you intend to approach?

Are they Lesbian professionals who are closeted, because they feel it is unsafe to be out? Talk to them about the need for increased visibility of Lesbians, about the need for Lesbian art to achieve the same standards of quality as mainstream art. Talk to them about the need for positive role models, the need for opportunities for the public to interface with our culture in traditional and comfortable venues. Talk to them about the need to rent a performance space that will not contribute to our marginalization.

Or maybe their bottom line is their fascination with theatre, their desire to be part of that world. For those of us who are slogging through rewrites, midnight rehearsals, set disasters, and the deadlines of press releases, we can sometimes forget the powerful mystique that surrounds our work. Theatre generates tremendous curiosity and excitement, and this is an angle to use when you approach potential backers. If stardust is their bottom line, consider a special preview night for backers. Do they want their names in the program? A T-shirt? A reception with the actors? The loan of some actors to perform at a soiree?

I recommend approaching individuals, rather than groups, for your start-up capital. You can also host a fund-raiser, but be aware that fund-raising events are a production in themselves, and my personal opinion is that they are a tremendous drain on an organization that is already in the business of producing. And they don't raise that much money. If you really want to hold an event to raise money, a far better use of time is the backers' audition for a carefully selected group of wealthy women. But if you have your heart set on fund-raising, there are plenty of books in the library about how to go about it.

And now a word about bookkeeping. Get someone with experience to set up your books for you. If you have the resources, you might consider using a computer program. In any event, have a system that is clear, detailed, and easy to teach to someone else. Since your publicist and designers are all working within a budget, it's useful to have a system that breaks down your expenses by "set," "publicity," "space rental," "lighting," and so forth. Past budgets are useful guidelines for comparing and for drawing up new budgets.

And have a separate bank account for your theatre, even on a first production. If you are incorporated with the state as a nonprofit organization, you can open a corporate account as long as you have a copy of your filing with the state. If you are being sponsored by another Lesbian organization, ask them how they would like you to set up your bookkeeping.

Even if you are not formally organized, get a separate account! Call yourself a DBA and get the account opened in your name, with the name of the theatre or production printed on the check as well. *Don't* try to operate out of your own checking account. No matter how carefully you keep your records, it's confusing and it leaves you very vulnerable. Also, if you open a DBA account, you will be able to accept checks made out to the theatre. This is a better practice than having to ask that checks be made out to an individual.

It's important to know how to budget money in theatre, but it's equally important to know how to budget your time. So let's look at the schedule now.

Chapter 14

The Schedule

The schedule for a production is very, very important. It is the principal instrument for coordination, and theatre is nothing if not the art of coordination.

The schedule will depend on many things. First and foremost, it depends on the dates for which you have leased the theatre. But it will also depend on the length of your rehearsal period. This varies from director to director. Four weeks is pushing it, but possible—especially for a two-woman show. Eight weeks for rehearsal is long, but justified if you are doing a musical, or if you have actors who have other commitments that preclude a normal rehearsal schedule. A rehearsal schedule of more than eight weeks runs the risk of demoralizing the actors or losing focus. But there are wonderful shows that have been "in progress" for over a year. The most important thing is that the schedule be comfortable for the director and feasible for the resources of the company.

The schedule is set by the director, although the producer, who pays the bills and schedules the theatre and rehearsal space, will probably have input. The schedule should be one of the main subjects of the first production meeting, because it will determine the deadlines for designers, the tech director, the stage manager, and the publicist. Let's take a look at the sample schedule in Appendix 6. Let's assume that today is January 1, a Monday. You have gotten some friends together, selected a play, drawn up a budget, and leased a performance space for the week beginning Sunday, March 17, eleven weeks from today. That's your Tech Week. You plan to open your show on Friday, March 22, and it will run for the next four weekends, Fridays and Saturdays, until April 14, the closing night.

Now, you need to work backward from the opening to set your other dates. Let's say your director wants a six-week rehearsal period, with Tech Week being the sixth week. That means you will need to start rehearsals on Monday, February 12 (six weeks from today). Auditions should be held close to that date.

If the first rehearsal is scheduled for February 12, a Monday, I would recommend that you hold auditions on Saturday, February 3, and Sunday, February 4. This will allow the director a week between casting the show and the first meeting with the cast. Some directors prefer to hold auditions just a day or two before the first meeting, but I find it helpful to allow the director a grace period for a number of reasons.

First, she has time to look around if there is some role she couldn't cast from the actors who showed up for auditions. Sometimes a director must cast an actor she doesn't want to work with, but in my experience, this is almost always a disaster. I prefer to spend a week making phone calls and inquiries about other options before I will cast someone with whom I am not excited about working. I have always been able to fill slots in the cast if I allow myself time.

Second, I like to give the actors a week to shift gears before we begin actual rehearsals. Theatre is a sacred activity, whether you choose to approach it that way or not (more of that later), and the actor/warrior should have some time to herself to consider the sobering responsibility she is undertaking.

Third, the director may need that extra week to draw up the rehearsal schedule, which she should be able to hand out to the actors at the first rehearsal. One of the biggest differences about working with Lesbian actors as opposed to non-Lesbian actors is that we tend to have full, active, well-rounded lives—and we are very adamant about keeping it that way. For the director who is coming from mainstream theatre, where you cast a show, tell the actors when you need them, and then expect them to quit their jobs, cut their classes, or hire a sitter, this difference can be a shock.

Part of creating Lesbian theatre is the need to critique the "business as usual" practices of heteropatriarchal theatres. Casting and scheduling practices in mainstream theatres make the same assumptions that all mainstream institutions do: Women will pick up the slack. If the actor is male, his wife/girlfriend/mother will do his laundry, fix his meals, and take care of the baby. He will probably not have any trouble working full-time and coming in after hours for evening or weekend rehearsals. If the actor is female, it is understood that if she is foolhardy enough to have a child *and* want to work in theatre, it is entirely her problem. Mainstream theatre does not make allowances for the needs of women. If they can't take the heat, they should stay out of the kitchen.

Lesbian theatre is woman-centered, and it is in the interests of the cast, crew, director, producer, and audience to make accommodation of schedules a team effort. I feel passionately about this, because inflexible scheduling is the cutting edge of discrimination against women in many, many areas. The Lesbian who can afford to commit six weeks of her time to a prearranged schedule of evening and weekend hours is going to be very, very rare. And the Lesbian with the tough schedule may be the best performer in your cast.

There is one area where I am inflexible: Tech Week. The rule is "Every actor, every day, for the whole rehearsal." If an actor cannot make time for this one week in the rehearsal schedule, I will reluctantly have to pass her up. Rehearsals during Tech Week that are missing an actor are essentially a waste of everyone's time at this level of production. And an abbreviated Tech Week is very stressful on the performers, if not fatal for the production. If you have scheduling bottom lines, like mine about Tech Week, be sure to tell the actors *at the auditions*.

The best way for the director to know what she's up against is to pass out a form at the auditions that has a grid of days of the week and hours of the day from 9:00 A.M. to 9:00 P.M. Ask the actors to mark an *X* in every block of time for which they are absolutely not available (see Appendix 23). This includes time in school, time in transit, time at work, or time they need to be with their children. Also ask them to write in any day or days between now and opening when they will be away or unable to rehearse. You'd be surprised how many actors will read for a show when they are planning a five-day trip in the middle of the rehearsal period. Get all of this information *before* you cast the show!

These grids with the *X*'s are easy to work with, compared to a written list of hours. I lay them on top of one another and hold them up to the light to see which hours are free for all the actors. Remember, in the first three weeks of rehearsal, you will not need the whole cast the whole time. This is the time of greatest flexibility. You can often find time for two- and three-person scenes.

When you make out your rehearsal schedule for the first meeting with the cast, be sure to detail not only the days of rehearsal, but who you need and which scene you will be doing. (See Appendix 26.) I like to use a calendar grid. I write the act and scene number in the square, the time and location for the rehearsal, and the names of the characters who are called for the rehearsal.

The calendar format is easier to scan than a list, and the actors are less likely to confuse Wednesday with Thursday, because days are not only listed by name, but they are also visually located on the grid. This format also provides an overview of the entire rehearsal process. I include on the calendar the dates when actors must be "off book" (able to rehearse without a script in hand) and "off prompt" (able to rehearse without calling to the assistant director for lines and blocking). The off-book date is usually the beginning of the third or fourth week, and off-prompt, the beginning of the fourth or fifth week. The photo call is also on the calendar, with the characters who will be needed for the shoot. Schedule your photo shoot early enough to allow another if the pictures don't turn out. The photo shoot should be done as early as you can schedule it. The second week of rehearsals is not too early.

The rehearsal schedule is the nexus of the production. Take time with it. As I said, one of the reasons I give myself a week between auditions and first rehearsal is so that I am not up all night trying to work out a schedule in one sitting. The larger the cast, the more difficult the task. With a ten-woman show, expect to have the kitchen table covered with ten personal schedules, while you attempt to draw up the one that will accommodate them all.

And I hate to mention it here, but if you have a musical director and a choreographer on the show, they too will need the actors on certain days, and probably in different locations. Now you have two more factors to multiply into the scheme of things.

Take lots of breaks and keep a sense of humor. If you believe in the Goddess, work with She Who Specializes in Logistics. And if that fails, trust that the schedule will come together simply because it must. That's always worked for me.

And while you're in the mood for thinking ahead, what about tickets?

Chapter 15

The Tickets

Ticket sales, like everything else in Lesbian theatre, is a political issue: What do you charge? Charge what you're worth.

In this country, art is tremendously undervalued. Theatres are not subsidized by the government. Artists rarely can make a living at what we do. Our government's decision not to fund the arts communicates a powerful message to everyone: "Art should pay for itself. It should be a marketable product, like a widget, for which there is a sizeable demand among the general public. And if art cannot survive in the open marketplace, then it deserves to fail." In other words, our government applies a corporate model to the art world. When it does fund the arts, as through the National Endowment for the Arts (NEA), it applies an abusive and controlling approach. The NEA treats artists as if we were deadbeat daughters asking Daddy for a handout, who then throw tantrums when he isn't willing to underwrite our "immoral" lifestyles. According to the government, the real grown-up artist understands that the bottom line for art should be an ever-increasing profit margin.

This model is obscene. It enforces conformity with the goals of patriarchy and privileges the electronic media, which can actually mass-produce its product as if it were a widget and distribute it internationally. The live performing arts cannot hope to compete financially. Our product exists for a brief period of time for the lucky few who happen to be in the right place at the right time to catch the show. The magic of the evening is the result of a collaborative effort between audience and performers, a phenomenon that does not occur with electronic media—with the possible exception of *The Rocky Horror Picture Show*.

So we have two major prejudices to overcome with live theatre: (1) the belief that ticket prices should be competitive with film prices or—Goddess forbid—video rental prices; and (2) the belief that, without subsidy, live theatre should be able to produce high-quality work, pay everyone at least minimum wage for their time, and cover production expenses solely through box office receipts.

These prejudices are stubbornly entrenched in the popular and even the unpopular mind, and they need to be actively and repeatedly challenged. It is imperative for your theatre's survival that you root out the myth that theatre should follow a corporate or even a small-business model.

It is very, very rare for live theatre to meet its expenses with box-office intake alone. When it does, the theatre is usually in a donated space, the actors aren't paid, or the run is unsatisfyingly short. Most theatres with any kind of longevity (more than two years), get 50–70 percent of their operating expenses from donations—either from private donations, corporate grants, or funding from agencies or foundations. Let me rephrase that: A successful theatre raises half its operating expenses from sources other than box office. Or, a dynamic and expanding theatre must have a clear understanding that fund-raising needs to be a major activity of the company.

Relying on fund-raising goes against the grain of capitalist philosophies. It also goes against the myth of the self-made businessperson. Worst of all, it goes against the natural inclination of most Lesbians, which is not to ask for help, to do it all ourselves, and then to feel terribly betrayed when we collapse from the effort. Very noble, very romantic, and very counterproductive.

It's important for us Lesbians to work with this idea of subsidy until it begins to feel comfortable and natural. Art has always required patrons, because art is about art. "Cost-effectiveness" is meaningless to the artist. Everyone in this country needs to be more educated about the value of art and its place in the human economy. Lesbians need to be educated about what it will take to have theatres with reputations for quality. And, of course, we need to understand why it is imperative that we have these theatres.

But weren't we talking about ticket prices? Well, yes. And now that we all understand that we can't build a dynamic and thriving theatre on box office alone, let's talk about those tickets.

As I said, charge what you're worth. Resist comparisons to movies. Don't make the mistake of believing that you can woo a theatre audience with cheap prices. A theatre audience is wooed by a great show, period.

So, what are you worth? Certainly you should be worth what the comparably sized mainstream theatres in your community charge. I would use that as a standard.

But what about a sliding scale? Sliding-scale fees are a time-honored tradition for Lesbian events. I am going to tell a sad truth here: The sliding scale doesn't work the way it's supposed to. File this fact under "Lesbian Family Secrets." Even if you look out over an audience and recognize half of them to be physicians and attorneys, don't be surprised when your take for the evening averages out to a few cents above the bottom of the sliding scale. Now, maybe the $100-per-hour attorney is paying off the Porsche and the mortgage, and she is confusing her cash flow problems with limited income, who knows? But all I can say is that I have seen this in my own theatre, and I have heard of it over and over again from Lesbian producers and conference organizers all over the country. I would advise that you gear the bottom of your sliding scale to meet the minimum amount you feel you need to gross from the production. Protect yourself from being hurt by the women who abuse the system.

Also, understand that the sliding scale is a headache in terms of accountability with your ticket outlets. Normally, they return the unsold tickets and hand you the money for the balance of those they sold. Simple arithmetic for both of you to verify. But with a sliding scale, the outlet must hassle with the bookkeeping nightmare that results from every customer setting the price of her ticket.

An alternative to the sliding scale might be to offer ushering or concession positions to Lesbians who would like to attend, but who can't pay. Many women feel that work-exchange is punitive and patriarchal, but from my own observations of the sliding-scale abuse, I guess I have become somewhat jaundiced about these arguments. Especially since nobody is going on Olivia cruises with what they make in Lesbian theatre.

My caveat about sliding-scale fees does *not* apply to discounts for seniors or people with disabilities. These are both instances where discount prices are appropriate and where the policy is not abused. Some theatres offer student discounts. My thought about this is that many students have more discretionary income than nonstudents and that student discounts are only valid if a business is specifically interested in attracting that population through special incentives.

Often theatres will offer other kinds of discounts. These include discounts for Thursday night or Sunday matinee performances, discounts for members of special organizations, special two-for-one coupon ads run in publications for targeted audiences, and block-seat discounts or theatre nights.

Discounting your less popular performances (Thursday, Sunday) is a fine idea, but it might be even finer to consider eliminating those altogether, especially if the space rental is high. Discounts for members of organizations or coupon ads can be an effective way to bring in new audience members, but be sure you're not preaching (or discounting) to the already converted.

Offering discounts for block sales is an interesting practice whereby a party of theatregoers can get cheap seats as long as they pay in advance for a whole block of seats, usually a minimum of eight. The discount can range from $1 to 50 percent off, and the minimum can be anywhere from six to twenty seats. This gives potential members of your audience an incentive to recruit other members; in other words, they are motivated to do some aggressive publicity for you. Because of people's theatre habits and Lesbians' tendency to avoid herds, you will probably not have too many takers, but you might want to try the policy out and see what happens.

Sometimes theatres will try to sell entire performances to organizations. This is called a "theatre night," and it can benefit both parties. Here's how it works: Let's say the theatre seats one hundred people, but the productions do not usually attract more than fifty people per night. So it sells a theatre night to the battered women's shelter for a flat rate of $500. The battered women's shelter does its own publicity among its supporters for the theatre night fund-raiser. The shelter sells the tickets for $15 each, instead of the theatre's usual $10, and it attracts seventy-five people from its mailing list. The gross is $1125, and the net is $625. The only work the shelter had to do was a special mailing (the theatre supplied the graphics), and the theatre sold what was the equivalent of a full house. In addition, many women who would not have seen the show attended in support of the shelter. They may become regular patrons in the future. The only thing to worry about with selling performances is to do it way in advance, in time to be able to include the benefit information in your publicity.

So what about complimentary tickets, or "comps," as they're called? Policies vary from community to community, but I have a strong personal bias in this area. I feel that any theatre company that is counting on making ends meet by being stingy with comps is a theatre company already in trouble. This is not to say that comps should be promiscuously distributed to anyone who asks for them—and even those who don't. (This is called "papering the house," and occasionally theatres will indulge in this activity as a last-ditch effort to create the illusion that the show is popular or to impress the critics with a full house. I have never seen it work.)

What I am talking about is being penny-wise and pound-foolish. Comping is good business. Comping can generate goodwill for the theatre, can allow women who might never have bought a ticket for themselves to see the show, and can give women the opportunity to feel that they are part of something very exciting that is happening in their community. Allowing women to identify with what you're doing is money in the bank in the long run. Use comp tickets to show gratitude, and include anyone who has donated *any amount* of goods or services to the theatre, even someone who only loaned a teacup or put in fifteen minutes of work at a mailing party.

It's traditional for the members of the cast and crew to receive a certain number of comp tickets in acknowledgment of their participation. Often, in community theatre, this is the only material form of remuneration they will receive for all their weeks of hard work. I feel strongly that this is the wrong area in which to cut corners. If you need the cast's comps to break even, your community can't afford the production.

If money is really tight, go ahead and give the cast and crew their two comps, and then explain the situation. Encourage them to share their comps with women who would normally not attend. If their close friends and family members can afford to buy tickets, suggest that the cast and crew solicit their understanding of the situation. It's a patriarchal model to assume that the actors are some kind of underlings who can be expected to tighten their belts to take up the financial slack—something along the lines of Reagan cutting the school lunch budget to balance the federal deficit. The actors carry the show, and they have as much of a stake in the success of the theatre as anyone. It's an insult to act as if they don't. Can you tell I feel strongly about this?

Comps can be handled a number of ways. The comp tickets themselves can be handed out in advance, in which case there is no need to hold them at the box office. These tickets should be marked on both ends with a *C*, so that the stubs will not be inventoried as paid tickets. When the "hard tickets" are handed out, it's the actors' responsibility to get them to the appropriate parties, and if the tickets are lost, too bad.

Another way of handling comps is to keep a list at the box office with the names of all cast and crew members. When their guests go to pick up the tickets, the box office attendant puts a check by the name. This is less hassle for the actors.

In addition to those for cast and crew, there should be comps for newspaper reviewers, who should have been invited by the publicist, as well as for those folks who loaned props, donated services, or gave the theatre money.

So . . . enough about free lunches. On to sales.

Making tickets available in advance helps with sales. First, it gives credibility to the production; and second, it allows your potential audience to make plans in advance. They know that they will get seating. Otherwise, they have to plan to get to the theatre close to when the box office opens (usually a half hour early), and this is a hassle. Some theatres will take reservations by phone, allowing the patron to pay for the ticket at the door. This is a courtesy to the patrons, but can be a headache for the producer. Frequently those who made reservations are no-shows, especially when they constituted a large party. My own feeling is that if they want us to hold the seats, they can buy the tickets. And until you can afford your own box office and credit-card account, this means using an outlet.

Most communities have a women's bookstore or coffeehouse that handles tickets for women's events. If you have booked into a performing arts center, the center frequently handles ticket sales in advance also. Sometimes these outlets will charge the producer a handling fee, or sometimes they will charge the customer at the time of purchase. This is a fair practice, because they are taking time out from their regular business to make money for the theatre, and they also have to do some extra bookkeeping. They should get something for their trouble.

If you are using an outlet, have a clear and preferably written agreement with the outlet in advance. This agreement should specify the price for the tickets, who pays the surcharge if there is one (customer or theatre), and how many tickets the seller has received. (The tickets should be in a numbered block.) The seller needs to tell the theatre if she will be running the money through her books, which means she will take checks and charges made out to her business, not to the theatre. It also means she will be liable for covering bad checks. If she is not running it through her books, you need to tell her how you want the checks made out. In the case of a discrepancy between amount collected and the number of unsold tickets, the seller will be responsible for making up the difference.

Accountability can break down at small ticket outlets where the sales staff has not been trained consistently about the procedures for handling your ticket sales. It may be that six different sales clerks have taken checks made out to the bookstore, to the theatre, or to you personally. It may also be that they have stashed ticket sale money in various envelopes and in various drawers, or dumped it into the register without recording it. The salesclerk who was never informed about the procedure will not be accountable. Be sure that your contact person at the outlet understands that you are holding her personally accountable for your agreement with the store.

Written contracts are impressive and incontestable. The woman who nods her head amiably, "Yes, yes, no problem," may take considerably longer reading a contract that says exactly the same thing. There is something very sobering about signing one's name to an agreement about money. Appendix 7 contains a sample ticket contract, taken from *Note by Note: A Guide to Concert Production*. (By the way, this book is an excellent resource for grassroots and first-time concert producers in the women's community. It was orginally published by Redwood Cultural Work, with contributions by a number of Lesbian musicians and organizers, with the particular needs of our community in mind.)

As I mentioned in Chapter 12, some rental halls operate their own outlets, especially the larger complexes. These halls should have their own contracts about carrying your tickets, and if they do, *read the fine print*. These halls may charge the customer as much as $2 for a handling charge *and* charge the theatre a percentage of the gross on top of that! Is it really worth it to let them handle your sales, especially when the alternative is a women's bookstore? And if you are going with the hall's outlet, find out when you can get your money. If you need your gross the day after closing, it's a shock to find out that it will be a month or more before the hall can get around to closing the books.

Be sure to list all your ticket outlets on your posters and flyers. Include the information in your press releases and calendar spots, including addresses, if possible.

When you sell tickets in advance, these tickets should be numbered for the sake of inventory, and they should list price, date, time, location, play title and author(s), and seat number, if you are selling reserved seats (see Appendix 8). Print shops carry ticket stock, and they can advise you on your layout. If you are leasing a 500-seat house, you probably won't need to print up 500 tickets in advance for each night of the run. On the other hand, if you are leasing an 80-seat house, there is a chance you might sell out. In that case, you may want to print 80 tickets per night. In any event, *never* print more tickets than your house will hold for a given night.

As for selling tickets yourself, you probably will not have the resources to do this until a half hour before curtain on the days of the performances. (See Chapter 19.)

If the theatre is using outlets, it's a good idea to call or drop by on the day of a performance to find out how many tickets have been sold for that night. This will give you some idea about the size of the audience you can expect. It may be possible that two hundred women will rush you at the door, when you have had little or no advance ticket sales. Possible, but not probable.

When should you put the advance tickets on sale? As soon as any of your publicity goes out. But that's another section of the book. Let's take a look at your staff.

Part IV

The Folks behind the Scenes

Chapter 16

The Designers

So far, you have a director and a producer. Hopefully, the auditions will bring forth the actors. Now you need to consider lining up the rest of the staff.

The first order of business is the designers. You may be lucky enough to know professional scene, costume, lighting, and sound designers who are Lesbian and who are dying to donate their time to your production. Then again, you may not.

Lesbians with carpentry skills, Lesbians who dress with a flair for the dramatic, Lesbians who love VCRs, computers, and other electronic gadgetry often turn up with brilliantly creative ideas for sets, costumes, and tech. Ask around. Just because a Lesbian has never done something before is no reason not to try it now. After all, how did she get to be Lesbian in the first place?

So . . . the designers. Who are they and what do they do?

The Scene Designer

The scene designer plans the stage set or sets for the play. She has to keep several things in mind.

First and foremost, she must know the space where the play will be performed. She needs to know the stage dimensions, which include the amount of space in the wings (if any), and the amount of storage space (if any). She needs to know the sight lines of the theatre, which means she needs to know if the person sitting down front on the far left side is going to be able to see all the actors changing costumes in the wings off to the right. Sometimes, it's not possible—or worthwhile—to mask the stage for those end seats, but it's better to know that up front and to be able to advise your ushers than to discover it on opening night.

The scene designer needs to know if the theatre has a curtain, if it actually works, and if the director plans to use it. She needs to know what kind of stockpile the theatre has in terms of flats, platforms, doors, stair units, rugs, curtains, furniture, and so on, if any. And she needs to have a general idea of the kinds of tools to which she and her crew will have access. What's the point of designing something that requires fancy lathe work, if nobody can get their hands on a lathe?

She needs to know if the show is supposed to tour, and she needs to know if the play is going to be produced in a space that needs to be shared with other events. In other words, does the set need to come down every night or every weekend of the run? And if it does, what will be the storage facilities? If the show tours, does the set need to fit into a station wagon, a van, or a one-ton pickup?

The scene designer should know the amount of her budget, and she should plan to bring the set in under this amount, because there are always unexpected surprises.

The technical director will be the Lesbian who actually builds the set. Sometimes this is the same woman as the scene designer. In this case, she will need to keep a record of her expenses, as well as hold on to her receipts. The scene designer/tech director should keep current with the state of her budget and be able to report on it at production meetings.

If the tech director is a different person from the scene designer, she will be responsible for keeping her costs within the budget for the set. The scene designer will need to work closely with the tech director, so that she does design a set that is feasible for the tech director's budget and resources.

Finally, and most importantly, the scene designer should know the script thoroughly and how the director intends to interpret it. She should have read it at least twice, better still, three times. It's not enough to design a gorgeous bedroom if that set will entail two lovers climbing in through the window, one player running out on the balcony, six hiding in the closet, and one crawling under the bed, which folds up into the wall. The set must accommodate the action as indicated in the script *and* as the director plans to block it.

The scene designer needs to submit floor plans and elevations (front views) to the director *before* the rehearsals begin. And she needs to have the director's approval before she begins ordering materials or constructing anything.

A word on Lesbian collaboration: Obviously, we don't like being told what to do, or we would all be heterosexuals. And, probably, with Lesbian theatre, most of us are working without pay. There's a strong temptation for Lesbians in situations like this to feel that whatever we do should be appreciated—as indeed it should. On the other hand, there's more to it than gratitude. Just because the director is grateful for the designer's help does not mean that she will find it any easier to work on a set that completely impedes the flow of traffic. Just because the designer is grateful for the director's commitment to Lesbian culture doesn't mean she will be able to design a a kitchen, complete with cabinets, appliances, and running water, within a budget of $50. Technically, the director has the last word, because she is in charge of what is onstage, but it's far more productive to work toward mutual agreement, mutual compromise.

The Costume Designer

The costume designer is responsible for the costumes.

Her job is similar to the scene designer's, in that she must also know the space for the performance (an audience for a 50-seat house reads detail much differently than an audience in a 500-seat auditorium), and she must have an idea of what the backstage space is like. If the action in the play requires quick changes, these will have to be performed in the wings, or behind flats, and the costume designer needs to consider the size and accessibility of these spaces (will the actor also need a dresser?) when she considers the costumes for these changes.

And, of course, the costume designer needs to have read the script three times: once for the gist, once for the job, and once for the juice. A costume plot is a graph, with a list of all the actors down the side and columns across the top for all the different scenes (see Appendix 9). The squares of the graph are filled in with the costume worn by each actor for each scene. The costume plot allows the designer to see at a glance all the costumes required for a specific actor, as well as what every character is wearing in a specific scene. This will allow her to coordinate color schemes and develop a certain consistency of style for each character.

The costume designer needs to consult with the director early on, and she needs to know her budget.

If several Lesbians volunteer to help the costume designer, great. If not, she should feel free to ask for assistance. In small productions, the costume designer may discuss her ideas with the cast, and often they are able to provide many of the costumes themselves, especially if the show is about contemporary Lesbians.

The costume designer, even if she is counting on renting or borrowing costumes, should still meet with the director to discuss her concept for the show and to get approval for her ideas. As with the set design, the director also has veto power over the costumes. Again, mutual respect is the key. If the costume designer has been unable to locate a free tuxedo in the right size for one of the actors and has thus had to modify a suit from a thrift store, it would be important for the director to understand the amount of effort and labor that went into this costume before she laughs it off the stage. Likewise, when the director insists on authentic period costumes, she needs to give the costume designer a budget that takes into consideration the high cost of rentals.

Costume rental is not a bad way to go, if you use your ingenuity. The commercial costume rental businesses should be the last resort. These places often charge by the night, and they are very expensive. Try the community college or the high school. Sometimes these institutions have an official policy of "no rentals," but often, if you know the right people, you can work something out. And try the other theatre companies. Whenever you get a "no," always ask, "Do you have any idea of other places I could try?"

If costuming for a period show is too expensive or impractical for other reasons, the designer might consider putting the actors in simple contemporary clothing as part of a design concept for the show.

It's a good idea for the costume designer to show up for the first rehearsal, to size up the cast, literally, and get measurements. These include waist, bust, hip, inseam, torso, neck, sleeve, and wrist measurements; waist-to-ankle length, and hat size, if hats are in the show. This might be the time to find out if the actor has clothing that might be appropriate for the character.

Traditionally, it is the costume designer's responsibility to have all costumes at the theatre, clean and pressed, in time for dress rehearsal. It's a better practice to have the costumes at the theatre for the beginning of Tech Week, especially if the costumes will restrict or otherwise affect mobility (long skirts, high heels, wigs, etc.). Actors need more than one rehearsal to feel at home in their costumes. The costumes should be on hangers and marked with the name of the character. It is the actors' responsibility to return the costumes to the hangers at the end of each rehearsal or performance and to notify the wardrobe manager or the designer if there is a rip, stain, or missing part to the costume.

The costume designer is responsible for keeping records and receipts. Like the tech director, she should maintain a running total of expenses, so that she can report on the state of her budget at production meetings. After the show, the costume designer will be responsible for returning everything in the condition in which it was borrowed. She should count on attending the last performance and personally checking off the inventory before the actors leave. Costumes have a way of straying after closing, so it's a good idea to get them before they walk off.

And, finally, a caution about costuming: Clothing is an emotional issue for most people, because clothing is a mark of class and status. Costumers need to be sensitive to what clothing symbolizes for the actors. In patriarchy, clothing carries a special charge for Lesbians. A costume designer for a Lesbian production needs to be sensitive to issues of identity and vulnerability, and she needs to be flexible.

Not all actors' objections to costumes are valid, however. Sometimes an actor wants her character's appearance to conform to standards that are not appropriate for the character she is playing or that are inconsistent with the period or style of the play. It's a tough call for the designer to determine which objections are valid and which are not. But an actor who hates her costume can be a dangerous animal, and it would be my suggestion to find some measure of compromise that won't violate the production values or raise cries of "special treatment" from the other members of the cast.

The Lighting Designer

The lighting designer is the person responsible for planning the lights for the show. This may be the scene designer, but it may be someone else. In smaller operations, the lighting designer may also double as the lightboard operator, running the lights during actual performance.

The lighting designer should have her own budget, just as the scene and costume designers have separate budgets. She should keep records, save receipts, and be able to report on the status of her budget at production meetings.

The lighting designer draws a light plot, which shows the setting and position of all the lights in the production (see Appendix 10). If you have rented a traditional theatre space, it probably comes with lighting instruments that hang from pipes running the width of the theatre. If this is the case, be sure you have permission to move the lights, and if you do, find out if you need to return them to the original positions at the end of the show.

If you rent a space that comes with a small supply of lights, think before you move them! Often they have been placed where they are for a good reason. There are not too many ways to light a stage when you have only a handful of instruments. Before you wear out yourself or your crew with climbing up and down ladders, consider making life easier and using them where they are. Then you will just have to focus and gel for the show.

If you have rented a nontraditional space, you may have to rent lights that will be on "trees." The use of trees narrows the options for positioning, but someone will still need to decide about gels, light levels, and angles.

And check the specs in the performance space! What does this mean? It means find out how much juice you can run off the outlets before you shell out the money for equipment that's going to blow the circuits! The building manager should have this information. And as a last resort, phone around to other theatre companies that have used the space and ask them what kind of lights they used. There is nothing worse than a blackout in the middle of a production, while the technical crew frantically goes off in search of the fuse box. And a warning about electrical circuits: If you have overloaded them, they may blow the second you throw the switch, but they might also wait until you are halfway through the first act before they short out. Just because all the lights are up is no guarantee that you are not overloading the circuit.

The lighting designer needs to be as familiar with the script as are the costume and scene designers. Obviously, she will need to collaborate with the director and the other designers. She needs to know which instruments are available to the theatre and what is affordable for rental. (Again, theatrical lighting businesses are usually the most expensive way to go. See if you can rent or borrow from other theatres. If there is someone in town who produces a lot of events, she may have her own supply of lights. Ask around.) The lighting designer also needs to know how much time the crew will have to hang and focus the lights during Tech Week.

Lighting designers have their own styles and preferences, as do all designers. The director needs to bear in mind that designing lights is an art, but the lighting designer needs to bear in mind that the most artistic effect in the world will not serve the play if it doesn't light the actors' faces. The motivational lighting of the late-afternoon sun slanting through the leaf gobos may be absolutely authentic, but if the angle is such that half the actors are in shadow and the leaf gobo creates a strobe effect as the actors move in and out of the light, better to trust the action and the dialogue to establish the environment. Ditto for moonlight trysting. Nothing is more unromantic than the indistinguishable features of an actor during a peak emotional moment.

Some of the greatest plays in men's culture came from the ancient Greek theatre and from Shakespeare's theatre—both of which produced their plays outside in broad daylight. When in doubt, light the actors!

The lighting designer also draws up the cue sheet that contains the setup of lights at the beginning of each act, the light changes, the warning cues for light changes, and the cues for the light changes.

The lighting designer should be present to check the lighting effects in Tech Week and at dress rehearsal. Either she or the technical director is responsible for the return of rented or borrowed equipment. Because of this, she may want to be present to train the light-board operators and set a few rules, such as "No Drinks in the Light Booth."

The Sound Designer

The sound designer is responsible for designing the sound effects and/or incidental music for the show. She may also double as the sound technician, running the sound during performances.

The sound designer should know the play. She works with the director to design a sound appropriate for the production. If the show has preshow music or music between the set changes, it should be consistent with the style of the show. Harpsichord music, for instance, might be out of place in a show about a Lesbian softball league.

The sound designer should be familiar with the resources for music and sound effects. Most colleges and universities have the BBC series of sound effects either in their libraries, their theatre departments, or their media centers. These include every conceivable effect from toilets flushing to World War I air raid sirens.

If the show is a musical that is using prerecorded music for the numbers, the sound designer will need to work closely with the musical director and the sound technician.

The sound designer draws up a cue sheet, with the warning cues and then the sound cues. She also attends tech rehearsals to see that the equipment is running and that the effects work for the show. If she does not run the sound for performances, she should train the sound technician who will. And she sees that everything is returned in good condition.

If the sound designer is also in charge of equipment, she will need to know what is available to the theatre and scout out the best deals for renting or borrowing. If she borrows or rents equipment, she will be in charge of returning it.

Chapter 17

The Assistant Director and the Stage Manager

The assistant director and the stage manager are key people on your production team. In small theatres, the same woman may take on both jobs, because the assistant director's main task is to cover the first weeks of rehearsal, and the stage manager's job doesn't begin until Tech Week, the last week before opening.

The Assistant Director

The assistant director (AD) assists the director and should be present at all rehearsals.

The AD takes blocking notes (notes on the actors' movements) in the prompt book, "holds book" at rehearsals (tells the actors when they forget lines or blocking), and runs general errands. If an actor is missing or late, the AD might be asked to fill in the lines, or even walk the blocking for the missing actor. The AD may be asked to tape the rehearsal floor and set up (and put away) the rehearsal furniture and props. She nags the actors to clean up after themselves, because if they don't, she gets stuck cleaning up after them. She sometimes acts as a gofer, running out for coffee or pizza during rehearsals. After the rehearsals, the AD should be the last to leave, checking that everyone is gone, that the lights are out, the heat or air conditioning is off, and the doors are locked. (During Tech Week in the theatre space, the stage manager is responsible for closing up.)

One of the most important aspects of the AD's job is the moral support she can provide during the early weeks of the rehearsal process. It is unethical for the director to discuss her doubts or problems with the cast when the issues concern other actors, and she will risk looking incompetent if she takes these daily troubles to the producer. This leaves the director with no one to talk to except her friends outside the production, and they can't really offer satisfying feedback, because they are not witness to the process and they probably don't understand the psychological complexity that goes into mounting a play.

So where can the director go for support when she needs to talk about how annoying it is when Louise keeps lapsing into that phony accent or when Melissa seems more interested in flirting than acting? The AD is the ideal person. She is involved in the show, but because she is not a direct participant, her job is not compromised by the director's confidences. Her function is to assist the director. She can serve as a sounding board for the director's ideas, she can be the sympathetic ear when the director needs to let off steam, and she can offer feedback and suggestions from an unofficial, but informed perspective. The AD's feedback at auditions can be invaluable.

The job of the assistant director is frequently tedious and thankless, requiring a high degree of responsibility (attendance at all rehearsals), almost no authority, and even less creativity—at least, officially. But as right-hand woman for the director, and even confidante, the job can offer an excellent vantage point for learning the business of directing. Describe the assistant directorship as an apprenticeship for directing, and you might be surprised how many Lesbians put in for the job!

The Stage Manager

The SM (stage manager, not sadomasochist!) is not a director, but she takes over the running of the show during Tech Week. Once the show has opened, the director should not even need to appear at the theatre.

The stage manager is the person responsible for everything—except the individual performances of the actors—that takes place onstage or backstage during Tech Week and during the performances. She is responsible for the *smooth* running of the production. She supervises the entire tech crew for the performance, as well as the house manager. Although she does not give artistic input to the actors, she is in charge of their logistics during performances. A good SM is responsible, cool, considerate, organized, efficient, punctual, and dependable. She thinks ahead and has a good sense of humor. Sounds like one of those unrealistic personal ads in the Lesbian paper, doesn't it? "Director seeks desirable stage manager . . . must be responsible . . ."

Actually, many Lesbians can meet these criteria, *if* (big "if") they are given the right conditions. If you want a good SM, be sure that she has an adequate and competent crew for running the show, that she has access to the theatre in plenty of time to move the set in and to train her crew, that she is given authority over her crew (the director should channel all technical notes through the stage manager), that she has access to the director, and that the director provides her with adequate rehearsal time for cleaning up technical problems. These rehearsals may include dry techs (rehearsals without the actors), cue-to-cues (rehearsals with the actors that skip from one light or sound cue to the next), and rehearsals that can be interrupted to make technical adjustments.

It's a good idea to have an assistant stage manager (ASM). Her job will be to perform whatever tasks the SM delegates to her. Often the SM and the ASM work as a production team.

Okay, let's look at exactly what the stage manager does. After the producer and director, she is the Third Most Valuable Player. It is her responsibility to see that all needed personnel are at scheduled production meetings. If someone is missing, the SM takes notes at the meeting and sees that the absent party gets them.

The SM should have complete lists of props, furniture, and costumes for the show. These lists may have been compiled by the prop manager, the scene designer (or tech director), or the costume designer. If you don't have personnel for all these positions, the responsibility will fall to the SM. Some one person must have all the lists, and that person is the SM. (The director should also have lists, but since the SM is the one who will be overseeing the storage, placement, use, and return of all materials, it is most important that her lists be kept current. The director is concerned with them only as far as approving design and directing how they are used in the course of the play.)

The stage manager has all the schedules, too. This includes the schedule of production meetings as well as the schedule for rehearsals and performances. She has current phone numbers and addresses for *everyone* involved in the production.

The SM meets with the director. It would be a good idea for the two of them to meet separately before the first scheduled production meeting, just to get clear about their expectations and responsibilities. The SM should also have a good working relationship with the technical director, who will be constructing the set and who will probably be involved with loading it in during Tech Week.

The SM needs to be at rehearsals during Tech Week at least thirty minutes before starting time. She needs to make sure that the stage is set up and that the lights and sound have been checked. The SM lets the director know when the actors are ready and the stage is set. She should always try to start on time. If an actor is late, the SM calls her. If there is a problem (car trouble, etc.), she is the one who is responsible for dealing with the problem.

During Tech Week and after performances, the SM is the last to leave. She checks the lights, makes sure everyone is out of the theatre, and locks up.

It is the SM's responsibility to make sure that the designers see the run-throughs as soon as possible. The crew needs to sit in on at least one run-through before the cue-to-cue. And the house manager should see one of the last tech rehearsals, so that she will know what to expect in terms of late seating and be able to anticipate the intermissions.

The stage manager runs the tech rehearsals. She calls the cues for lights, sound, and curtains (if there is one). She checks the stage before rehearsal, making sure that it is completely set a half hour before curtain. She calls "half hour," "ten minutes," and "places" (two minutes before curtain) to the actors before the show. It is her responsibility to check whether the actors are ready before bringing up the lights or curtain. She calls "five minutes" and "places" during intermission. She cues the house manager to blink the lights to signal the start of the show or the end of intermission. She makes the decision about "holding the house," that is, starting the play late. (It's a poor idea to hold the house more than five minutes unless there are unusual circumstances. If you habitually hold the house ten or fifteen minutes for latecomers, don't be surprised when your audiences become increasingly casual about showing up on time. On the other hand, keeping latecomers in the lobby until the first scene break tends to enhance their appreciation for your curtain time. Why should the innocent have to pay for the crimes of the guilty?) The SM also gives the calls for the next rehearsals or performances and informs the cast where and when notes will be given by the director.

The stage manager sees that all the technical mistakes are corrected by opening. She takes tech notes from the director, and she checks with each department head (costume, props, lighting, tech director) to see if she knows what has to be done and that she has sufficient help and equipment to accomplish it. She takes note of any damage that occurs to props, costumes, set, and so forth, during rehearsals or performances.

The SM organizes the strike (the dismantling of the production), which is traditionally held the night of the closing performance. It will be her job to assign chores and to make decisions about stripping the set (taking hinges off, removing windows, etc.). She will see that everything is stored or discarded, and she will send the workers home as their tasks are completed.

And all of this is the SM's responsibility. The secret of her survival? Delegate! Be sure that your stage manager is someone who can break a job down into specific tasks, can delegate authority, and can do follow-up with the people to whom she has delegated.

And, finally, a word about the psychology of stage managing: The SM comes in as a key player at a very critical point in the production. Until Tech Week, the actors have been working in seclusion with the director and the assistant director. Suddenly, during Tech Week, they move to the stage with unfamiliar furniture, props, and costumes and a number of folks who have not seen them work before: the set crew, the running crew, the light and sound technicians—and the stage manager. At this time, the director begins to let go of the production and turn it over to the SM. The reality of performance hits home: "We are really going to do this! People are going to come and pay money and sit there and watch us!" This period of transition can be pretty traumatic for the actors, and a stage manager who inspires confidence is an invaluable asset. She also has the tremendous advantage of being a fresh face and new blood.

The Tech Week period is a microcosm of adolescence: The actors are growing up in the parts. They are becoming responsible for themselves. The director, whose attention must now be divided with technical considerations, begins to wean them off her approval. This process, after the intimacy of the rehearsal room where the actors were the center of attention, can feel like rejection, or even abandonment. Actors, like teenagers, will act out. Sometimes they become excessively needy, seeking extra approval. Sometimes they become rebellious. Stage business that was never a problem before, is suddenly violating their characters. Costumes are suddenly cramping their style. Technicians may be accused of deliberate sabotage. And frequently, the director is the target.

A good SM understands actors—and especially actors experiencing their Tech Week growing pains. A good stage manager keeps the focus on the production, not on personalities. Her perspective and her professionalism can go a long way in putting out the Tech Week brush fires. Pick your stage manager as much for her people skills as for her technical ones. If you're thinking about a Lesbian who has a history of taking sides in conflicts, who gets her feelings hurt easily, who wants to be liked so much she can't be assertive, who has a short fuse, or who is a perfectionist, *keep looking!* Pick the most functional adult you know.

And a word of warning to Lesbian theatres operating on a shoestring: There is a temptation to cut staffing corners by letting the director perform the function of the SM. Bad, bad idea.

Chapter 18

The Techies

"Techies" is an affectionate term for those people who work on the technical aspects of the production: building and moving the set, running the lights and sound, keeping track of the props, and the like. How many techies does it take to put up a Lesbian play? It depends.

Bear in mind that the following list of positions applies to a best-case scenario. You may not be able to fill all these positions, some of them may be filled by actors or Lesbians who are already serving in another capacity, or you may choose not to fill some of them at all. Not to worry. The show will go on. But for now, let's assume that you have found Lesbians for every conceivable position on the tech crew. Your lineup will therefore include the following roles.

The Technical Director

If anyone reading this book is a technical director for a commercial theatre, she is no doubt wondering about her billing here. The tech director is the woman who is in charge of all the technical aspects of a theatre company. She is a permanent member of the staff (doesn't change for every production), and if anyone is on salary, it's going to be the tech director. If you look at the flowchart in Appendix 11, you can see that the tech director is accountable to the producer, not to the director.

The tech director, who is the woman actually in charge of executing the sets, is a tremendously important member of the team; but in Lesbian theatre, it is unlikely that she will occupy the key position that she does in commercial theatres. Tech directors are likely to change with each production, and since few Lesbian theatres can afford the rent for year-round leases (much less payments to buy the building), she will not be in charge of the performance space.

Anyway, the technical director is in charge of executing the set according to the specifications of the scene designer. This entails several different areas of responsibility.

In Lesbian theatre, the scene designer and the tech director are often one and the same woman. If this is not the case, it's very important that the tech director and designer be able to communicate their needs clearly and honestly. If the design is too ambitious for the space, for the budget, for the time line, or for the resources of the tech director, it's important that she make this known at the outset, in time for modification of the design. Better a simple, low-budget design that is fully executed by opening night than pieces of a more elaborate set that are never quite put together because the budget ran out.

The tech director is in charge of the shop and equipment. In Lesbian theatre, the shop will probably be someone's backyard or garage. The tech director will be responsible for scheduling the work parties and for collecting whatever equipment and supplies will be needed to build the set. She will need to assign jobs to the crew, and this means she has to know the skill levels of these women and possibly be willing to train them, if necessary. She will have the ultimate responsibility for all tools, many of which may be borrowed, and so it's important that she know how to supervise the women who use them. She is also responsible for the safety of the crew.

The tech director orders the lumber, fabric, paint, hardware, and so forth, for the set. She should be able to locate the most reasonable source and order in appropriate amounts. It's helpful to find a tech director who can network well with other theatres in the community, or with the theatre departments of the local colleges. Building from scratch should be the last option for a theatre on a limited budget. (If a set must be built from scratch, the scene designer and the tech director should look into the construction of basic flats and platforms that can be modified and reused in other shows.)

The tech director will be working within the budget given to her by the director (or the budget assigned to the scene designer, if there is one), and it will be her responsibility to keep accounts and make regular reports at the production meetings. Cost overruns happen most frequently in the building of the set, but if the tech director can anticipate them, often the director and the staff can come up with other areas where they can trim budgets to make up the difference.

The tech director is responsible for making sure the set is sturdy (i.e., safe) and complete. She should be familiar with the show and with the director's blocking, so that she will know which windows will actually need to open and close, if a door must be pounded on, which pieces of furniture will be moved during set changes, and other such actions. How the set is used has a lot to do with how it's built. The saloon bar upon which an actor leaps to belt out a song is not the same creature as the saloon bar that only has to support a few elbows and a glass of beer. Also, it's up to the tech director to remember the details like the doorknobs, the bannister, the frames on door flats. It's also up to her to see that the set's paint is dry before rehearsals and performances.

If the play requires special effects related to the use of the set (smashing a window every night or flying off to Never-Never Land), the technical director will be responsible for the special design and construction that go into these effects, keeping in mind the need for consistency every night and also for the safety of the actors.

And the tech director assists with the strike (tearing down the set) after the show is over, though the stage manager is in charge of the strike.

The Lightboard Operator

The lightboard operator operates the lightboard (what a surprise!). Sometimes she is the same person who designed the lights, but if not, then the designer or stage manager needs to train her. During Tech Week, the lightboard operator may be recruited to help hang, focus, and gel the lights. She should have copies of the light plots and the cue sheets for the lights. She is under the supervision of the stage manager for performances. She checks all her instruments a half hour before the show. If the hall is rented to other groups between shows, she should know whether or not the lights will need to be rehung, refocused, and regelled.

If the theatre is big enough to warrant headsets, she will wear a set during rehearsals and performances, so that she can hear the stage manager call the warning cues and the light cues. The lightboard operator should be the same person for Tech Week and all performances.

She checks all the instruments a half hour before each show, and she should have some skills in troubleshooting, so that if there are problems with the equipment—as there usually are—she will have some idea of what to do.

The Sound Technician

The sound technician runs the sound for the show. She needs to be familiar with the sound effects or music for the show and with the equipment. She should always check the sound system a half hour before each show.

If she didn't design the sound, she should meet with the designer to set levels and fine-tune the cues. In a larger theatre, she also will wear a headset to hear the stage manager call the cues.

The sound technician should also be able to troubleshoot problems during a run. She should have a backup tape, because tapes have a way of getting erased, unwound, or broken during shows. If the show is a musical that uses taped music, it's especially important to have extra copies of the master tape.

The Prop Manager

The prop manager is the person who buys, rents, borrows, or constructs the props used in the show. There are two kinds of props: set props and hand props. The set props are those used to "dress" the stage, such as mirrors or lamps. The hand props are those carried by the actors, such as umbrellas or pipes.

The prop manager needs to work closely with the scene designer and the costume designer in determining the style, period, color, and so forth, of the props for the show. It's a good idea to solicit input from the actors, also—especially in the case of hand props. The actor who is going to have to use one, may have special needs herself or a more detailed idea about the specs for the prop. Does the actor have to wear the steel-rimmed glasses? (If so, knock out the lenses.) Is the audience going to be close enough to read the titles of the books in the bookcase? (If so, make sure they're appropriate for the character's home. The actor playing the character may have valuable input on her character's taste in literature.)

Generally, there is a prop table set up during Tech Week. This is often a table covered with an old sheet or butcher paper. Each prop is outlined on the paper or sheet with a black felt-tip pen, and then the outline is labeled. This allows the prop manager (and the actors) to see at a glance what prop or props, if any, are missing from the table. Sometimes there is a different table, or sheet, for each act.

The prop manager is responsible for setting up the prop table a half hour before each performance and for storing the props, if necessary, after each show. And, of course, she will need to return them in good condition to their owners at the end of the run, preferably within three days of closing night.

If there are any props that require special instructions, she will need to instruct the actors in how to handle or care for them.

Locating props is a true art form, and the Lesbian who loves flea markets, who frequents thrift stores, and whose home looks like a museum is a good candidate for prop manager. The prop manager should also be a courteous person with good people skills. The folks who loan their property for theatrical productions are a rare and valuable breed of philanthropists, and it's important that they be treated with respect. Give them credit in the program—if they want it—and a pair of comp tickets. Their property should be treated with respect, so that they may be approached for future loans.

If the props are valuable, such as an antique gramophone or an authentic samovar, the prop manager may need to arrange for storage away from the theatre. In this case, she needs to be responsible for making sure that the prop is at the theatre a half hour before each performance. The prop manager should know if the theatre company is willing to assume the costs of repair or replacement for damaged, lost, or stolen props. Often, the owner will automatically assume that the theatre will be liable, when the theatre has no intention of paying a replacement cost—and in fact, wouldn't borrow the item under those conditions. Inform the owner up front about the theatre's policies. If the loan is at the owner's risk, she has a right to that information *before* she loans it. If the prop is cracked, dented, torn, or stained before borrowing, be sure to draw this to the attention of the owner before you take it to the theatre.

If food is used onstage during the show, this is the prop manager's responsibility. If the food is actually eaten by actors onstage, she needs to be sensitive to their concerns about the source and storage of the food.

And the prop manager needs to work with a budget, keep records, and make reports at the production meetings.

The Wardrobe Manager

The wardrobe manager takes care of the costumes during Tech Week and during performances of the show.

This includes repairs, washing, and ironing. She is responsible for seeing that each actor's costumes are put away at the end of each rehearsal or performance and ready for wear on the next night. She is under the supervision of the stage manager during performances.

When you are looking for production crew positions you can do without, there is a tendency to consider this position a luxury. After all, can't the actors take care of their own costumes? But before you skip over the wardrobe manager, I urge you to reconsider.

Don't underestimate the psychological role of this person! An actor during a performance is under tremendous pressure, and her support people are otherwise occupied: The director—if she's in the theatre at all—should be somewhere out front enjoying the show; and the stage manager is on headsets taking care of the tech. And the other actors, well, they're probably in just as bad a shape, if not worse!

It's a potentially volatile situation for actors to have to lean on one another for support at a performance, especially at an opening. Each actor has just about all she can handle. The presence of a production crew member backstage can provide a critical buffer for tensions. Here is a person who is involved in the production, but at nowhere near the same level as the actor. Here is a person who understands and who has the time to communicate her concern.

The wardrobe manager, whose whole job is the monitoring of costumes during and after performances, is in an ideal position to nurture the actors. This is especially true when an actor's anxiety takes the form of obsessing with her costume or her hair, as often happens. A button looks like it's going to fall off, the wig won't stay on right, or the shirt ruffles need a touch-up with the iron. The wardrobe manager, in my book, is one of the Most Valuable Players in terms of cast morale, and cast morale is one of the first things that comes across the footlights. Think of her as the one who helps the warrior on with her armor before battle; but pick someone who understands the psychology of small children, and you'll have a perfect wardrobe manager.

The Dresser

The dresser helps the actor or actors with costume changes. In contemporary theatre, dressers are used only when there is a costume change which cannot be executed by the actor alone quickly enough for her to make her next entrance. The dresser may be a member of the running crew, the wardrobe manager, or another actor who does not have to be onstage for a while.

The dresser is responsible for seeing that the costume for the change is prepared for the change (e.g., zipper already open, laces of the shoes undone) and set out in the right place. In the case of a very quick change, there is not time for the actor to return to the dressing room (assuming your space even has one!), and the change must take place in the wings, directly to the side of the stage.

A quick change must be carefully choreographed to minimize the time required. For example, while one dresser takes a costume off over the actor's head, another dresser can be changing her shoes. The dresser or dressers should have rehearsed the procedure with the actor to make sure that the change can be executed before the cue for her entrance. The dresser will remove the discarded costume pieces and store them in the appropriate place for the next performance.

The Set Crew

The set crew consists of the folks who build the set. Sometimes they are a steady corps, and sometimes they are whoever showed up for the work party. Occasionally, the set crew is made up of women outside the production, but more often than not in Lesbian theatre, it will be members of the cast and technical crew. The tech director assigns tasks to them, and it is the crew members' responsibility to tell the tech director about their bad back or their lack of experience with a drill press.

The Running Crew

The running crew consists of the folks backstage who move the scenery or reset the props between acts. Sometimes they operate the sound effect devices, such as rattling a sheet of metal for the thunder, or pressing a buzzer for the doorbell. The running crew may be composed of actors who are not on for a particular scene, or they may be friends and lovers who want to be a part of the show.

The stage manager assigns jobs to the running crew

and supervises them. In some cases—especially in theatres with thrust stages and no curtain—the set changes take place in full view of the audience. If the change is between scenes, the audience will be watching. For situations like this, the director may want to choreograph the change, so that it will have aesthetic value as an integral part of the show, instead of serving only to change the furniture. In this case, the director will supervise the actions of the running crew while they are onstage. She may also request that they all wear black, or baseball shirts, or something in keeping with the style of the show.

Chapter 19

The House Staff

The house staff are the people who will interface directly with the audience members before the show and between the acts: taking tickets, seating people, selling food and drinks, handing out programs, handling emergencies or disruptions, and so forth.

The House Manager

The house manager is in charge of everything that goes on in the lobby and the "house" during performances. She is in charge of training and supervising the ushers, the concessionaire, and the box-office staff. She herself is under the supervision of the stage manager during performances. She should coordinate with the stage manager to blink the house lights to signal the beginning of the show or the end of intermission. She should advise the stage manager of any emergencies that might delay or disrupt the show.

The house manager should know what to do if there is an emergency or a disturbance in the house. She should know the policies about small children and babies, and she should be prepared to enforce them—which is not always an easy task in a women's theatre.

The bottom line is that many Lesbians have rehearsed for many hundreds of hours to pull off the show, that many Lesbians have driven many miles and worked many hours to pay many dollars to see that effort brought to fruition, and that one fussy baby can destroy the whole illusion, just as thoroughly as if an audience member were to climb onstage and tear the set to pieces in the middle of the show. A play is not a lecture or a political rally or a dance.

If a Lesbian theatre can afford an evening that provides child care, that's a fine thing; but if not, it's only fair to the actors to have a policy about audience disruption. There are mothers who will not agree with me, but I will bet they don't work in theatre.

Every theatre should have a policy about beepers and about photographing or tape-recording during performances, and it is the house manager's responsibility to see that these policies are enforced. (If the cast wants photos of the show, have a photographer come in and shoot a rehearsal during Tech Week. Ditto for videotaping. Some theatres videotape a performance during the run, because they want the effect of the live audience's reactions, but I find this practice offensive, distracting, and exploitive of the audience. The show no longer exists for their benefit. Now, the audience exists for the benefit of the videotaping. If you are going to use your audience, comp them all in or pay them a wage for being "extras"!)

Another form of disruption is the kind caused by protest or heckling. In the case of Lesbian theatre, this can be confusing. There have been instances when Lesbians, offended by the content of some portion of a production, have shown up at the theatre specifically to disrupt the performance with a premeditated protest action. *Do not* leave the actors to deal with this.

Because of myths of sisterhood and because of codependency training, Lesbian actors have been known to attempt to dialogue from the stage with their hecklers. This is unfair to the members of the audience who want to see the show, privileging the interests of the disrupters. Besides, if your hecklers were interested in productive dialogue, they would have chosen another way to express themselves.

The house manager is responsible for dealing quickly and effectively (and as quietly as possible) with disruption in the house. If she feels it is never justifiable to call the police against a "sister," get another house manager. You owe it to yourself and your cast and crew to protect your production from disruption.

If the disrupters are men, the issue is often less ambiguous. But remember, any physical attempt to remove a persona non grata from the theatre can result in a charge of assault and battery. Don't touch them! Let the police handle it.

The Ushers

The ushers are often partners and lovers of the actors, who hang out for every performance, or women who prefer to do work in exchange for admission.

Ushers can be invited to the dress rehearsal. This will give your actors and the director a "test audience" to try out the jokes, to see what works, and so on. It will also familiarize the ushers with the show, because they might have to seat themselves late or leave the theatre a few minutes before intermission, so it's nice for them to know what they're missing.

Ushers hand out programs, direct people to water fountains and bathrooms, and answer questions about the seating. If the theatre has reserved seats, the ushers might need some orientation ahead of time. *All* the ushers should have *all* the information about accessibility. If there are alternate entrances and bathrooms for people using wheelchairs, the ushers should know these locations. They also need to know where the seating in the house is for wheelchair users. If the performance is signed, the ushers need to know which seating is reserved for deaf and hearing-impaired audience members. But note: Ushers should never assume that a deaf or hearing-impaired person will choose to sit in the reserved area.

With general seating, there are usually no problems with the tickets. First come, first served. But sometimes with reserved seating, there can be a problem with duplicate tickets, or people who are sitting inadvertently (or sometimes deliberately!) in the wrong seats. The ushers should be trained to handle these problems, or directed to refer them to the house manager or box office.

The Box Office Staff

The box-office staff are the women who sell tickets or hold the prepaid ones at the door. They also will keep track of the comp list (list of people entitled to complimentary tickets) and reserved tickets. The box-office staff will be accountable for the money. *Never* — yes, even at a Lesbian performance—leave the cash box unattended. Never.

Your box-office staff, under the supervision of the house manager, should arrive at the theatre an hour before the show, in time to set up their table. They will need a cash box with a supply of small bills (at least twenty ones and a couple of fives), pens for check writing, and the comp list. If your theatre has sold tickets in advance, they should have these tickets set aside in marked and alphabetically organized envelopes.

A special note for theatres that take reservations without preselling the ticket: Be prepared for no-shows! When people call to make these reservations, advise them that the theatre can hold their tickets only until fifteen minutes before the curtain. If the house is selling out, you will need to sell off the unpaid reserved tickets at that time.

Be sure that all comp tickets are marked on both ends with a *C*, so that the stubs will not be counted as tickets that were sold, if your theatre is using stubs for inventory purposes.

The box-office staff counts the money, submits it

with a written and initialed statement, and turns it over to the house manager at the end of the evening. If the show is still running, make sure the cash box has a stash of change to start off the next performance night.

The Concessionaire

The concessionaire is in charge of the food and beverages sold before, during, or after the performance. She can be a member of the theatre, or an outside caterer.

Sometimes a producer may invite a Lesbian caterer, bakery, or restaurant to handle concessions. Outside businesses might find the offer attractive, because it will allow them exposure in the community. They will get to display a sampling of their wares: tarts, quiches, pastries, cappuccino, and the like, to a targeted population of women who are obviously supportive of women's endeavors. The money made from selling concessions is minimal, and although the producer can ask for a percentage of profits from an outside caterer, I would suggest that she be satisfied with the prestige she gets from having her production associated with a quality line of refreshments.

If the theatre handles its own concessions, there is usually a Lesbian who is in charge of the concessions. She has been given a budget, and she also keeps track of her receipts and her bookkeeping. Generally, she turns in her money at the end of the run. The concessionaire recruits, trains, and supervises her workers, who—like the ushers—may be women doing labor exchange, or they may be the cast members' partners who don't like staying at home on weekends.

Because everyone has enough to worry about, the concessions—when they're handled in-house—are usually kept very simple: coffee, tea, sparkling water or soda, and some cookies or brownies. (See Appendix 4 for information on accessibility as it applies to food.) The concessionaire should check around for the best wholesale prices. She may get ambitious and want to do the baking herself, but this is certainly above and beyond the call of duty.

If the theatre is going to serve alcohol, be sure to check into the legal technicalities concerning licensing and insurance. As a director and a playwright, I am always against sale of alcohol in theatre lobbies, because it dulls the senses of the audience. When I put my best work up for show, I want everyone who sees it to be on their toes!

The concessionaire is responsible for having the food ready for sale a half hour before curtain, or in time for intermission—depending on the policy for the show. (This means that the coffee is made in advance.) If the concessions are inside the performance space, she should be sure that the noisy appliances are turned off during the performance!

And, finally, if food and beverages are not allowed in the theatre, it's only fair for the concession sellers to advise the patrons accordingly—especially if they're trying to buy a cup of steaming coffee at the end of intermission.

Chapter 20

Everyone Else

The Publicist

The publicist is in charge of the publicity: the photo shoot, the posters, the flyers, the press releases, the calendar spots, and the interviews. She should be someone who can work on deadline, because a missed press deadline can be fatal for a community production. She needs to be able to work within a budget, keep records, and make reports at the production meetings. She needs to have good communication skills, and she needs to be assertive, as in, "I need this done by *Thursday*."

If she isn't an artist herself or doesn't do typesetting, she needs to be familiar with the resources in the community, and she needs to know the best prices for printing. Frequently, the publicist is also the person in charge of putting together the program.

Since publicity warrants its own section in this book, there's no need to say much more at this point about the publicist. But pick a "people person" for the job!

The Sign-Language Interpreter(s) and Sign Master

Consciousness is changing rapidly in the deaf community as well as in the Lesbian community; and as consciousness continues to change, new questions are being asked about the politics of interpreting art forms that belong to a hearing culture: Is sign-language interpretation of music or theatre emerging as an art form in its own right, one that transpires simultaneously but with a different aesthetic from the forms of the hearing culture? Or is it unprofessional of the interpreter to incorporate her own personality, creativity, and theatricality into her signing, because it might distract from, or even upstage, the performers? And, finally, is it even appropriate for interpreters and deaf people to validate for themselves these culturally bound art forms that exclude deaf people?

These are serious questions that require dialogue between the members of the deaf community, the interpreter, the producer, and the director.

If a theatre company decides to have a show interpreted, it needs to give careful consideration to the logistics of the play. If the performance is a one-woman show, the show can probably be interpreted in a format similar to that used for most concerts: A single interpreter stands to one side of the stage, often with her own light, and signs everything that is spoken from the stage.

However, most plays—even two-person plays—have dialogue that is too rapid and too dramatic for one interpreter to sign effectively. In this case, the producer will need to hire two or more interpreters. Not only does this raise budget issues, but it also raises the question of whether or not it's desirable to have what amounts to two dramas taking place simultaneously on separate areas of the stage. Is it preferable for the interpreters to place themselves in the scene, standing beside the actors they are interpreting? And if it is preferable, then what degree of identification with the character's role will constitute an act of "upstaging" on the part of the interpreter? Or is the whole notion of competition with the interpreter an artificial and arrogant construct of the hearing culture? If the deaf and hearing-impaired audience must focus on the interpreter in order to understand the dialogue of the play, how much opportunity would they have to experience the actors' expressions and gestures anyway?

Tough questions with no easy answers. But one thing is certain; if your play is interpreted, you will have special technical and artistic requirements that will involve the cooperation of the director, the stage manager, the technicians, and the actors. Be sure these folks are all in on the decisions that will affect their areas of responsibility—and the sooner the better.

In the past, deaf people have been excluded from decisions regarding the interpretation of performances. Because they are the creators and consumers of deaf culture, there is a growing acknowledgment of the need for their inclusion in the process. The hiring of a sign master is becoming an accepted practice. The sign master is a deaf person who studies the script and observes the interpreters in rehearsal. She gives suggestions and corrections on the signing. If a sign master is hired, it is important for both the sign master and the interpreters to have a clear understanding of their roles. Is the sign master in charge of the interpreters, or is she acting in an advisory capacity? Also, the sign master is *not* a co-director, unless that has been the understanding from the conception of the production. She works in cooperation with the director, who has the ultimate responsibility for everything that takes place at rehearsals. Again, good boundaries and clearly defined roles can eliminate many potential areas of friction in a situation where new paradigms are evolving from rapid changes in consciousness.

The sign master and interpreter(s) will need copies of the script as far in advance as possible. They should be paid for time spent preparing as well as for the actual performance time. If the interpreters will be working on the set with the actors, the sign master and the interpreters will need to see one or more rehearsals during Tech Week, and they should be included in at least one rehearsal during that week. They will need to become familiar with the blocking and comfortable with moving on the set, and the actors will need to get used to the adjustments in blocking mandated by the presence of extra people on the set. Even if the interpreters don't plan to rehearse with the actors, they should be invited to see the show during Tech Week, to hear the timing. The director decides which rehearsals to open for the inclusion of the interpreters.

And, finally, if the actors or technicians have concerns about working with the interpreters, they should take them to the director. It's not their place to give direction or even advice to the interpreter.

The Volunteer Coordinator

If your theatre is really successful in establishing itself, you may find yourself fortunate enough to need a volunteer coordinator. This is a Lesbian who is the contact person for people who want to get involved. She keeps the lists of those who have worked in any capacity for the theatre in the past. When a tech director needs a crew, or the costume designer needs an assistant, she can give them some possible names of women to contact. She also routes the volunteers in the direction of their interests, giving their names to the appropriate designer, house manager, or other staff person. The volunteer coordinator is accountable to the producer.

A good volunteer coordinator takes care of her volunteers. She runs interference when they are having trouble with their supervisor, she organizes parties for them, she makes sure they are all thanked for their good work. And she might be in charge of outreach in the community to recruit more workers (press releases, announcements at women's gatherings, etc.).

Even if your theatre is too new and too small for a volunteer coordinator, consider naming a volunteer contact person, who at least provides the central phone number for volunteers and staff looking for help. A Lesbian who wants to get involved in a theatre can be overwhelmed by all the activity, the "glamor," or by her own ignorance of the business. It's important to nurture these first tentative contacts and to help potential volunteers feel that they belong and are needed. Theoretically, anyone in the theatre company could do this; but in reality, most of the staff in the heat of production will consider nurturing a volunteer to be more trouble than it's worth. A volunteer contact person who has focused on building skills in this area is probably going to be in a better position to respond to the needs of the volunteer. (See Chapter 9.)

The Professional Fund-raiser

Although Lesbian theatres are a long way from being in a position to hire full-time or even part-time professional fund-raisers, you might still want to hire one for consultation or for writing the occasional grant. There are more and more foundations and funds being established all the time for Lesbian organizations and projects. If you have 501(c)3 status, or if you can come under the umbrella of an organization that has that status, then you can apply for grants.

A professional fund-raiser can be a valuable mentor for a new theatre group. She can proof your promotional materials, help you with marketing strategies, and give you many ideas about ways to raise money. Remember, the majority of theatres in this country are subsidized by public foundations or private donations. Box-office receipts alone are never going to be enough to keep your theatre operating on more than a production-by-production basis. The average theatre budget is 50–70 percent subsidized. It's never too early to start considering alternative sources for funding.

The Office Manager

This is a position you don't need to worry about until your theatre is tremendously successful and has a long track record, which is to say, until your theatre can afford an office and pay a salary. The office manager takes care of the daily business of the theatre including phone calls, bookkeeping, filing, and correspondence. But hold the vision!

The Others

Finally, there are, of course, the other nameless positions for those who show up for mailing parties, for strike, for mounting flyers around town, etcetera, etcetera. *Comp these folks into the show!* And consider these helpers part of the theatre, because they are. The theatre that sets rigid boundaries and criteria for who is a member and who is not is a club, not a theatre—and not one of which I want to be a member!

All of the above obviously has outlined an ideal staff. Small theatres and new productions often double, triple, or quadruple up on jobs. The scene designer may also be the tech director, who may also be the stage manager and the lightboard operator. The actors may be responsible for getting all their own costumes or props. And all of this can work out fine. But before you figure out a way to work with a skeleton crew, try to fill as many of these slots as possible. For one thing, it helps your theatre grow. For another, it allows other staff members to focus their priorities. A director who is handling box office, publicity, and training volunteers on the lightboard will have a tough time giving the actors the attention they need.

When you recruit the staff, don't be afraid to give out written job descriptions, including your own. This can be more helpful than intimidating, because people like to know exactly what is expected of them in terms of budgets, deadlines, and mandatory production meetings. People like to know the limits of their authority and responsibility. The prop manager will be relieved to know that the props are loaned at the owner's risk. The costume designer will find it helpful to learn that it is the director's responsibility to field the actors' complaints about their costumes. And for absolute clarity and consensus, nothing beats having things down in writing.

If all of this seems terribly structured, that's because it is. Live theatre, even when it is collective or improvisational, requires a high degree of coordination and accountability. Some kinds of women's events and women's organizations work best without a lot of structure, where spontaneity, flexibility, and trading off responsibilities are the order of the day. But live theatre, because of the number of elements that must be coordinated in a compressed amount of time, requires structure. A full production crew actually reduces friction and frees the actors and crew members to focus on their work. (See the flowchart in Appendix 11, showing the lines of accountability among cast and crew for a production.)

And a final word on hierarchy and division of labor:

Supervision does not mean dominance, and accountability does not mean subservience. In patriarchal organizations, it is almost impossible to separate these functions from their connotations of power-over; but in Lesbian theatre, it is not only possible to separate them, but it is essential.

Too often, Lesbians stampede toward anarchy in an effort to avoid a structure that could lend itself to power abuses. This is counterproductive, because anarchy is the breeding ground for covert power structures. On the other hand, Lesbians burned out on collective chaos may in despair revert to patriarchal structures, without bothering to critique the attitudes or patterns of dominance that have been associated with these structures.

The women who are technicians are just as important as the women who are actors. The *roles* they serve in a particular production may not be as important. Certainly, the sound technician who came on board five days before opening is more easily replaced than the lead actor. But this does not mean that her concerns for safety or comfort, or her need to be treated with respect and dignity, should weigh any less than those of the lead actor.

Part V

Putting out the Word

Chapter 21

The Press Kit

Publicity is the advance guard of self-esteem, and it should be taken very seriously. Good marketing will probably not save a bad show, but on the other hand, an excellent show will not be able to override the effects of bad marketing. Put your best foot forward!

The publicist will need to generate materials for publicity. Let's start with those materials: the accessibility information; the theatre logo; the press release; the publicity photos; the calendar announcement; the public service announcement (PSA); the flyer/poster/postcard; the paid ad; the Internet web page.

The Accessibility Information

Accessibility information will need to be on all of your publicity materials: the press release, the calendar announcements, the flyers and posters, and so forth.

If your performance is going to be interpreted, your press should say so. If only one performance of the run is going to be interpreted, specify which night on your publicity. If your performance is wheelchair accessible, say so. If only some parts of the hall are accessible, say so. (See Chapter 12 for some of the specs on accessibility.)

Your publicity might read: "The Friday, May 16 performance will be sign-language interpreted. The theatre is wheelchair accessible, bathroom is not." Or it might read, "Wheelchair accessible entrance on North Street."

To save space, you may want to use graphics that are gaining acceptance as universal symbols of accessibility (see Appendix 12). If you use the graphic denoting wheelchair accessibility, be sure that the performance is entirely accessible!

The Theatre Logo

A theatre logo may be the last thing on your mind when you are mounting a production, but if you plan to be around for a while, it's a good idea to start thinking about one. The logo for a theatre is a symbol or a special design for the lettering of the name. It will appear on all your publicity materials for all your productions, and this repeated exposure to a consistent graphic will help establish recognition for your theatre.

The logo should say something about the goals of

the company. If it's a theatre where community actors get together to have a good time, then a lighthearted logo might be in order. On the other hand, if you're going for semiprofessional quality and big bucks, you might want to use a graphic design that is a little more distinguished, or should I say stodgy?

You can hire a graphic designer to come up with a logo, or you could hold a contest or schedule a company brainstorming session. The logo is useful for stationery (press releases, calendar spots, PSAs), for flyers, for audition notices, for tickets, for ushers' name tags, for T-shirts, for program covers—for just about anything you can think of associated with your theatre. It increases the public's familiarity with your organization, and it lends some continuity to your press materials, which will vary widely from show to show.

The Press Release

The press release is a brief (no more than two double-spaced pages) article about the production. This is sent to newspapers and magazines. It can also be included in a press kit to radio or TV stations if you are trying to get an interview or a talk show spot.

Press releases are very important, and if the publicist does not possess good writing skills, she should delegate the job to someone who does. The press release tells how seriously you take yourself. Your production may be absolutely wonderful, but nobody in the media is going to take it seriously if your press release shuffles its feet and crams its hands in its pockets and says, "Well, gosh, gee, some of us Lesbians thought we'd get together and do a show . . ." A press release is a declaration of self-esteem, and it's my experience that if you are doing Lesbian theatre, it is not possible to have too much self-esteem.

Many papers, especially the alternative papers (which would include the gay-and-Lesbian and the women's presses) tend to run press releases with little or no editing. If your release is well written, the mainstream paper may run it unedited also, but this is less likely. In any event, write it as if it's going to run verbatim.

The press release goes to the news editor. (And before you mail or hand-deliver, find out that person's name, and address it to her personally.) She may choose to run it as is, or she may rewrite it or cut it, or she may give the contact person a call for more information because she has decided to do an interview or a special feature article.

Every press release has an angle. The angle is the aspect of the story that you choose to emphasize. For most Lesbian theatre productions, the angle will probably be what the play is about. But if the play features the Women's Philharmonic in the pit, that might be a more important angle for publicity. If the play is a world premiere and the playwright is flying out from New York to attend, that might be your angle. If your theatre is brand-new and this is its first production, you might make the launching of the theatre the angle.

The angle will determine what you describe, who you quote, and what kind of quotations you use in the body of the press release. But the most important thing to keep in mind is that the primary purpose of the release is to get people to the theatre, and the most important information is the who-what-when-where-how logistics.

There are many books on publicity and writing for newspapers, but the rules are based on a simple fact of human nature: People skim newspapers. If the headline interests them, they'll probably take a look at the first line. If that interests them, they'll maybe take a look at the first paragraph. But, frankly, they will probably not read the whole article. They will read enough to get what they want, and then move on. So this is no time to save the best for last. Another reason not to do this, is that editors tend to chop off the ends of articles when they are abridging them. Put your filler at the end.

With all this in mind, write a real grabber for the first sentence (remember your angle!). And then pack all the information about who, what, when, where, and how much into the first paragraph. After you've done this, go back to the angle and give details about the play itself, or carry some quotations from the playwright who is flying in for the premiere, or give information about the brand-new Lesbian theatre in town. (See the sample press release in Appendix 13.) And always send a photo with the press release.

The Publicity Photos

A picture is worth a thousand words; I would rather have an exciting picture run with a calendar spot than have the whole press release appear without the photo.

Why? Because everyone who looks at the page will notice the photo (especially if it's dramatic), but not everyone will read or even skim or remember the press release.

A good publicity photo for a play is one that conveys a sense of drama. This can be achieved through dramatic tension among the subjects, or through an element of surprise. The actors might be engaged in an unusual activity (or one that is seldom seen in the media, e.g., women embracing), or perhaps there is a juxtaposition of incongruous elements in the composition itself.

Use a good photographer. That doesn't mean you necessarily have to hire a professional, but do hire someone with experience, preferably someone who has her own camera and understands all its quirks. Often the photo shoot is scheduled during a rehearsal time. This means the director will be present. She probably has a good eye for dramatic tableaux, because she's a director. Get her input. Again, she also has an idea of how she is going to interpret the material, so she may want to see that interpretation expressed in the photos taken. Also, especially with Lesbian theatre, you may want to take different shots for the different newspapers. The gay-and-Lesbian paper may run the photo of two women in passionate embrace, but it's probably a waste of the print to send it to the mainstream daily paper.

And, remember, photos can go on location. One of the most effective publicity photos I ever saw was one for *The Madwoman of Chaillot*. It was being produced by a summer-stock company at a beach resort. The madwoman, in full turn-of-the-century regalia—parasol and all—was stepping out of the surf. The poster was arresting, because the imagery was incongruent; and yet at the same time, it conveyed very clearly two ideas: the beach and classical repertory.

A warning about action shots: Don't pose for action shots! If two actors are fighting, don't have them raise fists at each other and hold. These photos always look stagy as hell. Have them play the scene, and a good photographer should be able to catch the action on the fly. Also, don't let the actors wear makeup designed to be seen by gaslight in the last row of the balcony, unless you plan to put the photographer in that last row for the shoot. I don't know why, but actors seem to have a thing about wearing too much makeup for a photo call. If you are trying to capture the emotional relationship among the actors in the photo (jealousy, lust, rage, etc.), keep it subtle. If the actors are mugging, the photo will come off looking like a still from an old two-reel melodrama.

When you look at the contact sheets, pick your shots for clarity and focus. The actor with the black hair standing in front of the dark curtain may come out looking bald in the newspaper. Look closely at the contact sheets—use a magnifying glass, if you can—to see if the shot is out of focus, before you pay to have it enlarged.

And get some feedback. The photographer, the publicist, the director, and the actors will all have interesting things to say.

If your theatre can't afford to pay a professional photographer, you might be able to work out a deal that will make it worth her while anyway. If the photographer shoots portraits of the whole company during the shoot, the cast might be interested in buying prints. This is a deal for the cast, who can get professional quality portraits without a sitting fee, and a deal for the photographer, who can shoot the whole company in one afternoon. These photos can also be used for the lobby shots of the company, which are a nice touch to any production. (It's generally the publicist's job to put together any displays for the lobby.)

If you plan to use the photo on flyers or posters, have a half-tone made. If you've ever tried to photocopy a photograph, you know how poorly it copies. The half-tone converts the photo image into an image composed of little dots, like the kind you see in newsprint. This makes a world of difference when it comes to copying. Some laser printers can reproduce sharp images directly from the photo, but these are more expensive than standard copiers. Also, you can have the image scanned by a computer and stored to disk. This may be worth the extra cost if you plan to post on the Internet, or generate a variety of different publicity materials using the same graphics.

It isn't necessary to order half-tones for your press kits. Newspapers are used to working off glossies, and the quality of printing in a newspaper is not going to be that great anyway. Besides, if you sent a half-tone to every newspaper, it would be very expensive, as opposed to the regular old 5×7 prints. (Newspapers don't need 8×10's.)

Also, be sure the actors understand that the photo may be used on posters or flyers and may be sent to the mainstream press. Request that they sign a model release form (see Appendix 14), just to cover yourself legally. Alas, some Lesbians are still closeted at work or at home. Better to find out before the shoot than to realize you have a roll of film you can't use.

And a final warning about the photo call: Plan it early. The first week of rehearsals is generally not too early, once you figure in the time it takes to develop and check the proofs, to order the prints, and to mail to the press. The photos are so important that you might want to allow enough time for a second photo call, in case you can't use any of the pictures from the first shoot.

The Calendar Announcement

The calendar announcement, or "spot," contains the bare essentials, the who-what-when-where-how of the production. You can sometimes add a sentence about the play itself, but most editors will not run more than the minimum information to allow people to get to the show.

Calendar spots should organize the information with the calendar editor in mind. She gets a zillion of these things in the mail every day, and each one is formatted differently. It must drive her crazy!

Make the information easy to scan. I use a who-what-when-where format myself, which may seem simplistic, but my spots always run, and the information is rarely misprinted. I also repeat the information in paragraph form at the bottom of the page, because some editors will want to present the information that way. It's a good idea to read the calendars of the publications to which you're submitting, and try to tailor your spot to their formats. If they don't have to re-write, that eliminates a step; and every time you eliminate a step, you eliminate potential errors. (There is a sample calendar spot in Appendix 15.)

The Public Service Announcement

Radio stations and cable TV stations frequently have a policy concerning the airing of PSAs. Sometimes they have a "Community Calendar" or "Arts Calendar" feature, where they run theatre announcements. Again, it's a good idea to research the policies of the media in your area before you submit your PSA.

The PSA is similar to the calendar announcement in that it sticks to the basics: who, what, when, where, and how much. Write the information out in paragraph form, and monitor the time it takes to read it out loud.

The PSA can take three different forms: the ten-second PSA, the fifteen-second PSA, and the twenty-second PSA. The longer ones can include an extra sentence or two about the play, but you won't have time for this in the ten-second PSA.

The Flyer/Poster/Postcard

The flyer should be dramatic. After all, this is theatre. It should also be well done.

That doesn't mean that a flyer about a comedy can't be zany and wild. And it doesn't mean that a show about Bloomsbury Lesbians needs to be boring and stuffy. The flyer should reflect the style of the show, should give the audience some idea of what to expect when they get in the theatre, and it should be exciting. Juxtaposition of incongruent images is one way to generate excitement. Photos on flyers can also be exciting, depending on what the actors are doing. Be sure to check with the director. She may have her own ideas based on her interpretation of the show.

What's on the flyer? The title of the play, playwright(s) (if it's a musical, then the bookwriter, lyricist, and composer are credited), director, theatre company (with logo, if it has one) or producer, dates and times, location of theatre, ticket prices and where to get them, and accessibility information, including dates of signed productions. If the theatre is accessible to wheelchairs, you should use the symbol for accessibility on your poster or flyer. (See Appendix 16 for some sample flyers.)

The flyer, if it's going to be posted on bulletin boards around town, should be clearly readable from a distance—or at least the title and graphics should be.

Flyers are a very versatile tool for publicity. They can be used as posters, in windows and on telephone poles. They can also be sent out as mailings or enclosures. They can be included in press kits and left in stacks at various events.

Posters are sturdier and larger than flyers, which makes them easier to read and less likely to get dog-eared, but it also makes them less likely to be posted. Most bulletin boards for women's events are crammed with notices, and often there is a policy about size of notices. This is true for merchants' windows also. You may have gone to all the trouble and expense of printing posters only to find that you can't put them up. If you need to cut publicity costs, then cut printing posters and stick with flyers.

Another way to go, especially if you don't have a bulk mailing permit, is to shrink your flyer design down to postcard size and print it on card stock. These can be mailed cheaper than flyers, and they don't require folding or stapling.

The flyer design may also be sized down for the cover of your program (but that's the subject of a whole different chapter!)

The Paid Ad

Paid advertisements are a low priority because the most effective place to run them are the papers that are probably already running your press release, your photo, your calendar spot, and maybe a review—in other words, the women's presses or the gay-and-Lesbian papers. If you have a tight budget, skip the ads.

One instance where it might make a meaningful difference would be if the women's press or gay-and-Lesbian paper for your area is weekly or biweekly and you have a long run for your play. In that case, there might be no mention of the show after its initial announcement in the paper even though it's still going on. (There *should* be a calendar spot, but maybe you feel this isn't enough. And, it's true, an ad is more eye-catching than a calendar spot.)

Another situation where paid advertising might be in order is for a large women's concert, where the producers are printing a program. Since this is a very targeted audience, you might want to take out an ad in their program.

If a paper has been exceptionally supportive, you may want to take out an ad as a way of thanking them. A nice gesture, but costly. Comping in the reviewer or the writer who did a special feature is probably a more direct and cost-effective way to grease the wheel.

If you do run an ad, you should be able to size down graphics from your flyer or poster, or you can use the theatre logo. (If the ad is business-card size, you may not have the space for this.) The ad should carry the same information as the flyer, including ticket outlets and accessibility. If space is really limited, you can resort to a "For information, call . . ." line.

The Internet Web Page

More and more businesses are making their presence known on "the Web"—in other words, on the Internet. The marketing advantage of the Internet is its capacity to disseminate information quickly to the far corners of the world. Since attending a live theatre event is a geographically-bound activity, advertising on the Internet has limited application for a Lesbian theatre company.

Most of the theatres with websites are professional theatres with full seasons, and their URL (Uniform Resource Locator, or address) appears at a variety of other websites. If you do establish a web page for your Lesbian theatre, there are a number of websites for Lesbian resources that would be happy to list your URL. At this point, having an Internet presence is about exposure, about establishing membership in a fledgling cyberspace community. Being able to list your URL in your printed publicity or refer to it in a grant application may be impressive, but don't count on it for bringing in an audience.

You can design your own web page with one of the many do-it-yourself manuals for constructing a web page, or you can hire someone to do it for you. The web page can be as simple as a press release, or it can include graphics, sound bites, or even animated video clips. The web page can be filled with "links" that will take the viewer to excerpts of local reviews, biographies of your cast, the history of your theatre, or even an interactive form by means of which they can be added to your mailing list. The possibilities are intriguing, even if the results do not translate to box-office receipts.

And that's it for materials. Now, what do you do with them?

Chapter 22

Publicizing Auditions

The publicist for a Lesbian play must actually gear up for two events: the auditions and the performance. Both require good publicity, and good publicity requires good planning.

But the director already knows who she's going to cast! But our theatre company wants to have closed auditions! We don't need/want to publicize!

Oh, yes, you do. You may know all your actors. You may even know whom you want to cast, but it doesn't hurt to post your auditions in the press. For one thing, it makes Lesbian theatre visible. For another, it puts your production on a par with the other theatres that post their auditions publicly. It says, "We're competitive, we're authentic, we have just as much a right to be here as you do." And it reaches Lesbians who might not otherwise show up for auditions. If your chosen actor is really the best, then open auditions will only strengthen your convictions. On the other hand, someone beyond your wildest dreams may walk in the door. Don't limit your options in order to take care of your actors' insecurities or to protect your status in a theatre "family."

Many Lesbians believe that women's culture should be kept private, with the only advertising being word of mouth or mailings to listed members of women's organizations. Without going into the politics of this, I would just say that you will forgo a lot of talent, a lot of money, and a lot of exposure if you go this route. You will gain a measure of privacy, and some will argue that there is safety in this. I believe that privacy for an actively oppressed group has its place, but that theatre should be a public activity. The more oppressed we are, the more public our theatres should be.

Have I convinced you?

The publicity for auditions is not as extensive as that for the production itself, because you are targeting a much more specific audience—potential actors and volunteers—and because the auditions themselves do not generate money.

From my experience, the most cost-effective ways to publicize auditions are (in order of effectiveness):

1. Press releases and calendar spots to the local women's press or newsletter.
2. Press releases and calendar spots to the local gay-and-Lesbian paper or newsletter.
3. Calendar spots to the mainstream daily paper and alternative paper.

4. Flyers at theatres, theatre departments, women's community events, and bulletin boards at the women's bookstore, coffee shop, and the like.
5. Announcements made at gay-and-lesbian events or women's events.

Let's use the same time frame mentioned in Chapter 14 for the schedule. Today is January 1, the auditions are scheduled for February 3 and 4, and the opening night is March 22.

If you live in an area where there is a gay-and-Lesbian paper or a women's paper, these will be your cheapest, least labor-intensive way to reach the women most likely to be interested in auditioning. These papers are usually monthlies, and here you have to pay attention: If your auditions are February 3 and 4, you should probably announce them in the January paper, because most people don't pick up a free paper the day it comes out. In order to get the notice in the January paper, you will need to mail out your press release by mid-December. This may seem ridiculously early for a show that goes up at the end of March, but when you use the monthlies, you learn to think far in advance. You can also run the notice again in the February paper, just for the heck of it.

In order to set up your press calendar, you will need to call around. Find out the deadlines for the papers in your community. And when you call, be sure to ask for the deadline for press releases *and* for the community calendar. Sometimes these are different, because the calendar spots don't require a lot of editing. Often they can be added at the last minute. The news editor, on the other hand, may need press releases considerably earlier, because she needs to decide which ones to run "as is" and which ones to follow up with an interview or full feature article. And be sure to get the name of the editor for each and her specific mailing address. Also, call the radio and TV stations and find out their policies and deadlines about public service announcements. (Your theatre will need to be nonprofit in order to qualify.)

Let's assume that the deadlines in your community are similar to those in mine. Here is what your calendar might look like for audition publicity:

December 10: Mail press release and calendar spots to monthlies (women's and gay-and-Lesbian presses).
January 8: Typeset the audition flyer and make copies.
January 10: Mail the second round of calendar spots to the monthlies and weeklies.
January 15: Mail the press releases and spots to the dailies. Mail PSAs to TV and radio stations. Mount flyers at theatres, theatre departments, women's coffeehouses and bookstores.
January 15–February 3: Take flyers to any event in the community for women or Lesbians.

So what about this audition publicity? What should it look like? Well, audition notices don't need to be anywhere near as sharp as your publicity for the show. You don't need fancy graphic art designed to attract a targeted audience. You don't need a clever angle to catch the attention of the jaundiced consumer. The population you want to attract will be grabbed immediately by one word, in plain bold type: AUDITIONS.

Don't spend money on your audition flyers. Find someone with a minimal graphics program on her computer, and pay her $5 or $10 to type up all the information—maybe with a border if you're feeling daring. If your theatre has a logo, you might want to paste that up on the flyer. But stick to basics. Anyone who comes to auditions because of the pretty colors on a flyer should probably stay in the audience anyway.

And don't print a lot of them, even if there's a women's event that is going to draw 1,000 women. Audition flyers are for those who are interested. If you want to reach every woman at that event, try writing up a brief announcement for the emcee to read—more efficient and lots cheaper. Post the flyers only in areas where they are likely to be seen by actors or Lesbians, or both. If you take them to events, take a small quantity. Don't hand one to everyone who walks through the door.

What's on the flyer? Basically, the flyer should say who's producing, who's directing, what play (include the playwright), when, where, what actors you're looking for, and what kind of auditions you're holding. (See Appendix 17 for sample audition flyer.) When you list the available parts, keep it simple: "Six women, all ages. Open casting." If your casting is not open, specify: "Three African American women in early twenties; one white woman in sixties." And you should tell the auditioner what to expect: "Readings from script" or "Two contrasting monologues, under three minutes" or "Song from a musical, bring sheet music (or taped accompaniment)." If your auditions are going to be private, then your flyer should say, "Call for appointment" and list a phone number. If you have already booked your space, put the dates of the run. If this seems like a lot of copy, you can simplify by listing only time, place, and "For information, call . . ."

That's it. No glitz, no glamour. The stardust is between the lines.

The calendar spot for auditions contains the same information, but it's laid out in a different format. (See Chapter 21 and Appendix 18.) Now, the press release for auditions. If the article is for the women's press or the gay-and-Lesbian press and you are concerned about the turnout for auditions, you could use the press release to reassure potential actors that the auditions will be user-friendly. You could describe the process and carry some reassuring quotations from the director: "Some of the most interesting actors I have worked with are Lesbians who have never been on a stage before. Let's face it, as Lesbians we've all had to learn to put on an act at one time or another." (See Appendix 19 for a sample audition press release.)

I encourage Lesbians to come to the auditions, even if they're just curious about the process. This is a good place to recruit volunteers for tech positions, but also many women will decide to audition after they get there and see that it's not all that scary. If they feel they have to commit ahead of time, they may decide not to show up, and that's a loss for everyone. And if they do decide not to audition, it hasn't hurt anyone. Some directors may take issue with this policy, but I feel that any practice that demystifies theatre for Lesbians is a positive step.

If the company wants to make scripts available in advance, put that information in the press release. (You can include it in the calendar spot, but it probably won't run.) And a word of warning: If you do check out scripts, ask for a deposit that is refundable at auditions. Otherwise, you probably won't get them back, and the costs add up.

It's doubtful that the TV or radio stations will air a PSA about auditions, but you can try anyway. Again, write up the PSA with the same information as the calendar spot, only in paragraph form, and then time it. (If there is a women's radio show or a gay-and-Lesbian show, you have a much better chance of getting it aired.)

Well, so much for auditions. On to the main event . . .

Chapter 23

Publicizing the Show

The outlets for publicity for the show itself are somewhat different than those for auditions. Here are my suggestions, in order of effectiveness:

1. Direct mailing to a targeted women's or Lesbian mailing list.
2. Enclosure in another organization's bulk mailing to a targeted mailing list.
3. Press releases, photos, calendar spots to women's and gay-and-Lesbian presses.
4. Press release, photos, calendar spots to mainstream and alternative presses.
5. Flyers at targeted locations (bookstores, coffeehouses, etc.).
6. Sales of block tickets or special theatre nights.
7. Interviews or segments of the show on women's radio programs.
8. Paid advertisements in special mailings or women's and gay-and-Lesbian presses.
9. Radio and cable TV PSAs.
10. Announcements and flyers at women's or Lesbian events.

And don't forget the most important publicity vehicle of all: *getting reviewed!*

The first three priorities listed above target the women's and Lesbian community. At this point in history, no matter how excellent your production or how much it may speak to mainstream concerns like ableism, the environment, or violence against women, the majority of your audience will still be Lesbian. This can be frustrating, especially when you don't see the same standard applied to gay male theatre (notice that *Torch Song Trilogy* and *La Cage aux Folles* have both been made into mainstream hit movies—and in the case of *Cage*, even sequels!). You don't see non-Jewish people shunning *Fiddler on the Roof*, or white people avoiding *A Raisin in the Sun*. But for reasons that could take up the length of another book, men and heterosexual women are not crossing over in droves to our theatres. This can be discouraging, but it does help us focus more clearly on our own culture. The very few Lesbian plays I have seen produced in mainstream venues have been written with the biases of straight people in mind, and they were—quite frankly—boring: Lesbianism 101.

So, for better or for worse, our people will be the majority of our audience. Gear your publicity accordingly.

Now that you have some idea of where you're going to publicize, you're in a position to draw up a budget. This will include typesetting, graphics, flyer and/or poster costs, paid advertising, photo costs (including making the half-tone, if you are using a photo on your flyers), and postage fees to organizations that will include your flyer in their mailings. (There is a sample publicity budget in Appendix 20.)

Now, on to the calendar: It's January 1, auditions are February 3 and 4, and the show opens on March 23. Here is some idea of what your deadlines for publicity will look like:

January 15–29: Copy to graphic designer. (January 15 is very early, but since you have almost a month before production elements begin, this is a good time to get your poster out of the way. It's also a good time to do layout for the program, if you are in charge of that.)

January 22: Contact a photographer and schedule a shoot in two weeks.

January 31: Contact women's and Lesbian papers about a special article. Contact radio show hosts about scheduling interviews with the director or with the actors.

February 6: Photo call. Drop off the film and rush-order the contact sheet.

February 7: Order prints from the contact sheet.

February 9: Proofread the graphics for posters and flyers.

February 11: Draft press releases and calendar sports.

February 12: Pick up the photos.

February 13: Mail press releases with photos to weeklies and monthlies. Place ads (optional).

February 14: Place the order for posters, flyers, and tickets.

February 16: Pick up the posters, flyers, and tickets from the printer.

February 19: Ask for cast and crew biographies for the program.

February 20: Begin selling program ads to merchants and patrons.

February 25: Hold a mailing party for the bulk mailing of flyers or postcards.

February 26: Deliver tickets to the designated outlets.

March 1: Collect and edit cast and crew biographies.

March 2: Distribute the flyers to cast members.

March 4: Take the program copy to a graphic designer.

March 5: Mail the press releases with photos to the dailies. Mail PSA's to radio and TV stations. Mount the flyers around town.

March 13: Deliver the rough draft of program to the director.

March 17: Ask the cast and crew to approve the program.

March 18: Take the amended program to the typesetter.

March 19: Place the order for printing the programs.

March 21: Pick up programs.

At any and all times: Distribute announcements and flyers at community events. Contact mainstream editors to encourage them to review or run a feature on your show. Meet various deadlines for arts council newsletters, local entertainment guides, and so forth.

As you can see, being the publicist entails a lot of responsibility. You may want to delegate chunks of tasks to different women. It's a good idea to have one woman in charge of drafting and assembling the press materials (the photo, the press release, the calendar spot), then distributing these materials and delegating the different areas of publicity to individuals: a woman in charge of mainstream presses, a woman in charge of the monthlies, a woman in charge of out-of-town presses (especially if your town is an hour or two away from a large city), a woman in charge of radio contacts. You might also want to put one woman in charge of distributing flyers, or have a group of women divide up the key locations in a community. Still another woman might take charge of the mailing party. Whether or not she does it all herself, the publicist will need to be very organized and comfortable with deadlines.

Chapter 21 specifies the composition of these materials. Here let's talk about how to use them.

Direct Mailing and Enclosures

Most communities have some kind of women's mailing list. Sometimes they are willing to sell this list outright, but because of many Lesbians' concerns about being "outed," many organizations have a policy not to sell their lists. If their policy is to use it only for their own mailings, often they will be willing to enclose a flyer about your production—if they approve it—and charge you a percentage of the mailing costs. They may ask that you send a volunteer to help with their mailing, as part of your contribution. But, as I warned above, check the timing of their mailing: Too far ahead or too short notice may both be a waste of your money. Another option is to rent a mailing list from a particular community on a case-by-case basis.

Large mailings by nonprofit organizations probably use a bulk mailing permit, which is cheaper than regular postage. Your theatre, once it becomes established and develops its own mailing list, may eventually want its own permit, but the permits are expensive, and in order for it to pay off, you will need a large list and frequent mailings. The post office is very picky about the procedures for a bulk mailing. If you do not observe its procedures, your mailing may not be delivered. Be sure that you have the appropriate stamps and stickers, and that you follow the correct procedure for bundling by zip code.

Contacting the Press

Make telephone calls! Before you send out your carefully prepared press kit (flyer, photo, press release, calendar announcement, etc.) to appropriate parties, be sure you know to whom to send it, the accurate mailing address (which might be different from the address on the masthead of a publication), and the deadline by which the kit is needed. Mailing to the "Arts Editor" is better than nothing, but an actual name is even better. If you're very close to deadline, better to drive by and deliver the kit in person. But if you do this, don't expect to have contact with the editor herself. If it's a large newspaper, there will be a receptionist on the ground floor who intercepts these kinds of deliveries.

If you want to speak in person with the editor, call to find out the best time to reach her. Then, when you do reach the editor, find out when she can meet with you or conduct a phone interview. Editors don't owe you any free publicity, so it pays to be polite and persistent.

Posting Flyers

There are services that will post your flyers for you, but they cost money, and they won't necessarily know where to reach the targeted audience. Better to divide up the territory among actors or volunteers and have the company members post the flyers themselves. I like to recruit the cast for this job, because it's not that difficult (I don't ask the actors to do anything else related to publicity, unless it's a public appearance), and because they always come up with creative ideas for locations. In addition to the local gay-and-Lesbian church, coffeehouse, bar, women's bookstore and dance hall, there may be women in the cast who have a line on Lesbian organizations or organizers in the small towns outside your area. They may have contacts in other places. They may be members of a specialized Lesbian business group or softball team. Ask the actors. They are a great resource and highly motivated to have their friends come see them.

If you are canvasing a university campus, keep in mind that such places frequently have a policy requiring prior approval of anything posted on their bulletin boards. Sometimes, the college requests that you leave the flyers with someone there, and it has its own staff who will post them. Find out the policy before you waste your time posting flyers that are just going to be torn down the next day.

Block Ticket Sales and Theatre Nights

Block sales and theatre nights are two special methods of selling tickets that can generate publicity for your production. Both were addressed in Chapter 15, but I will mention them again here in terms of their publicity value.

In a block sales situation, there is a discount for a party of a certain size that buys its tickets in advance. The block-sales policy should be made known to the members of the cast and crew, because they will be contributing to the publicity as they spread the word about the play. If the theatre is using a mailing list that includes women's businesses and organizations, it might be a good idea to include block-sales information in those materials.

If your theatre is attempting to sell entire performances to organizations—a theatre night—this requires some special targeted publicity efforts. The publicist could take this on herself, designing a special letter for the organizations the theatre is hoping to attract, or making personal contact with these organizations. Since this is a sales job, it might be a good idea to offer a 10–15 percent commission to whoever can sell a theatre night.

Interviews

Find out what kind of women's programming or arts programming is on the radio in your area. If your theatre is just opening, or if homophobia has been an issue for your community, you may be able to get on the air for a mainstream talk radio show. Scout around.

Give yourself plenty of lead time (around two months) to line up the interview. If you want to send the host a press kit, include a photo, press release, flyer, a bio on whom you have selected as the interviewee, and a sample of the segment you want to perform, if applicable. Follow up with phone calls. Be persistent.

You can send the performers, or the director, or the director and the producer, or the producer and playwright. And a word of warning to the women being interviewed: Stay in control of the interview. Know what you want to talk about, and find ways to come back to these points. Often, the interviewer will have some angle of interest, but one entirely irrelevant to your theatre. For example, it's not uncommon for those of us working in women's culture to encounter representatives of the media who are obsessed with "what about the men" questions. Responding to these is always a dead-end situation at best, and a trap at worst. Keep it light. You can always say, "Well, maybe the men should answer that. But the challenge *we* find in our work is to take this play about Amazon warriors and . . ." Know what you want to say, and make sure you say it. Don't give your power away!

If the interviewer is openly hostile and persists with sidetracking questions, don't hesitate to use some verbal self-defense: "When did you get the idea that men are uncomfortable with women's theatres?" Keep asking questions about her questions until she is on the defensive and relieved to let you change the subject.

Most interviewers, especially if they're on women's programming or Lesbian programming, are wonderful. But, occasionally, you will find someone who throws you a curve. Sometimes the host is just wonderful in the reception area but then turns into a barracuda on the air. Keep your cool; and remember that you read about this type of person in this book. You're not crazy, you didn't cause the behavior, such people do exist. Who knows why?

Paid Advertisements

There's not too much that needs to be said. Find out advertising costs, sizes, deadlines. That's about it. And do follow-up work. Check to make sure the publications in which you decided to buy space actually ran the ad.

Special Events Publicity

If there is a women's dance, or concert, or other special event scheduled in your community prior to the play's run, there will probably be a table there for printed materials. Leave a stack of your flyers. Since these are for the show, not the auditions, you can afford not to be stingy. In some cases, depending on the event (I'm thinking of International Women's Day), there may be staffed information tables for different organizations. Consider having someone, like a volunteer coordinator, staff a table to represent your theatre. In addition to flyers for the show, you could have general information about the theatre available, as well as volunteer sign-up sheets or a mailing list roster.

Getting Reviewed

Last but not least is the question of getting reviewed. A good or even mediocre review can be one of your most effective forms of publicity.

As opposed to the other forms of publicity, however, this is the one area where you have the least control. You *should* be able to get a review from the women's press or the gay-and-Lesbian paper, but sometimes even in these special interest papers there will be competition for space for the performing arts write-ups. And watch out for lesbophobia, if your show opens at the same time as the new drag revue and the AIDS benefit! Be assertive!

Even if you do get supportive reviews from the women's press or gay-and-Lesbian paper, these are usually monthly publications, so chances are that the review will come late in your run, or even after the run, in which case it's nice for everyone's ego, but doesn't do much for your box office.

Far more helpful is a review from the mainstream daily paper in your town, the "legit" paper. These reviews are read by far more people, and they either come out weekly in a special arts section, or they may come out on any day when the editor has the space. In other words, your chances of a timely review are much greater in the mainstream press.

But what about these guys (and guys they usually are)? Aren't they likely to cause more trouble than they're worth?

Well, first, the *Times* (*New York*, et al.) they are a-changing. Feminist concerns are being addressed in more and more legit film and theatre reviews. And so is racism, and even classism. A critic who glorifies a woman-hating work is likely to hear from more than just the radical dykes these days.

And a good review—or even a mediocre review—is excellent publicity for a Lesbian theatre. Our audiences, with their incredible loyalty, bless their hearts, will often come just because we're Lesbian and we're doing it. A mixed or poor review will still generate a certain amount of curiosity.

So, yes, invite all critics. (As theatre people, we all know they're idiots anyway, right?)

To garner reviews, use the same approach you did with the press releases, only be even more assertive. Find out who any particular drama critic is. Read several of her reviews. Send her a press kit. Call ostensibly to verify that she received it, and then pitch like hell whatever angle of the show you feel will have the most appeal to her readers or to her own pet areas (you can deduce these from her reviews). Talk to her in her language. You both must love theatre, so try to find the common ground. Don't hesitate to talk about the difficulty in getting the word out to heterosexual audiences that Lesbian theatre offers an exciting, competitive, cutting-edge alternative to mainstream culture. Tell her that you are holding two comps in her name at the box office. And if there is *anyone* in your theatre company or associated with it who has connections, use them. Ask the connection to put in a good word. Drop names. Schmooze or lose.

What about a bad review? Don't give up. Call and request to meet with the reviewer about it. Listen to her objections, even if they're completely off the wall. Explain your point of view. Explain what part of the review you may have felt was unfair or unreasonable. Explain the important aspects that you felt were overlooked.

Sometimes this is a tricky area, because Lesbian theatre may have one-tenth the resources of a mainstream community theatre, and yet you will probably be judged by their standards. You may want to talk about how affirmative-action principles are applicable. But keep in mind that a theatre critic is not usually a political activist. She is primarily an entertainer herself, and she will lose her credibility if she recommends poor productions by worthy organizations. Show respect for her position, but don't lose respect for yours. (There are some critics, of course, who are arrogant bigots. In that case, you might want to consider a letter-writing campaign to the editor in protest of the misogyny or homophobia of the critic.)

So . . . you've got your materials, your calendar, and your technique down. What could possibly go wrong?

Chapter 24

Troubleshooting

Accountability

Publicity can be a touchy area in theatre, because everybody likes to be represented favorably and accurately in the media. The publicist should be aware of the problems, both internal and external, that can arise around publicity for a play.

The biggest cause of internal friction is lack of accountability. (Where have I heard that before?) I'm talking about misspelled names in the paper, leading actors seeing what they consider smaller parts given more credit, erroneous dates, missed deadlines, expensive typos detected after the flyers are printed, and so on. Nobody is perfect, but since publicity is an area that is so important and that will involve so many egos, it's good for a theatre company to have a system of checks and balances to protect both itself (from expensive mistakes and angry actors) and the publicist (from criticism burnout).

In the first place, it's bad process to have one person solely responsible for the content of all the publicity. There should be someone else who has approval rights. It could be the director, or the executive producer, or someone appointed by the executive producer. This person should review all the materials before they go out to printers and the press.

Whoever reviews the publicity materials should not just proofread the spelling (which, by the way, includes knowing how to spell names), but this Lesbian should also check for accuracy, check for inclusion of all pertinent information (accessibility information, for instance), and check that the material is of an appropriate quality to represent the theatre company: Is it handwritten or typed? Is it well written? Does it highlight what the theatre company wants to highlight? Is it feminist?

The flyers are a special case, because of the money involved in having to reprint them in the event of error. Be sure to proofread the work *before* the printing is done, because graphic designers make mistakes, too. Don't stand at the counter and scan the flyer. Walk over to a corner, sit down, and read it word by word, even moving your lips or tracing the words with your finger. Check the dates against a calendar. When the date says Saturday, May 9, but May 9 is actually a Sunday, don't expect your audience to guess what you really mean. If your flyer is being typeset at the same print shop that is going to do the printing, be sure to ask them to hold off until you've had a chance to drop by and proof the job. (Many print shops have that policy anyway, but if they don't, be sure to make the request.)

Homophobes, Lesbophobes, and Woman-Haters

Yes, they're out there. And you'd be surprised: They're not all right-wing Christian heterosexuals. Believe it or not, there are Lesbians who don't like women, there are gay men who don't like Lesbians, and there are all kinds of people who can't stand the thought of people putting on plays. Go figure . . . and figure good, because you may have to deal with these folks if you're doing publicity.

Many people don't consider theatre important or serious. This is more of a problem in grant writing than it is in media contact, because most papers are used to reserving space for news on plays, movies, etcetera. But it can be a problem in terms of whether or not you can get an interview or an appearance on the air.

The most important thing is for the publicist to be aware of this prejudice and, when the manifestations of it surface, not to allow herself to internalize any of it. No, you are not wasting the busy and important news editor's time. No, you are not being pushy. No, you are not demanding an inordinate amount of space for an event that won't be seen by that many people. Lesbian theatre is on the cutting edge of women's issues. There has not been a women's culture in thousands of years. This is the arrival of a new era on the planet. This is probably the most significant story the paper will run all week, even though they may not know it.

What about Lesbophobia? Well, a gay man may not have a prejudice against his brothers, but he could be harboring a real antipathy for Lesbians—which is not to say that he will be overtly hostile. He may just be oblivious to the fact that his supposedly gay-and-Lesbian paper runs six gay male articles for every one Lesbian article. He may not understand how man-boy love violates Lesbian values. He may really believe that AIDS should be a priority issue for Lesbians. Yep, Lesbophobia. Ignorance is but one of the disguises of prejudice.

It's sad to say it, but most of the gay-and-Lesbian papers (and theatres!) heavily favor the gay male agenda over the Lesbian one. For instance, if your play is running at the same time that the newest drag show about Bette Davis opens, guess who's going to get the review?

Know the paper you're lobbying. Scan a copy. How many articles on AIDS? How many on Lesbian health care? Look at the staff masthead. Who are the editors? How many are men, and what are their positions? Forewarned is forearmed. If the paper is top-heavy with men's news, you may have to be a little more firm, or even aggressive. In fact, you may need to call this to the paper's attention.

In approaching mainstream newspapers, it's difficult to separate the woman-hating from the homophobia, and often the two are combined. Let's say that your theatre opening was "accidentally left out" of the mainstream daily. You contact the appropriate editor and he tells you it was an oversight—these things happen. What do you do? Consider pursuing the matter further. I have frequently had to do a little consciousness-raising when this happens to my publicity.

One of the slimier characters is the editor who "hasn't got a problem with homosexuality myself, but my boss does." Fine. Go find the boss.

One secret about Lesbophobes, women-haters, homophobes, and art bigots: They are cowards. They are living their lives according to someone else's code, and that's why they have such bitter hatred for those of us who choose to define ourselves. Cowards are easily intimidated by the faintest whiff of appealing to higher authority, of litigation, of any kind of trouble. They hate that. Avoiding confrontation has been the rationale for their lack of self-realization. Because of this fact, when in doubt, I always speak up. This usually scares them and occasionally even makes them ashamed. Sometimes they will attempt to attribute their discomfort to my nasty personality, but the truth has a way of seeping through the layers of bedrock, and I always leave these encounters feeling that what I have said is going to stay with them and continue to work its way between the strata of their thinking. And, you know, just a little layer of truth, like water, can expand under the right conditions and split off the whole face of a mountain.

Your publicist needs to be someone who interfaces comfortably with a wide range of people, who has good communication skills, who can "chat people up," and who can remain diplomatic but firm under fire. Good publicists are often women with experience in sales, or those with a good understanding of the white male business world. It goes without saying that she needs to be proud of her Lesbianism.

Well, that's it for publicity, except for one more last-minute bit of business . . . the program.

Chapter 25

The Program

The final item on the publicity agenda is the program. The program is very important, at least in my view, for in all-volunteer companies, it may be the only public recognition the cast and crew receive. Take it seriously!

Programs can be inexpensively photocopied on 8½″ × 14″ paper, then folded into booklet format; or they can be glossy, stapled, custom-sized, multicolored affairs. They can be a real moneymaker for the company, or they can be one more budget item. Again, make some bottom-line decisions about the program before you even begin your publicity calendar.

If you decide to sell advertising space in the program, price it so that it will at least pay for the program. You can sell full-page, half-page, quarter-page, and business-card-size ads. You can also run a list of "Friends of the Theatre" and charge by the line. (This list can be expanded creatively to include sponsors, benefactors, etc., and categorized by the size of donation.) I recommend charging $5 a line for inclusion in the "Friends" list, and $25 for running business-card-size ads. Larger-sized ads should be priced higher accordingly.

The publicist may be the person in charge of the program, or maybe it will be someone else from the company. There may be one woman who sells all the ads, or maybe the cast and crew can be recruited to solicit their friends and their favorite businesses. If one woman does the selling, the company might want to allow her a 10–15 percent commission. After all, the money she raises is money you might not have otherwise. It's just good business to provide her with some personal incentive.

The program should have its own budget, based on the cost of graphics, the quality of paper, and the quantity. If your theatre is producing a longer run, you might consider printing a conservative number of programs, because you can always print more during the run, as the need arises. On the other hand, if the price break for printing 1,000 at a time is substantial, it might not be so smart to run two orders of 500. Cover graphics for the program are often taken from the flyer or poster graphics. Sometimes the entire flyer is sized down for the cover. (See Appendix 21 for a sample program.)

The program should always include the following information:

- The same information as on the flyer: who, what, when, where, and how.

- The names of all cast and crew members and the titles of their positions or names of their characters.
- The location and time for every act (taken from the script).
- Information about the number and length of intermissions.
- Acknowledgment of those who lent their support through goods or services to the production (This can be a simple list of names of individuals or businesses, in alphabetical order, or it can be more specific: "Special thanks to Jill Trainer of Ritz Designs for the evening gowns, to Lisa Moore of Shears for hair styling, to Morecambe Bay Antiques for the furniture . . ." And, note, you should acknowledge advertisers in the program, even though their ads simultaneously appear in the program.)

In addition, the program can include the following:

- Cast biographies. (Note: Please, don't make them cute! I.e., don't let the actors write them themselves. They vary too much in quality, and distract from the focus on the show. The actors can *submit* bio material, but have someone edit the material for consistent length, quality, and style. It's bad form to have one bio list Actors' Equity Association credits, while another is full of self-deprecating absurdities. Limited bios include those on the cast, director, musical director, choreographer, and sometimes stage manager. If you want to go further than that, it's up to you.)
- Cast photos.
- Director's notes.
- Playwright's notes
- Names of "Friends of the Theatre" (i.e., donors).
- Upcoming auditions and/or productions.
- Calls for volunteers, wish lists, etc.
- History of the production or theatre.
- Playwright's bio.
- Advertisements.
- Clip-and-mail forms for donations, volunteering, or mailing list inclusions.
- Beeper and/or camera policies.
- The URL to the theatre's web page on the Internet.
- Inserts with last-minute changes or credits. (And, yes, it's better to include inserts than to omit someone's name!)

The program should be one of the last items of business to complete before opening, because there are so many last-minute additions to the crew, to the thank-you list, to the names of advertisers, and so forth. And even with the most last-minute printing, it's common to see a little slip of paper fall out of the program that reads, "Please note that the stage manager for the Friday, March 23 performance will be Julie Jacobs."

I have a program policy that is taken from my own experience in Lesbian theatre. Many producers or directors will probably consider this a headache, but here it is: I always get a copy of the rough draft of the program during Tech Week and circulate it among the cast and crew. I ask them to make changes or additions right on it, and when they are done, I ask them to initial next to their names. When I get the draft back, with all the little initials, I know I have a program that every single member of the cast and crew has amended and approved. There are not going to be any unpleasant surprises, at least from the program, on opening night, when everyone should be feeling happy and important. An actor whose name is misspelled or who feels undercredited in the program can be bad news. The actor's or technician's worst fears can crystalize around this "evidence" that she has been abused, neglected, exploited. And on opening night, no one is going to be in a position to take this individual's concerns personally. We'll talk about this phenomenon later when we get to curtain calls, but never underestimate the significance of billing.

So, I give each member of the production the chance to edit the program. And there are *always* many changes. The actor who sewed the Velcro on her gown for the dream sequence, for instance, might really want a costuming credit. Or the actor who showed up for one work party might feel that a "set crew" credit is important for her career. The actor whose partner has done six solid weeks of child care may feel that giving her program credit under "Special Thanks" will help mend some fences. And then there are the Sues and the Chrises who suddenly want to be listed as Susan Marie or Christiana—even though no one has ever heard them go by those names in their life. But this is their night, and I feel that the program should reflect the cast and crew's wishes for recognition. It's the least I, as director, can do.

Then there is the issue of hierarchy. The cast list is not a problem, because it's customary to present it "in order of appearance" (and say so!). The designer and tech credits are not that simple. I try to use an order that will reflect (in general) the lines of accountability (see Appendix 11), and here it is: playwright (bookwriter, lyric writer, composer), director, musical director, choreographer, scene designer, costume designer, lighting designer, sound designer, assistant director, technical director, lightboard operator, sound technician, house manager, wardrobe mistress, prop manager, set crew. If this is too hierarchical, you could list designers and crew in alphabetical order. In any event, if you have the cast and crew proof the program before it goes to the printer, you should have time to field whatever objections may arise from how you organized the information.

The director should approve the program. If she is responsible for drafting the copy for it, it should also be approved by the publicist. If there is information about the theatre itself, the producer should see it before it goes to press. And be sure that your donors want their names in print. Some Lesbians are very touchy about this. (You can always acknowledge anonymous supporters in an additional line, since—to paraphrase Virginia Woolf—" 'Anonymous' was a woman!")

And that's it for the publicity. Whew!

Part VI

On with the Show

Chapter 26

Approaching Sacred Ground

If you've come this far in the book, you have to know by now that my approach to Lesbian theatre is nothing if not pragmatic. I believe that those of us working in theatre have to work with *what is:* the frailties of human nature, the realities of oppression, the process of the actor, and so forth. And one of the facts we need to work with is that live theatre is a sacred activity.

Before we look at what it is the director *does*, we need to look at this aspect of theatre, because the artist who tries to work in the theatre without understanding the spiritual nature of her practice will find herself in a predicament similar to that of the sorcerer's apprentice. If you saw the movie *Fantasia*, you will remember that Mickey Mouse tried to clone the sorcerer's spell without any understanding of how or why magic works. Not surprisingly, his cloned spell began to clone itself, and pretty soon Mickey was up to his Mouseketeer ears in buckets, brooms, and water. The sorcerer, literally, had to bail him out. Theatre without magic is also a cloning activity. If you don't believe me, just turn on your television and look at all the little phallic clones mindlessly carrying their buckets of slop into the world.

Good theatre is conjuring and spell casting. It is bringing a spirit or spirits to life to tell a story, to warn an audience, to exorcise demons, to inspire with examples of courage or messages of hope. It is putting the audience under a spell, bewitching them with the performance, so that the truth of the play can go to work on their psyches. You could think of the actors as being possessed by spirits from another world and the audience as being in a state of trance. The success of your conjuring and spell casting will depend on the precision of the spell (the play), on the clarity and focus of the channelers (the actors), and the receptivity of the participants (the audience).

If you are a director or producer, pay attention to your spiritual hygiene. Whatever your practice—twelve-step, Wicca, meditation, the Metropolitan Community Church, body work, or distance running—*don't* let it lapse during production! Spiritual poise is a concomitant of good leadership.

Purify: A good director serves the script. She does not use the script as a vehicle for her ego, for her reputation, for her politics. This is not to say that she can't select a script for its social change potential or put her own stamp on the production. Good directors are creative interpreters of the written word, and they should never back off from that aspect of the job with a false sense of humility. But the director needs to be honest with herself about her motives. Does she really believe in what she's doing? Is she really open to casting the best people, or does she have a girlfriend to whom she's promised the lead role? Will she be ready to take charge of the production, even if it means facing off with the producer or the actors? Can she find the time in her personal life for directing without compromising those around her? Directing is a sacred trust, and one not to be taken lightly. Whatever impurities of motive a director carries into the theatre with her, she can expect to see them precipitate during the intense heat of the rehearsal process. It's far easier to get rid of these impurities ahead of time, in privacy and at leisure, before their appearance involves the other members of the production in a crisis situation.

Banish: Theatre, and especially auditions, can be a real convention of "evil spirits." I am talking about jealousy, betrayal, low self-esteem, self-doubt, paranoia, envy, and malice. If the director is threatened by another actor and feels that archetypal impulse to check another woman's momentum because her own has been so painfully checked, she can take a good hard look at that impulse—and she can banish it. The director can set a firm boundary between her personal life and her role as a director. She needs to do this, because she endangers her actors if she doesn't. This is the aspect of theatre that protects actors from sexual harassment or emotional harassment (being expected to meet the director's emotional or social needs). This is an essential part of theatre that has been lost by the secularization of patriarchal theatre.

Cast the Circle: The casting of the circle to me is the casting of the show. And it is one of the most sacred aspects of directing. In the next chapter, I will talk about the process of auditioning, but I want to take a minute with the metaphysics here. Casting a show takes humility. It takes open channels. It takes a willful setting aside of preconceived notions, stereotypes, and prejudices.

So far, the director has been working with the script at home, developing her own ideas. She may have evolved a concept, and she may have been working with some of the designers already. But she's not really going to know what she's got until the auditions. At the auditions, the show begins to reveal itself to the director. She needs to pay attention.

The auditions will test how well the director has purified her motives. Is she imposing her bias on her perceptions? Is she so invested in certain actors she's overlooking their limitations in the part, the clues they may be giving off that this is not the part or the time for them, for whatever reason? Is she ignoring a newcomer? Are the actors showing her things about the play she might have missed? Has the director gone into auditions identifying with her role in the community or her role as a teacher, instead of her role as the director? Has she set a tone that is focused on personalities and not performance? Has she set a tone for the auditions (either intimidatingly authoritative or trivializingly social) that will impede the actors' attempts to focus on their own spiritual/artistic process?

The casting of the circle will define who is in the ritual and who is outside it. The responsibility is awesome. The priestess who attempts to cast a circle from a sense of personal power invites challenges to her position, jealousy, and resentment. The same goes for the director who mistakes her personality or her achievements as the source of her power during the auditions. The purity of the director's motives will be her protection.

Invoke: Intentionally call in the qualities you want realized in your direction and in your production. Contact your emotions. Recruit your subconscious. It takes inspiration, passion, emotion, intuition, and integrity to put up a show.

The director who is not in touch with her emotions will have a hard time interpreting the play or relating to the actors, especially during Tech Week. The director who does not acknowledge or honor her subconscious mind will be losing out on one of her best resources for solving problems, and most likely her show will lack dimension. The director who is all intellect and no passion will have a very dull show, and the director who does not trust in her own inspiration is going to spend her time referencing to the work and opinions of others, depriving the show of essential vitality. The director with no integrity is the sorriest creature of all, because she will do more damage than good; may the Goddess help the actors who find themselves under the leadership of such a one.

I use specific Goddess imagery in my own rituals, and there is a Goddess I invoke who has a special relevance to Lesbian theatre: Sedna. Legends among the Eskimos tell of a woman who refused to marry, who flew off to live with the birds; but when she found herself trapped in a nest, she took flight again—this time to her father's boat. When the seas became rough, he threw her overboard. When she tried to climb back in, he cut off her hands and shoved an oar in her eye. Sliding into the icy waters of the ocean, Sedna became transformed, regenerated. She made the sea her matriarchate, and she became the great protector of the creatures of the deep.

I also tried to escape in my father's boat—the patriarchal theatre—which was the only theatre I knew about growing up. I studied this theatre; I joined it. But when I began to insist on putting women front and center, the waves began to get choppy and it was no longer smooth sailing. I lost job after job in patriarchal theatre—some of them before I even had time to start! I lost jobs teaching in the public schools. I went up against a state university in a huge lawsuit—and lost. The work of my hands, my plays, were violently rejected. My vision was nullified. I sank back into the icy waters, feeling there was no place for me, no life for me.

But to my amazement, I didn't die. I discovered that there was a whole unexplored universe of women's culture waiting to be celebrated in theatre arts. I laugh now at the memory of my fixation on my father's boat! What treasures are ours in this sea of women! This eye they tried to put out, these fingers they tried to render useless—I have never had such keen use of my faculties! And so when I think of Sedna, with her enormous fish tail stretching across the oceans, I am reminded of what is just below the surface of men's history, men's reality. I remember my home, my place. I know that the theatre of which I dream is unfolding beautifully in a deep and mysterious realm. I laugh at the little men in their limited vessels who presume to chart our waters. Sedna divides my firmament. Sedna remembers the agony of the passage. And Sedna shows me the wonder.

Another part of my personal ritual is the "Charge of the Goddess," read on full moons and Sabbats (Wiccan holy days). It reads: "If that which you seek you find not within yourself, you shall never find it without." And if that's not a rationale for method acting, I don't know what is. If the interpretation does not have roots in the actor's own truth, it will have a false ring no matter how technically polished. I think this also could apply to the play itself. It is the playwright's vision, but something about the play must resonate with the deep truths of the director in order for the director to give the thing life on the stage.

Guided Visualization: I consider this the script itself. It will take us all into a wondrous imaginary world. We will see strange visions, meet wondrous creatures here. And we will come together to reenact this journey on the stage. But it happens to all of us first in our minds, in our private interaction with the written word where we see the play in our mind's eye first.

The Ritual: In theatre, this would be the rehearsal process. That is what we will be doing for six weeks. We will enact and reenact the scenes, over and over, until we understand them in all their significance, until we have perfected the method to communicate this understanding to others. And in repetition, we will be increasing the power of the ritual.

Raising the Power: In theatre, the cone of power is raised during live performance. All the rehearsals are moving toward this point, and during Tech Week, there is a rapid escalation of activity as the technical crew joins the cast and the production moves into the theatre space. Everything intensifies. The pace picks up. The pressure builds. And then, opening night, the intention, pure as a laser from all the weeks of hard work, travels out across the stage, into the house, and into the mind of the audience where it will have the power to move thought. And moving thought is the whole purpose of theatre, real theatre. Yes, a play should entertain, it should engage intellectually; but if it doesn't move thought, it's nothing more than a staged narrative, a baby-sitting device. Real theatre is magic, and magic is the art of changing consciousness at will. Magic changes the world.

Self-Blessing: The ritual ends with a self-blessing. This is important, because after the release of all that energy, the actors or the director may be looking to the audience, to one another, or, Goddess help them, to the critics! for their blessing. No one can give us what we need after a performance except ourselves. And we need to give ourselves that blessing. Otherwise, the experience can be disorienting, depleting, and leave a morass of uncomfortable feelings that can crystallize around irrelevant issues.

Performance is a great feat, and it deserves colossal recognition. Trust me, the world will never give it. The audience is too busy figuring out what hit them (if the play really did its job). To them, the actors, no matter how dazzling, were just the messengers. The audience leaves the theatre grappling with the message. Someone has rearranged their mental furniture during the last two hours, and now they have to figure out what to do about it—move it all back again, or get used to the new arrangement? The critics are on deadline, often looking for ways to use the performance to make themselves look clever in print. In other words, no help here. And the director has her own demons. Every member of the ritual or the production must know how to bless herself, whether it's taking herself out for dessert afterward, or buying herself a nice gift, or just looking in the mirror as she takes off the makeup and saying, "Well done, my dear. Very, very well done."

Grounding: The grounding means finding some way back to the here and now, so that you don't go home and keep your partner up all night talking about the show. So that you don't go into a major depression two weeks after the show closes. In rituals, the grounding can be touching palms of hands or foreheads to the ground, or eating. Personally, I favor eating. Go out afterward. Or raid the kitchen. Have a cast party—a big one—at the end of the run.

Open the Circle: The show is over, but it still lives. Witches, at the end of a ritual, say "Merry meet and merry part and merry meet again," which means, "See you at the next auditions." The post-production meeting is another way to "open the circle."

And that's it. Rehearsal as ritual. Director as priestess. Actors as witches. Performance as magic. Theatre as sacred.

Blessed be.

Chapter 27

Auditioning Lesbians

Auditions are scary for every actor, but there are reasons they are especially scary for Lesbians. We are not supposed to be here.

We are not discriminated against by traditional methods of exclusion. Our very existence is literally denied. We are the women who "want to be men." We are the women who just "never met the right man." If we are considered biological freaks, then our political struggle is erased. If we are seen as political dissidents, then our sexuality is erased. Women preferring the company of women is such a threatening concept in patriarchy, it must be depicted as deviant. We are explained away on a case-by-case basis—and always in relation to the dominant culture. We are perpetual exceptions, and we are seldom acknowledged as a community with a culture of our own.

Lesbian women who reject the trappings of "femininity," or the emblems of sexual subordination, are frequently made to feel like freaks. The woman who does not shave her facial hair, the woman who refuses to diet, the woman who wears clothing that is comfortable and practical—all of us who have reclaimed our identities—are depicted as extreme, when in fact the woman who acts out her fear and shame of her own body is really the extremist.

And Lesbians are under very real attack. Our doors are spray-painted. We are yelled at on the street. People throw things at us. We are harassed at our gathering places. Religious and political organizations wage very real and very serious campaigns to deprive us of our rights. Our expressions of intimacy are still illegal in many states.

There are good reasons for a Lesbian to have qualms about getting up onstage, where she will be judged for who she is. And for this reason, directors of Lesbian productions should take special care to see that their auditions are humane and user-friendly.

Also, many Lesbians who have considerable dramatic ability have never performed before. Again, there are reasons for this. Traditional acting schools and college acting programs are extremely homophobic. The roles, since 99 percent of the canon of classical and contemporary plays are by men, reflect stereotyped images of women. A Lesbian in a four-year college program can expect to play wives, girlfriends, and mothers of men in plays where the male and his interests take center stage. She can expect to be an obstacle or a reward. If she is fat, older, physically challenged, or a woman with a non-Anglo-European background, she can expect to be relegated to minor roles and character parts. For most Lesbians, the price of acquiring the training is simply too high. Directors auditioning Lesbians need to honor the fact that some of our finest talent has gone without training, not because of low self-esteem or fear of success—to the contrary!—but as part of our ongoing Lesbian resistance to the roles that degrade and demoralize women. Every effort should be made to locate the women who felt a love of theatre, but who saw themselves disenfranchised by mainstream institutions. Our refusal to practice our art under the conditions established by patriarchy is a testimony to our integrity as artists. We will not allow mainstream society to drive a wedge in our identity to split off the word "Lesbian" from the word "artists."

What does it mean to be born an artist, but to be denied the opportunity to practice that art? For some women, it has meant repression and sublimation. For others, it has contributed to addictive patterns. Artist Elizabeth Layton has written movingly of her own history of severe mental illness, until in her sixties she discovered her calling as a visual artist. In my own history, my coming out as a Lesbian was simultaneous with my discovery that I was an artist. Western culture does not place a high value on art except as status symbols for the wealthy. The United States places even less value on artists than do other Western countries. Coming out as an artist is an act of courage and defiance almost as great as coming out as a Lesbian. To choose to make art the priority, given the grim economic reality for artists, is a great act of integrity.

Because of the political climate of misogyny and homophobia, the terms "professional" and "amateur" do not carry their usual connotations for Lesbians. The so-called professional actor who is Lesbian has probably never been allowed to perform Lesbian art. So what does that say about her credentials? The so-called amateur actor who is Lesbian has probably never had access to the resources that would allow her to achieve a high level of exposure or proficiency. On the other hand, she may have performed nothing but Lesbian art. What does that say about her seeming lack of experience? It is time that we break down the barriers that have divided Lesbians, forcing us to choose between our art and our Lesbianism.

So . . . how do you get the Lesbians to show up? If your audition notice is public, you will increase your chances of reaching more Lesbians. Also, if you are able to run a press release about your theatre and about your auditions in the gay-and-Lesbian or women's papers, you will have the opportunity to demystify the process for women who might be intrigued, but who may believe that auditions are only for those who are already in the theatre. It's a good idea in any publicity relating to the auditions to specify that the auditions will consist of readings from the script, that women with no previous experience are encouraged to try out, and that women of color or old women or young women or physically challenged or fat women are especially encouraged to try out. It goes without saying that Lesbian theatre practices open casting.

Auditions should be held in a space large enough to accommodate the number of women who will be trying out. It's a good idea to use the space where you will be performing, if possible, because you will need to see if the performers who will be using their voices can be heard. This is especially true with a musical.

If it's not possible to rent the performance space for auditions, then look at community centers, schools, and the like. The space you will be using for the first five weeks of rehearsal is the second-best option. Auditioning in a home is a poor choice, because the space is small; furthermore, it is not as comfortable or as professional as auditioning in a more public space.

The director and assistant director should be present at the auditions, and no one else—unless, of course, it's a musical. In that case, the choreographer and the musical director will be auditioning the actors as much as the director. The producer should not be there under any circumstances. This is the director's time, and she needs to stay focused exclusively on the integrity of her vision. Casting is a highly intuitive process, and the director needs all of her own attention.

The director should not have to be involved with greeting the auditioners or calling them. The assistant director should be the greeter. She should give the actor the audition form and explain what the procedure will be.

Sometimes auditions are closed, which means that the auditioners wait in another room or in a hall while the actors are called one at a time into the performance space. Here they perform their "audition piece," a prepared monologue *not* from the current show, in front of the director. Professional actors come to auditions of this type with "contrasting pieces." This means they will have a serious dramatic three-minute monologue and a three-minute comic piece. Often they will chose from a classical and a contemporary source, for additional contrast.

This type of audition is most often private. Closed auditions requiring audition pieces are not a good idea for Lesbian theatre, because they heavily discriminate against the actor with no formal training. To select, block, and polish an audition piece requires considerable background in theatre and access to resources. And closed auditions are very, very scary. The actor does not see the work of other women, and she has no way of judging the reactions to her work. Unless you want to keep Lesbians waiting for hours, closed auditions should be scheduled in advance, usually allowing twenty minutes per auditioner. "Call for appointment" needs to be on your publicity if this is the kind of audition you are holding.

One exception: If the show is a musical, it is almost imperative that the auditioners bring a song they have worked on. In this case, either there should be a piano player at the audition or you should let the auditioners know they need to bring a tape of their accompaniment. The same is true for dancers. They should come prepared to perform. In addition to the prepared piece, many choreographers will also want to teach the auditioners a simple sequence for them to perform, either with other auditioners or solo.

In an open audition, the actors sit together in the room where the auditions are taking place. The director or the assistant director calls specific actors up on the stage. If the auditions are in the form of readings from the script, the director will choose combinations of actors that she wants to see. This format is much less intimidating, and it provides a learning experience for the actors who will have the opportunity to observe one another. The drawback for the director is that she does not have the opportunity to see what the actors consider their best, most polished work—which is what audition pieces are all about. At the level of a cold reading, all of the performances are rough, and the director will have to use her intuition to assess how much can be accomplished in the rehearsal period.

Another drawback of the cold reading approach is that many women have poor reading skills. For some, English is a second language. Encourage women to let you know if this is the case. Make it known at the beginning of the audition that actors who are uncomfortable with reading from the script can request to improvise it. If possible, allow the actors to look over the material before they get up to read it. If scenes are repeated, this will also help familiarize them with the wording. I have cast women with severe dyslexia, women with literacy problems, and women who could not read English at all. Since reading has nothing to do with the final performance, it is a shame to allow it to prejudice the casting.

Another option is to allow actors to perform audition pieces in addition to their reading from the script. The director can ask if anyone has a prepared monologue they would like to perform.

The audition form is for the use of the director. This is her opportunity to get all the information from the actor that might help her in making a casting decision. The form should include name, address, phone number, previous experience (including singing and dancing, if relevant), which roles (if any) the actor would prefer, which roles she will *not* accept, and complete information about her schedule and calendar during the rehearsal and performance period. (See Appendix 22 for a sample audition form.)

I also include a sheet for information about other skills: carpentry, sewing, designing, painting, and so forth. I include a description of the technical jobs in the theatre, and I ask auditioners to put a check by any in which they might be interested. This sheet is invaluable in filling positions on the tech crew, because actors who are not cast are often very willing to work on the production in some other capacity. This is especially true for Lesbian theatre, because many of these Lesbian actors will not consider performing in other theatres. But people are shy about their skills, and they need a little prompting.

Before auditions, the director needs to have spent some time with the script. Often a superficial reading of the script will lend itself to stereotyped ideas about the casting. There is a tendency to "get on with the show," but the director who puts in her time studying the script will cast more creatively, direct with more confidence, and infuse her production with the many levels of meaning that are inherent in a good script.

Here is a general outline of some of the things a director needs to notice or make choices about, preferably *before* the auditions:

1. Given circumstances: geographical location, including climate; date, including time of day; economic conditions; political climate; social systems and class backgrounds; religious backgrounds and influences; things that have

happened prior to the opening scene; how the attitudes of the characters change—if they change—from the beginning of the play to the end.
2. Dialogue: imagery used by each character; style and rhythms of each character's speech.
3. Characters: each character's main objective in life (control? approval? freedom?); each character's primary needs, the obstacles to these needs in the play, the adjustment to the obstacles; suggested images for characters (bulldog? old slipper? snake?); contradiction in each character, which will be her source of fascination for the audience (cowardly heroine? fierce femme?); relationships among characters at the start of the play.
4. Theme: the spine of the play, in less than ten words ("Sex is not intimacy," "Loving oneself is the ultimate radical act," etc.); meaning of the title; philosophical statements in the play (pick them out); how the action states the theme.
5. Flavor: abstract and sensory images for each scene; abstract and sensory images for whole play.

Performing an analysis like this will enable the director to become familiar with the structure of the play and with what the playwright is trying to achieve. The final production will be a synthesis of the playwright's intention and the director's interpretation. Doing this kind of analysis, the director begins to formulate her own ideas about the material written by the playwright. This work, especially the character analysis, is invaluable preparation for the auditions.

In addition to analyzing the play, the director also needs to study the script in order to select the scenes she wants to hear read at the auditions. The more characters in the play, the more scenes she will need to select. A handy way of organizing these scenes for quick reference is to make a grid.

To make the grid, write a list of all the characters' names down the side of the paper, and then write the same list across the top. Rule these columns and rows to create a grid, and then fill in the squares of the grid with the page numbers of the scenes that show the two characters together. Where the line and column for the same character intersect, find the page for a monologue and put it in that square. (There is a sample audition grid for the play *Little Women* in Appendix 23.)

Probably not every character will have a scene with every other character, so your grid will have a lot of blanks. Also, you may want to see two characters read more than one scene together, especially if they are the leads. In that case, put the page numbers for more than one scene in the grid. Make notations by them, so that you can remember which scene is which ("comic," "romantic," etc.). If there are scenes in the play with more than two characters that you want to see read at the auditions, make a note of these at the bottom of the page. For the most part, however, one- and two-person scenes make the most effective audition material.

The grid is one sure way to guarantee that you will be able to see every character in every possible two-person combination. The grid enables the director to find at a glance the page numbers for reading any two characters together, if such a scene exists. This takes some time to draw up, but it is invaluable in the heat of auditions. I have always resented directors who made me wait around for them to do their homework.

The director should leave the auditions confident that she has seen everything she needed and wanted to see. She should have seen the actors in all the roles in which she wanted to consider them, and she should have seen all the actors in combinations that would give her an idea of how they will fit the roles. In my opinion, a well-cast show is always cast as an ensemble, even if there are one or two so-called starring roles.

"Ensemble" means more than a show where the actors all have the same number of lines. In every show, the actors should achieve the same level of excellence whenever they are onstage, regardless of the size of their part. The actor with the walk-on role should receive the same quality of direction as the leads, because her believability will affect the believability of the other actors, the credibility of the action, and the overall pacing and style of the show.

The ensemble approach accords every actor the dignity she deserves and gives the highest priority to the play, not the stars. If you want to be in the business of showcasing performers, open a talent agency. In live theatre, how the actors work together is as important as their individual performance skills.

This raises the question of precasting. Precasting is something Broadway producers do when they need a name to get backers. There is seldom any need to precast at the community level, and it works against building an ensemble. Any actor worth her salt should understand the need for the director to see her with the other prospective cast members before the final decision. If she's too much of a prima donna to audition, who wants to work with her anyway? You can always tell an actor, "I would really like to see you read for this part," which lets her know she's got a good chance, but which also leaves the door open for those last-minute surprises that have a way of happening at auditions. And be sure when you tell an actor you'd like to see her read that she understands you mean just that—no promises!

At auditions, after the auditioners have been greeted and given the forms to fill out, it's a good idea for the director to introduce herself and make some comments about the show. Chances are, if it's Lesbian theatre, the auditioners will not know the script. It's appropriate to describe the story line briefly. It's also important to stress the need for them to fill out their schedules as accurately as possible. Give them the dates for Tech Week and stress that *every actor* will be needed *every night* of Tech Week. If they cannot give you that commitment, they should know they will not be cast in the show. This is also a good time to make your pitch about filling tech positions.

When I audition, I explain how I work. I tell the actors that I will interrupt a scene when I have seen what I want to see and that I do this so that we will not be there any longer than necessary. I advise them to try not to second-guess the director. I may interrupt a scene after one minute, because I have decided to cast both the actors. "Thank you" doesn't necessarily mean I didn't like what I saw. I have also been known to let actors go on for five minutes, and then decide not to cast either of them. Actors can tie themselves up in knots trying to read the mind of a director during auditions, and this will only distract and demoralize them. I suggest they resist the temptation and focus on their own ideas about the work.

I also invite the actors to tell me if I have not read them for a part for which they want to audition. At the end of auditions, I will ask if anyone has any requests to read for something else.

It's a poor idea to give direction at an audition, unless there is a specific reason. If an actor is way off the mark with her interpretation, for example, and you really want to see her read with a specific intention—"You want to kill her"—then you could request that the actor try working with that suggestion. Otherwise, it's a good idea to watch what the actors do on their own.

I do give one general direction at the beginning of auditions. I remind the actors that we will have six weeks to develop character. I am not interested in full-blown character interpretations at this stage. In fact, that could work against them, if the interpretations are not what I envision for the show. Instead, I encourage them to really work off the actor with whom they're reading, to show me that they can hit the ball back wherever it lands. I'm not nearly as interested in form as I am in how well they can keep the ball in play. If one actor gives another a line somewhere she didn't expect it, she should go where she has to in order to return it—even if it's coming from out-of-bounds.

The reason I give this direction is that many actors can look impressive in a vacuum. Unfortunately, these actors often stay in a vacuum. You can put them in the hottest love scene on earth, and they are basically still running monologues. This kind of actor is extremely difficult to work with, and the root of the problem is often too deep for the director to access. When I see an actor who cannot work off a partner at a reading, I have learned to assume that six weeks of rehearsal will not cure the problem. On the other hand, questions of timing or style or interpretation are relatively easy to work on. If two actors are really sparking at the reading, I don't care if they are reading each other's lines, mispronouncing one-syllable words, or even breaking character from the pleasure of working with each other. I'll cast that pair every time over the polished technical performer who treats her partner like some kind of automatic ball boy, lobbing lines to her so she can show off her form.

In Lesbian theatre, there's a good chance that some of the actors will be your good friends, ex-lovers, etcetera. There might therefore be a temptation to run the auditions informally and to interact on a personal level with the different women there. I do not recommend this, because the bottom line is that the director is going to cast as a director, not as a friend. Turning the auditions into a social event sends mixed messages, sets up the auditioners for a sense of betrayal, and establishes an unprofessional tone for the whole production. The closer your friendship with the auditioner, the kinder it is to keep a professional distance for this activity. It's also an act of consideration for the strangers among the crowd, who could be very intimidated by the director's familiarity with the other women.

And, finally, a word about attitude. This is for the actors, not the director. An actor who is a bad sport will sabotage her own audition just as surely as the tennis player who is a bad sport will sabotage her own game. A bitter or resentful actor cannot project effectively from the stage. Her energy is all pulled in by the turbulent emotions she is experiencing. She has very little left over to commit to the character she is attempting to portray.

If, as an actor, you feel the audition is not going your way, if you're feeling jealous, at an unfair advantage, or betrayed by the director, then pull back. Excuse yourself, take a break, take a walk, pull out something inspirational to read, *get over yourself*. If the auditions run for more than one day, go home and come back the next day. The actor who believes that "bad vibing" the director will influence the casting in her favor is sadly mistaken—unless her director is a hopeless co-dependent and a rotten artist. A good director who sees an actor attempt this kind of emotional blackmail at the audition stage, can only expect to see more of it later. By dress rehearsal, this actor could be a full-blown tyrant, threatening to sabotage the performance unless she gets her way. The director would be wise to pass over the actor, no matter how impressive the actor's previous track record.

Auditions may be held on one day or over two. Occasionally, a production will schedule two days of auditions and one day of callbacks. For Lesbian theatre, I usually have one day of auditions and schedule the callbacks for the next day. That way, women who could not make the first day of auditions can try out at the callbacks. If an actor can't make any of the dates, I am willing to schedule a private audition, but she must understand that she is at a disadvantage, because I will not be able to read her with the rest of the auditioners.

When in doubt about a performer, call back. It doesn't hurt, for even if you are 95 percent sure you can't use the actor, you can still take that one last look at her. There may be something you overlooked. You never know—maybe her cat died the day before.

The actors are usually called the night after auditions, or the next day. If there is some centrally located bulletin board at the community hall or the cafe where Lesbians congregate, you can post the callback list there. The actors should have the phone number of the assistant director; and if they are afraid they might have missed the call, they can phone her and ask her to read the list. This is less painful than having to identify yourself and be told you didn't make it. Instruct the assistant director not to ask who's calling. Or just put the cast list on your message machine and let all the calls ring through the next day.

In situations where the first round of auditions was private with audition pieces, the callback is the time for the director to read the actors against each other. In Lesbian theatre, assuming the auditions were readings, the callback is a time for the director to do more of the same mixing and matching, but generally with a tighter focus. Certain actors have been eliminated. Certain choices have been narrowed down. It's still a good idea to ask the actors if there is something they have not read for that they'd like to show you.

At the end of callbacks, when I have a strong idea of who I will cast, I ask these actors to stand together onstage. Some directors do this to get an idea about heights, but that is not my reason. I am looking for the feel of the ensemble. I consider this an important part of my last look at the actors, but it does have one drawback: It makes it evident for the first time who the director is favoring, and that can be very painful to the actors. Although I will usually call up a number of different combinations in an attempt to keep the actors guessing, it has always been my perception that, by this time, the actors can tell. It's difficult for actors to have to confront rejection in the presence of other actors, and I take pains to avoid that dynamic; but ultimately my obligations are to the show, and that's why I do a lineup as the very last order of business at the audition.

Now, the actual casting. This is an intensely private process. It's a commitment. It's like moving in with a lover: You can ask your friends' opinions all you want, but the bottom line is that you will be the one stuck with the consequences of your decision, and so you are the one you really have to ask.

I like to spend a little time "debriefing" with the assistant director after auditions. We sit in the empty theatre, or we go out for coffee. We talk about what we've just seen. Her feedback helps me articulate my own perceptions and sometimes can call attention to something I overlooked. We have a good time judging the contestants, as it were. It breaks the tension for me, and I like that second opinion—but notice it's from my assistant, not my boss.

I encourage directors to trust their intuitions, to play the long shots. There is a certain spark of excitement I get when I make a casting decision. If that spark is not there for you, I suggest you keep looking. Trust the universe. Take that extra week and call around. Don't cast someone out of duty or necessity, because you will not be able to work with her with any real conviction—and, sister, believe me, she's going to feel that, and she will not like you any better for it than the rebound lover enjoys spending time with a woman who wishes she were with someone else. Casting without conviction puts a ceiling on an actor's performance. You will be the coach. You cannot possibly coach an athlete beyond your own perception of her abilities. Don't even try. And have the humility to realize that another coach may get a gold medal out of her. Not every director is tailored for every actor, and vice versa. Keep this in mind when you run across an actor with an impressive resume but who doesn't do anything for you.

So trust your intuitions—and then read over the information sheets, *carefully*. If certain actors specified that they wouldn't accept a small part, don't count on talking them into taking one. Move on to your other choices. If one auditioner is going to Disneyland the week before Tech Week, forget how perfect she was for the part. She's not perfect anymore. If an actor you wish to cast works a night job four days a week and works in a group home on weekends, find a cast with exactly the same schedule or forget her.

As far as actors' previous experience—or lack thereof—goes, don't let it weigh as much as your own perceptions. We all know how to pad resumes, and actors are no exception. Without knowing the company or the director, what looks like a star turn may have just been a hack job. Extensive experience racked up under poor directors may be as much a minus as a plus in casting an actor. These actors may have all the bad habits of a novice, but all the attitude of a veteran.

And, finally, sleep on it. See if you feel the same toward your choices in the morning. Don't be afraid to leave holes in the cast, especially if you have a week before rehearsals start.

When you have your cast list, call the assistant director and give it to her. Ask her to read it back, just to be sure. Actors should be notified of the final casting as soon as possible, preferably the morning after the final audition or callback. Again, post the list if that's appropriate, and make it possible for the auditioners to phone the AD for the cast list. Often the auditioners will want to know who did get the part, even if they didn't. The AD should be the one to notify the actors who were cast, but it's a poor idea to notify those who didn't get cast. When the AD calls with the good news, she should provide the cast with the time, date, and location of the first rehearsal.

And then take yourself out for lunch. You deserve it. The die is cast, for better or for worse. You have cleared your first and, in many ways, most important hurdle: You have your actors.

Chapter 28

Production Meetings

Production meetings are meetings the director holds with the staff. These generally begin around the time of auditions. Obviously, the director will have already met with the producer about the script, budget, and performance space. The director will also have met with the publicist to get the notices out about auditions. She should also have met with the scene designer, because she will need to have her floor plan in time for the first rehearsal. She may have met with other designers, and she has probably met with the assistant director.

But we are talking about the first "Big Meeting," the first production meeting. Try to have everyone there: producer, director, choreographer, musical director, designers, tech director, publicist, stage manager, assistant director, assistant stage manager, house manager, prop manager, lightboard operator, sound operator, wardrobe manager. You won't need to see some of these folks again for a month or even more, but have them come to the first meeting. This will help them feel like they've been in on the production from the start, which is important for team morale.

If you don't have a full staff before auditions, I suggest you hold off the first production meeting until after you have had the chance to recruit from among the would-be actors. Remember the skills/interest form you had all the auditioners fill out? Give them a call. They'd love to be asked!

The purpose of the first production meeting is to generate excitement. You are all on a mission together. This is a time for introductions, for budgets, for scheduling, and for procedures. But it is also a time for vision. Everyone should feel that they are part of a very exciting and very important enterprise and that there is no limit on their participation or input.

As the members of the staff introduce themselves, allow them the opportunity to talk about their fears or their lack of experience. Many people on your staff will be doing something they have never done before, and it's helpful for them to understand there are others in the same boat. Transform their sources of anxiety into causes for excitement. This is a time for the designers to present their ideas, to pass around their sketches—but remember, it is not appropriate for staff to have input on design decisions. These are made strictly between director and designers. Too many cooks not only spoil the soup, but they can make the chef resign in disgust. Input should be given only if solicited.

You may not have worked out all the details of the rehearsal schedule yet, but you should have the schedule for Tech Week and performance nights (the space should have been reserved by now!). For most of the staff, the Tech Week schedule is the only one that concerns them. (The musical director and the choreographer will obviously be concerned with the entire rehearsal schedule.) The deadline for sets, costumes, props, technicians, and so forth, is the first rehearsal in the theatre, the beginning of Tech Week. This is also the day that the stage manager begins her duties. The house manager should attend at least one run-through during Tech Week, but her deadline is really opening night. The publicist's deadlines were discussed earlier.

The director should also have a schedule of production meetings available for the staff. For the first month, these can be every two weeks. Closer to opening, the staff should be meeting weekly. The director may choose to schedule separate meetings with each of the designers.

Production meetings should always start on time and stop on time. Have an agenda, give everyone a copy, ask for additions or changes, and then *stick to it*. Allow two hours for each meeting, and *never* go over. Schedule additional meetings if you have to. Nothing is more demoralizing than open-ended meetings that go on and on. Staff members should be prepared to come to meetings with the most current update on their budgets, with their projected expenditures, and with a report on the work they have done since the last meeting and the work they anticipate doing before the next meeting. If they have problems—or even if they just anticipate problems—they should bring these to the meeting. If any of the staff are having personnel problems, it is appropriate to take these up at the meeting—unless the conflict is with another staff member!

Production meetings are a "check-in" time, where the staff can update one another on the progress of their work. The tech director can talk about her anticipated cost overruns, because the community college changed its mind about loaning the platforms. The costume designer can report on the status of her search for gorilla suits. The lighting designer can discuss the implications of eliminating the follow spot. The publicist can check with the costume designer about the feasibility of having costumes in time for the photo shoot. Everyone can compare notes on how their budgets are doing. If costumes are going over budget, maybe the prop manager has some money to spare. Production meetings offer a good place to brainstorm creative solutions to problems. These meetings should be fun and exciting.

Production meetings can be held at the performance space, at the space being used for rehearsals, in a restaurant or other public facility, or in a home. It's a good idea to provide beverages and snacks. And it's okay to be silly. Some of my best times in theatre have been production meetings with a staff that's really bonded.

Chapter 29

The First Rehearsal

The first rehearsal is often called a "read-through" because traditionally at this rehearsal, the actors only read through the script. Before we talk about the read-through, however, there are several other things that need to be covered at the first meeting of the cast.

First and foremost, tell the cast that each and every one of them has gotten the part because they were the best. That may seem like a given, but it's important for the actors to hear that and to know that they were not "mercy-cast" or leftovers.

Introduce your assistant director, and tell the cast what her role will be. Pass out the contact sheets, which should list the names, addresses, and phone numbers of the cast, the AD, the tech director, the stage manager, and the director. The designers can also be included, as well as technicians and crew.

Sometimes the costume designer will be at the first rehearsal. If she is, introduce her. She may want to get everyone's measurements at this meeting. If she needs the cast to help costume themselves, allow her a block of time to talk about her needs. She can also come to a later rehearsal and talk privately with the actors when they are between scenes. (The read-through requires everyone's ongoing attention, and this is not an appropriate time for private meetings with the costumer.)

Next, you need to discuss your contract with them, because the director's relationship to the actors is a contractual one. This contract is seldom written and often taken for granted, but the bias of this book—if you haven't noticed—is for clear and up-front agreements. If there are any surprises in store, better to discover them at the first reading than later.

Here are some of the things that may be included under the director's contractual obligations:

1. She will show up on time and be ready to work at all scheduled rehearsals. She will be prepared for the work of that day's rehearsal. She will not change the schedule without consent of the cast, unless there are compelling reasons, such as changes in access to the rehearsal space. She will not take company time for business not related to the directing of the show. She will not waste the actors' time.

2. She will not allow her actors to look bad onstage: She will help them with motivation, with blocking. She will see that they have adequate and responsible tech on the show. She will make every effort to see that they have appro-

priate props and costumes early enough for the actors to be comfortable with them. If an actor is unhappy with any part of the direction, she will be as responsive as she can to the actor's needs, without sacrificing the performance of the other actors or the integrity of her vision.

3. She will exercise approval rights concerning the publicity for the show, making sure the actors get the best possible coverage—and coverage that represents the show accurately.
4. She will be available to actors to listen to their problems with the part or with other actors, crew members, or designers, and she will take responsibility for facilitating communication about problems within the company.
5. She will treat all the actors impartially, with respect for their dignity as women and respect for their commitment as actors. She will not give direction that will violate the actors or jeopardize their health or welfare. She will not indulge in favoritism.
6. She will not show up for work under the influence of drugs or alcohol.
7. Until Tech Week, no one else has a right to supervise the actors. During Tech Week, the stage manager begins to take over the running of the show. By opening night, the stage manager is completely in charge of the performances.

And here are some things that might be included under the actors' contractual obligations:

1. Actors will show up on time for rehearsals, *ready to work*. If they need to eat their dinner, change their clothes, make a phone call, they should arrive in plenty of time to take care of their personal needs before the scheduled time for the rehearsal. If an actor is going to be late, or even if she just knows she's cutting it close, she will contact the assistant director or director, or she will call the rehearsal hall.

A footnote to this clause: One of my first directors had a policy that an actor who was late for a rehearsal would need to apologize to the company, not just to the director. This is actually an excellent policy, even though it might at first seem like a punitive discipline. Acting is not a regular job where the absence of one employee may have a minimal effect on the other employees. At best, being late can cause other actors to worry, and at worst, it can stall the entire rehearsal. The situation is everyone's business, because of the high degree of collaboration in theatre.

It may seem like nitpicking to spend two paragraphs on the issue of tardiness, but live theatre is a mission wherein a number of women suddenly find that their success or failure rests on the shoulders of women they have never met before. In real life, we rarely give strangers or acquaintances that degree of power over our lives. In live theatre, we have to. Friendship and long histories cannot be relied on for good communication. Extremely clear lines of accountability and authority need to be established quickly, and any policy that facilitates this process is valuable.

2. Actors will show up on time for "the call"—the time designated for cast and crew to be at the theatre for performances, usually one hour before curtain. (When an actor is casual about this commitment, it can cause unnecessary anxiety for cast members.)
3. Actors will attend *all* rehearsals for which they are scheduled. If there is an emergency situation, the actor needs to let the director know as soon as possible. Actors may not be excused from any rehearsals during Tech Week. Actors should not ask for special days off, because if every actor did that, the schedule would be a shambles.
4. Actors will be off book by the date on the schedule. They will be off prompt by the date on the schedule. (An actor who is slow to get off book holds back all the other cast members who are ready to begin fine-tuning their timing and motivations. She forces them back to her level of performance, which isn't fair.) The actor will learn the lines *as written*.
5. Actors will take their complaints about the set, costumes, props, or the other actors to the director or the assistant director.

This fifth clause is probably the most important one in the contract: There is a chain of command in theatre, or if that term has too many patriarchal associations, try "chain of accountability." When a link in this chain is bypassed, it always causes problems. We have already seen what happens when actors go over the director's head to the producer. If they go "under" the director's head to the other actors or the technicians, it is equally unproductive. Other actors or technicians are not in a position to do anything more than listen or sympathize—or tell other actors.

What might have been no more than someone's thoughtless mistake can then take on the proportions of malicious sabotage in the high-pressure environment of Tech Week. Nervous actors looking for somewhere to project their fears can become vulnerable to gossip and rumors. Factions can form, and scapegoats can be created. These situations, once they get going, can be very difficult to contain. A good director tries to catch the miscommunication or the dissatisfaction before it escalates into mutiny.

The director needs to be accessible to the actors. She needs to continue to encourage them to come to her with their problems or complaints. As actors, they should be encouraged and reinforced for speaking up about blocking or direction that doesn't work for them. If an actor does not feel comfortable going to the director, she can be encouraged to go to the assistant director. The assistant director could pass on the suggestion or complaint anonymously. The most important thing is that the information gets to the person who is responsible for dealing with the problems: the director.

If a director senses a change in attitude from one of the actors, it might be a good idea to ask that actor to meet for coffee. If she feels that part of the cast or crew is beginning to form a faction, she should make an effort to determine the cause. Nothing diffuses anger like asking, "What would you like to see me do?" That does not commit the director to action, but it does get the dissatisfied party to commit to the specifics of her complaint.

But let's get back to the actors' contract with the director:

6. Actors agree to treat their co-actors and tech people with respect and consideration. They agree to go to the director, not the designer or technician, with suggestions or objections.
7. Actors will take responsibility for getting to and from rehearsals and performances. Any individual actor will not make her personal problems the responsibility of the cast. If she has a physical condition, or something going on emotionally that will affect her performance, she needs to tell the director or the assistant director. Sharing this information with her fellow actors, especially on performance nights, can cause them to lose their own focus. (Who wants to be waiting in the wings for the start of the comedy, and have their scene partner brush by them with the comment, "My lover just moved out"? I mention this because there is a certain breed of actor who seems to thrive on causing anxiety for other actors. It's easy to spot them: They're the actors who show up on opening night whispering "to save their voice." I suppose these actors have been around since Sophocles, and they're probably still going to be around when Lesbian theatres become mainstream, but perhaps they'll check some of their more flamboyant impulses if you let them know at first rehearsal that you're on to them.)
8. Actors will treat their work in small parts as seriously as their work in large parts.
9. Actors will not show up for work under the influence of drugs or alcohol.
10. Actors accept that the stage manager has absolute authority at the performances when the director is no longer directly involved.

In addition to discussing these agreements at the first rehearsal, I also include a few warnings about the way that I work and the environment for rehearsals. If the actors are uncomfortable with these, I advise them that it would be a good idea for them to excuse themselves from the production:

1. I talk about sexual harassment. It is legally defined as any unwanted sexual attention: jokes, comments on appearance, touching, innuendos, inappropriate questions, and so forth. I point out that these behaviors are illegal and that they will not be tolerated at rehearsals. Often Lesbians consider sexual harassment something that only happens in heterosexual environments, but that is, sadly, not true. Aside from the effects of these behaviors on the victims—who might be survivors—harassment tends to sexualize the environment for the whole cast.

Because actors are using their own emotions and their own bodies in their work, a sexual environment is as distracting and inappropriate in theatre as it would be in a massage therapy workshop. Often actors "fall in love" in the charged atmosphere of a production. Behaviors that sexualize the environment are unprofessional, disrupting the ensemble dynamic and requiring all of us to become an audience for the actors' personal theatre.

2. I warn cast members that there will probably be days when they are called to a rehearsal but only get to do ten minutes of work—or maybe they won't even be called onstage at all! I try very hard to draw up a schedule where this will not happen, but sometimes it can't be avoided. I ask the actors to bring something to do at rehearsals and to understand that this is just part of theatre.

3. I tell the cast that when an actor and I cannot agree about the blocking or the interpretation, I will try very hard to work with the actor to find something that will make us both happy. If this is not possible, however, I will use my prerogative as the director, and I will insist that the actor take my direction. Some actors feel that they should have the right to block themselves. I empathize with the actor who is stuck with an interpretation of her part that she feels is unactable, but on the other hand, the actor does not have the responsibility for the whole show, as the director does. If she is as focused on her part as she should be, she will not have the perspective to take into consideration the coordination of all the other actors' performances. This becomes increasingly true for most actors as they approach Tech Week. The director begins standing farther and farther back, while the actor is tightening her focus more and more.

Perspectives aside, in a situation where the actors have the right to direct themselves, the role of the director becomes reduced to that of an adviser. This puts a terrible burden on the other actors, whose only recourse now is to upstage before they become upstaged. A director who abdicates this area of control, in my opinion, is not acting professionally or responsibly. The reason I give this warning at first rehearsal is because it is much more difficult for the director to take back power once she has given it away.

The last matter for discussion at first rehearsal is the ultimate contract: the schedule. In theory, the actors gave you an accurate report of their personal schedules at auditions. In theory, you have spent several hours drawing up a master schedule that takes their individual schedules into account. In practice, however, there will probably be the need for some adjustments. Tell the actors to speak now or forever hold their peace. You will probably not have the entire cast together again for a few weeks, because you will be blocking small scenes. This is the time to make changes that require consensus.

Also, draw their attention to the dates for the photo call, for being off book, and for being off prompt. Stress again that you will need everyone every night for Tech Week.

So, finally, you're ready for the read-through. This can be done sitting around a table, or with actors sprawled on various pieces of furniture, or the floor.

The read-through is *not* a performance. This is a time for the actors, many of whom will not see one another again for several weeks, to experience the entire play together. In the old days, the playwright would come to the first rehearsal and read the play to the actors. This practice was very offensive to many directors and also to some actors, who would be doing their own interpretation, thank you, of the material. But there was some value in having the actors listen to the play, instead of to one another.

I ask the actors not to focus on performance or dramatic interpretation at all, but to focus on the actual words of the playwright. This is a time to let the play tell us about itself. We will have six weeks to impose ourselves on the text. This rehearsal is for listening. Nobody should be acting yet.

The actors should not leave the reading during scenes where their characters are not present. They should not be skimming ahead to practice their lines. They should *listen* and *think*.

And that is the first rehearsal. You've covered a lot of ground, and the cast has begun to bond.

Chapter 30

Blocking the Show

Every director has her own style of directing. Some directors will spend the first weeks of rehearsal sitting around a table, reading sections of the script and discussing the character motivation. Other directors begin giving blocking at the first rehearsal after the read-through. (Blocking is the direction for the actors' movements on the stage.) There is no right or wrong, except when a director adopts a mode of directing that is not her own in order to please someone else (i.e., an actor or the producer).

Proponents of the sitting-around-the-table method (and some of the greatest directors in the world work this way) claim that this enables the actors to make their characters their own, so that when it's time to block the show, an actor will already have a powerful sense of motivation, which will make the movement more organic. They feel that giving blocking too early can stunt the actors' creative process and might pressure them to build the characters from the outside in, instead of from the inside out.

This is a sound theory, but again, I believe it assumes a certain level of training and maturity that most amateurs—and some professionals—do not have. It has been my experience that just because an actor can make a brilliant intellectual analysis of character motivation doesn't mean she'll necessarily have the faintest clue how to bring any of those insights to life on the stage.

Giving the blocking early can free the actor to work psychologically. Not having to worry about when to stand or sit or make a cross, the actor can focus on the character's interior process. Also, good blocking can stimulate appropriate emotional states.

Whether you are working from the outside in or the inside out, the goal is for the actor to access the emotional truth—which must be hers *as the character* for the scene she is playing. This will not happen at every rehearsal or even every performance, and it doesn't need to. Often, when a scene is particularly charged, the actor will lose herself to the emotional truth only once during the rehearsal process. She will become overwhelmed; she may lose control; sometimes she can't do any more work that day. Contrary to what some method actors may tell you, it is not desirable for the experience to become this real during performance. It's scary, for the actor and her fellow actors, and sometimes for the audience. It's out of control, and theatre is nothing if not control. I will talk a little more about this in Chapter 31. Anyway, if you are a director and you see this happen in rehearsal, understand it is a stage in the process, not an end in itself. It's a wonderful point of breakthrough, and it will allow the actor to replicate the experience night after night, and that's what you're looking for.

As a director, I choose to move right into the blocking at the second rehearsal, with one exception. If the characters in the play have met one another before the opening scene, I take some time at the rehearsal after the read-through to ask them a little bit about their history with one another, and how they feel about one another's characters. In one show I directed, the opening scene included all the characters in the play, who were all members of a Lesbian softball team. Obviously the women knew one another, but the script did not give details about how long. At this second rehearsal, all of the team players talked about their characters (in the first person), and one by one each Lesbian described her relationship to the other members of the team. This process took an entire rehearsal, but it was well worth it, because otherwise some of the actors might never have given that much thought to their background with the other players, and the actors who did do this work might not have shared it with one another.

Whether you go directly into blocking or whether you choose to sit around the table, the director needs to have spent quite a bit of time on the script. I made this point earlier in the chapter on auditions, but it also pertains to the first week of rehearsal. This is not the time for a director to be just figuring out what's going on in the play.

Analyzing the script is the subject of numerous books on directing, and I would recommend that the novice director check out some of these books. The outline for preliminary script analysis in Chapter 27 is a good start, but blocking the show will require a more specific breakdown of the scenes.

A good analysis of the script will allow the director to break the script into coherent "units" of dramatic action, which may then be broken down into what Stanislavsky called "beats." There are many ways to describe a beat of dramatic action, but one of the most efficient ways is to think of it in terms of rhythm. A beat, like a passage of music, has a certain rhythm. This can shift abruptly—as when a character enters an ongoing scene and the entire direction of the dialogue changes—or it can undergo a quieter change. The dialogue can reach a sort of impasse and then begin a polite shift in another direction.

The beat is a very useful unit for the director, because the rhythm and movement patterns of a dramatic scene should be in tune with the beat in the script. The subtle (or not so subtle) shifts in rhythm should be reflected by the blocking, or the director will end up flattening all the peaks and valleys of the drama—kind of like what Muzak does to a dramatic piece of music. Also, the beat changes should be "clean," that is, clear and intelligible, not muddied with extraneous motion or incoherent blocking.

The beat is the basic building block of the play. It usually lasts only a minute or two. In a beat, there is a primary action (Jan hints to Kelly about spending the night together) and a primary counteraction (Kelly, ignoring Jan, keeps looking for her keys). The beat ends with some kind of resolution: A new primary action occurs (Kelly, giving up her search for her keys, asks if she can spend the night with Jan), or there is an interruption that triggers a new beat (Kelly's girlfriend enters).

Several beats go into making up a unit. A unit can last anywhere from five to ten minutes. A dramatic unit of action might be "Jan Tries to Seduce Kelly." This might be made up of six or seven pages of dialogue, including the beats where Jan picks Kelly up in a bar, walks her to her door, and then tries to talk her into spending the night with her.

I like to take the script and draw double lines across the page for every unit. I title the units. And then I draw single lines to divide the beats. Often these will change during the course of rehearsal, but at least I have a strong idea of what's going on before I undertake the blocking. There is a sample segment of a script divided into beats and units in Appendix 24.

And while I'm on the subject of script analysis, I should mention the director's notebook. Buy a large, three-ring notebook and a set of dividers. Label the dividers: "Addresses and Schedules," "Script" (for the director's annotated copy, *not* the prompt book!), "Analysis," "Publicity," and "Records." (The "Records" section is where you can file miscellaneous memoranda, receipts, projected budgets, old audition forms, design sketches, etc.). You will have a lot of loose papers to which you will need to refer frequently, and the notebook will make life a lot easier.

But let's get back to blocking. Blocking has something to do with traffic patterns, yes. And it has something to do with what is called "balancing the stage," as in not wanting six people in the downstage left corner for thirty minutes while no one else is onstage during that time. It also has something to do with creating "tableaux," which means making pictures on the stage. In the old-fashioned melodramas, the action would freeze in tableaux at the end of each scene: the hero down on his knees proposing to the ingenue, her head turned to the side in bashfulness; or the heroine headed for the sawmill while the villain twirls his mustache. (Tableaux making is held in contempt by some directors, but in my experience, the director who can go from one dramatic tableaux to another is probably very good at translating dialogue into action.)

But good blocking does a lot more than route traffic, distribute actors, and make pictures. It underlines the dramatic action. A spoken line of dialogue, especially in an unfamiliar play, goes by very fast—and it will not return again. Good blocking provides conditions that make those lines intelligible, even unforgettable. Think of Laura in *Tea and Sympathy* delivering that immortal line to the schoolboy she's about to initiate sexually: "Years from now . . . when you talk about this . . . and you will . . . be kind." What is her blocking? She stands in the doorway to his bedroom and unbuttons *one* button of her blouse. Blackout. That line was so memorable it even turned up in a Bugs Bunny cartoon ten years later. Trust me, without the blocking, Bugs would never have remembered it all those years.

Good blocking can also establish character. Remember when Stanley Kowalski in *A Streetcar Named Desire* makes his first entrance tossing meat covered with blood? A director can also use blocking to provide motivation in areas of a scene where the dialogue leaves something to be desired.

Most scripts will have some blocking notes written in: "Moving a step above armchair" or "Sways, covers face" or "Fumbling to embrace her." These are written in parentheses, and they are *not* gospel. Often the stage directions were taken from the blocking of the first production, and they are not part of the playwright's vision. They have been added to printed editions to help the reader (and potential publisher/producer) envision the action. Whereas the director has a legal and ethical obligation to perform all of the lines of the script as written, she has no obligation to use the blocking. Feel free to pick and choose among the stage directions for your interpretation.

At the point in rehearsal when the director will be giving blocking, she needs to know the dimensions of the playing space and the dimensions of the furniture, doors, and so on, that will be on the set. The rehearsal floor may be "taped," which means that the assistant director marks the edges and corners of the playing space with masking tape and "spikes" the furniture, that is, puts little tabs of tape where the corners of the furniture will be. She also tapes the markings for doors, indicating which way they will open, and for stairs, indicating how many and how wide.

Taping is a great idea if you are using the same rehearsal space night after night and if nobody minds leaving the tape on the floor. If you are renting a space where taping is impractical, however, have the assistant director bring lengths of string that correspond to the dimensions of the playing space. These can be laid down and taken up very quickly. Whether you use tape or string, it's very important that the actors work from the start in the right sized space, because distance will affect their timing and movements.

And just a note about set design (again, there are many books on the subject): If you can work with your designer to create a set with furniture, or platforms, that will allow for several "acting areas" and different levels, go for it! These are a great help for amateur actors. The actor who is compelled to work on a flat, bare stage will face many more challenges to her skills than the actor on a full set of furniture. Help your actors: Give them a set that allows for many choices.

The more acting areas the better. An acting area consists of two sit-down spaces that are not right next to each other. (A sofa, even with two actors sitting on it, is not considered an acting area.) Some designers insist that the spaces be six feet apart to constitute an acting area, but for smaller stages this is a luxury. A footstool and a chair two feet away from it constitute a perfectly fine acting area. As a rule of thumb, aim for a set with five acting areas.

The director can plan her blocking at home with the script. Some directors work with a model or floor plan of the set and actually move miniature figures around to test their blocking. Other directors invent the blocking at rehearsals, working as they go. The advantage of the latter method is that much of the blocking will change in the rehearsal process, and what you might have spent hours planning at home might all have to be changed two minutes into the scene.

Giving the initial blocking is time-consuming. For the first weeks of giving blocking, break the play into acts and the acts into scenes. If you are meeting to rehearse five times a week, you can probably block one act a week. I like to run the act with the blocking—no matter how ragged—as soon as it's all been given, and then move into the blocking for the next act. I do this so the actors will have some sense of how the scenes fit together, and also because the actors may not be seeing that act again for two more weeks if it's a three-act play.

I block scenes according to which actors are called for rehearsal. For instance, if I have the two romantic leads, I will block all the scenes they are in for the first act at the same rehearsal—if I can get to all of them. If possible, however, I try not to block scenes from different acts at the same time, because often each act has a different flavor all its own. I think it's a good idea to keep the scenes in one act discrete from the scenes in another.

When the director gives the blocking notes, the actors should be on the set walking the blocking, so that the director can see how it works. The actors should be taking notes on the blocking in their scripts *in pencil*. These notes will help the actors when they are learning lines, because the actors will be able to visualize where they are and what they are doing.

The assistant director takes down all the blocking notes in what is called the "prompt book." The prompt book is a notebook that holds the pages of the script. The script in the prompt book should be *single-sided*. If it isn't, make a copy that is. The reason for this is that there will then be a blank page facing every page of dialogue, which provides space for additional notes. (See Appendix 25 for a sample page of script with blocking notes.)

"Stage Left" and "Stage Right" refer to areas of the stage from the actor's point of view. Although a stage can be divided many different ways, a standard convention defines six areas: upstage left (UL), downstage left (DL), upstage center (UC), downstage center (DC), upstage right (UR), and downstage right (DR). The direction to cross is indicated with an *X*. If the actor is to cross upstage right after she says, "Go to hell," then the actor and AD will write "XUR" in pencil on the script after the line. Sitting or standing is indicated by up or down arrows, respectively.

The AD also writes in the "business," by which busy-ness is meant: lighting a cigarette, putting on a hat, loading a gun, and so forth. And the AD also writes in the lighting notes or sound notes as they come up. Often the director will have a flash of technological inspiration, and unless the AD takes it down, it's lost forever.

It is very important for the AD to take down all the blocking notes and to keep current on the changes. (That's why she uses a pencil!) The actors are often negligent or preoccupied when it comes to taking notes in their own scripts. They may forget to make the changes. If a scene has not been rehearsed for a while, they may have forgotten the blocking. If the scene has been reblocked several times, they may be confused about the final version. At a time like this, the prompt book is consulted as the authoritative version.

The prompt book notes are invaluable if an actor leaves the cast. The replacement can take the blocking from the AD. Also, if an actor is absent from a rehearsal, the AD can walk the blocking for that character, using the prompt book notes for blocking.

Actors can and will ask for their blocking notes during rehearsals—up until the date on the schedule marked "off prompt." After that date, they will need to struggle as best they can from memory. After the off-prompt date, the AD will give the actors notes at the end of the rehearsal about wrong lines, missed cues, or wrong blocking.

The director or the AD takes the prompt book home every night. It should never be left at the theatre or the rehearsal hall. It's too valuable.

And that should take us to the end of the third week of rehearsals, midpoint. This is where things begin to get interesting.

Part VII

Into the Vortex

Chapter 31

Some Notes on Acting

Acting is highly subjective. There is no right way to do it. The way that works is the right way. A good director should know several approaches to acting, because what is helpful for one actor may not be at all helpful for another.

Theoretically, there are two approaches to acting. Rather than try to put actors into one category or another, it's more useful to think of these two approaches as ends of a spectrum. Most actors are somewhere in the middle, combining techniques from both schools.

The first style is called "representational" acting. This is considered an old-fashioned approach, where the performer imitates or illustrates the behaviors of the character. This style is associated with mannerisms and stylized inflections.

The "presentational" style of acting is one wherein the actor uses an understanding of herself and of the character to reveal the behaviors. In other words, she works from the inside out, trusting the form to come out of her identification with the character, instead of adopting a form to be a vehicle for the character.

Let's look at an example: Lorraine was given a performance exercise. She's in a fancy restaurant, on a first date. She notices that she has spilled something on her pants.

The first time she performed the exercise, Lorraine relied on representational acting techniques. When her partner was concentrating on her plate, Lorraine would surreptitiously dip her napkin in her water glass and scrub frantically at the spot, freezing in a charming pose whenever her dinner partner looked up at her. The acting class roared with laughter. It was a situation-comedy scene, and Lorraine's timing and facial expressions were reminiscent of the best of *I Love Lucy*.

The second time she performed, she had been instructed to close her eyes before she began and remember an episode of shame from some period in high school or junior high. She was to envision this actual event in detail: where it occurred, time of day, furniture in the room, who else was there, what they were wearing. And then, having fully accessed the emotional memory of the event, she was to begin the scene again. This is called an "emotional memory" exercise.

This time, Lorraine came from a place of absolute terror. Her face was set in a tense, intentionally neutral expression; but the eyes, which were fixed on her date, were those of a woman who was terrified. Under the table, she was rubbing at the stain with her napkin, but slowly, as if she were afraid to move. There was nothing funny about this woman. Her shame was devastating. It was as if the stain on her pants carried the guilty secret of her innate worthlessness. Even her attempts to remove the stain seemed halfhearted and doomed from the outset. Needless to say, nobody laughed.

Lorraine was using her own shame, remembered from a period of painful self-consciousness. Her choices were unique to herself, even though she was playing a character in a scene. Any actor could have replicated her actions from the first portrayal and probably elicited the same response from the audience. The first exercise had been largely a question of comic timing.

On the other hand, few actors could have re-created what Lorraine did in the second scene. Lorraine's actions had been the tip of the iceberg. Her gestures and expression were the outcome of having achieved a state of overwhelming *personal* shame. It was this state that the audience was registering. And because Lorraine's experience of shame was so realistically based on her own past memory and her personality, imitation of the actions by another actor would not have achieved the same effect on the audience.

If a different actor had been asked to access a similar emotional memory of intense shame, she might have remembered an incident in which she responded to her discomfort with denial and exaggerated activity. Perhaps this actor, remembering that state, would choose to draw her date's attention to the stain, just to prove that it was not an issue for her. If her experience of shame was authentic, and if the actor had thoroughly accessed the emotional memory, her actions would have the same degree of power, even though they might be completely different from Lorraine's choices.

From this example, it might be easy to conclude that presentational acting, also known as "method acting," is superior to representational acting. Certainly, it has been the direction actor training has taken for the last fifty years. On the other hand, acting is not the same as real life, and completely presentational acting would not be effective at all.

There is an audience sitting out front. The actor is *not* in a real living room. The furniture more or less faces in one direction. The actor must be heard; the words must be intelligible. Moving on another actor's lines *does* distract. Speaking upstage is frustrating for the audience. Scenes of prolonged intimacy or prolonged violence may occur in real life, but onstage, they will quickly lose their impact.

Timing has its place and so does a certain understanding of stage conventions. It's no accident that some of the greatest comedians in the old films came out of vaudeville theatre. Vaudeville was nothing if not a discipline in reading and responding to an audience.

From the director's point of view, it's important to know about the ways that actors work, because you will need to help them when they are in trouble. I have given an example of emotional memory work. Often this is an effective technique for breaking through "staginess," but if you have an actor who is emotionally repressed, this technique can be risky. In fact, if you push it, you may precipitate a major life crisis for the actor, and your chances of getting the performance you want out of her will become very slim—assuming she even stays in the cast.

Know how to give representational blocking directions. An actor can also find her way into the character from the outside. A good director has a variety of approaches, because every actor responds differently. Also, it's important to remember that every actor has her own process. Laurette Taylor would not act until dress rehearsal. During rehearsals, she would walk the blocking and speak the lines—often stumbling over them—because she was still observing, thinking, planning. This would make her fellow actors very nervous and her director desperate, but when she finally kicked in, she was so uncompromisingly brilliant that no one dared take issue with how she got there. Often, the actor who is continuing to grow in the part will look the most tentative during the rehearsal period. On the other hand, the actor who seems more professionally consistent could be lazier and less creative.

And a note on stage violence or sex: The stage is not film, and scenes that might play like gangbusters on the big screen will have a radically different effect onstage. Realistic violence onstage defeats its purpose, because if it really looks convincing, the audience will forget the play and begin to speculate on whether or not the actor is really hurt, or how the effect was achieved.

I will never forget a scene in a production of *I Am a Camera*, where one of the characters has to drink some kind of morning-after concoction containing a raw egg. Everyone in the audience was suddenly aware that the actor had to do this every night. The actor never broke character, but the action had the same effect of taking the audience out of the play. The audience let out a collective gasp, *not* because they were identifying with the character—who actually liked the concoction, but because they were identifying with the actor. The spell was broken, and the scene shifted from a Berlin rooming house to an amateur stunt night. The same thing happens when live animals are used onstage. They do not know they are in a play, and the audience will frequently become caught up identifying with the experience of the animal. Too much reality is unreal, and a good stage fight is one where the punches are subtly, but visibly, pulled.

When a director makes the mistake of using graphic violence and sex on the stage, she destroys that essential dividing line between the actor and the character. Suddenly, we are worried that our friend Joanne got hit with a wine bottle, not the character in the bar. We are aware that a woman in our community is standing on a public stage with no clothes on, not the character in the play. When this boundary is violated in performance, the audience pulls back into their "real-life" reactions to situations, the magic spell is broken, and whatever the show gains in sensationalism, it loses in art. This is by no means an issue of puritanism or prudery. It's an issue of artistic integrity. Total realism has never been a goal of live theatre, because—quite simply—it isn't dramatic.

And finally, a word about Lesbians as actors: Heterosexualism puts pressure on women to live our lives as a performance. Women's sexuality is supposed to be for men's pleasure. Our anger is always unjustified, unfeminine, inappropriate. Our resources should be for the enhancement of a husband's career, the harmony of a home, or the glory of a patriarchal god. Our tastes and sense of humor should reflect the tastes and sense of humor of men. We are supposed to view male art, male literature, male plays as our own culture by extension. And so on. The Lesbian actor has a set of handicaps and advantages that derive directly from the fact that heterosexualism is a performance art for women.

The Lesbian actor has probably been discriminated against in traditional acting programs, because these are geared around the canon of traditional plays—which is to say, plays by, for, about, and serving the interests of men. The roles for women are what men fear we are or wish we were. Women are obstacles or rewards. We are universally stereotyped. And when the occasional heroine, such as Hedda Gabler, or Thelma or Louise, breaks through with some genuine feminist resentment, she is expected to pay for her enlightenment with her life, because you can't beat city hall. Lesbians who have obviously broken the first rule of patriarchy by saying "no" to male sexuality have a difficult time playing these roles.

Many Lesbians have resisted the makeup and costumes of heterosexualism. We have not starved our bodies to fit a stereotype. We wear sensible shoes. We let our facial hair grow. Casting directors and acting instructors don't know what to do with us. They give us directions like "Reclaim your pelvis," when they want us to wiggle our hips when we walk. They tell us not to be afraid of our femininity, which is idiotic. We should be terrified of what that term means to them. They tell us to flutter, to wilt, to glide . . . either that, or we are expected to play the character roles that spring from stereotypes about fat women or older women or "spinster" women. We are asked to degrade ourselves, betray our gender. This is all really too depressing for words.

So, yes, Lesbians have been terribly discriminated against in theatre. Sadly, many of our gay brothers, who have always held positions of power even in mainstream theatres, seem more comfortable with heterosexual women than with "out" political Lesbians. I have my own theory about this, but then, you probably do, too. The point is, the discrimination against us in theatre is everywhere.

Oppression is not particularly creative. Oppressors use the same strategies with depressing consistency. The same mentality that created "blackface" theatre to reassure those in power that the stereotypes about African Americans were authentic also creates the stereotyped roles for women in theatre—and for the same reason. The blackface minstrel show stereotypes depicted blacks as slow-moving and dim-witted. African American women were frequently depicted as promiscuous moral idiots. What the oppressor failed to note is that moving slowly and pretending not to understand are two of the only strategies of resistance available to enslaved people. And, obviously, the stereotype about black women's sexuality was an attempt to mask and justify the violence white men directed against black women. Mainstream theatre's stereotypes of women of all colors serve a similar purpose. These construct drag images of women as bitchy, self-absorbed, and/or promiscuous. Again, the oppressor fails to notice strategies of resistance among a population that is controlled and dominated through sexual terrorism and exploitation.

But there is good news for Lesbian actors: We don't have to unlearn so many of the bad habits that heterosexual women have internalized as part of their socialization/indoctrination. We also will not have to undo the damage of years and years in the professional theatre playing caricatures of ourselves.

Lesbians, having decolonized our bodies, are in a unique position to create the new theatre that will speak for all women. We have the potential to tell the truth.

Why is this in the chapter about acting? Because the director of Lesbians in theatre is breaking ground all the way around: with women-centered scripts, with Lesbian actors in Lesbian roles—many of whom have never acted before—with establishing a theatre without dominance. In directing actors, keep an eye out for the bad habits, the stereotyped mannerisms that the actors may have picked up from heterosexual theatre or from hours of imbibing televised images. Women living the truth have been absent from the media, and the Lesbian actor faces both an unusual opportunity and a major challenge in being true to herself and her gender.

Chapter 32

Advice to the Director

Being a director is a difficult job, because acting is dangerous. Like a good coach, the director needs to have a sixth sense about when to push and when to ease off. She also needs to have a very solid ego that can weather a number of challenges.

When an actor challenges the director in front of the company, there is a temptation to interpret it as an attack on the director's authority. This may be a mistake. Most likely, the challenge springs from a genuine concern. Actors, projecting their fears or mistaking the director for some authority figure from their family of birth, may demonstrate a lamentable lack of skill in communicating their concerns; but a good director who understands the enormous pressures on the actors should be able to interpret without allowing her ego to become engaged.

Showdowns in front of the company are almost always disastrous. If the director "wins," then the actor can play the misunderstood martyr, the violated artiste. If the director is seen to back down, she loses credibility. The best approach is to refuse to allow the actor to engage you emotionally, to address the immediate issue about blocking, props, whatever, and to table a final decision. ("Let me see what you have in mind," or, "I'd like you to try it this way for today," and so on.) Meet with the actor later in private, where you are less likely to be treated as a figurehead and the occasion will not lend itself to grandstanding.

If rumors begin to circulate, confront them. It is a serious mistake to attempt to rise above them by ignoring them, or to cultivate an attitude of aloofness as a buffer. Communicating to a cast that you are above an issue that concerns them will only add fuel to the fire.

Power-over is unhealthy, and so is power-under. This would be a good place to say a word about mentoring. The subject was touched on in Chapter 8 in the context of betrayal, but since the director so often falls into the role of mentor, it would be appropriate to look at this dynamic as part of the notes to the director.

Mentoring is a very, very poor model for a business relationship. Unfortunately, it's also one of the most common among Lesbians in organizations. I am talking about the older woman with more experience taking the younger, less experienced woman in hand for a kind of mother-daughter exchange. The mentor trades her expertise and her connections for the mentoree's company and appreciation. Notice the rotten boundaries in this exchange: career skills traded for social/emotional gratification. What happens with mentorships is that usually the mentoree gains the level of expertise and self-confidence to move on. Occasionally, she will replace her mentor.

The mentor feels used, taken advantage of, exploited. The mentoree feels the mentor is trying to own her, to hold her back. Both perceptions are justified. The fault lies not in the individuals, but in the dynamic of the mentorship. They signed a contract that was guaranteed to self-destruct. The more the mentor gives, the less the mentoree will feel overwhelmed with gratitude, because the more the mentor gives, the more the mentoree will become a peer. The mentoree, if she has been well mentored, will become less and less dependent on her mentor and more and more desirous of carving out her own territory. Sometimes a mentor relationship can survive the transition into a peer business relationship. This is more the exception than the rule, however. Most often, the two parties separate with acrimonious feelings, and the organization can be polarized by the division.

Does this mean that Lesbians with professional skills should never share them with less skilled Lesbians? No, of course not. It just means we need to have better models for that exchange. The bottom line should not include having one's social or emotional needs met. If an unskilled Lesbian is helping a more skilled Lesbian, there is a potential for a healthy trade: The director gets an assistant who will take on many of the rehearsal responsibilities in exchange for learning how the director works with the actors. The technical director gets help with the building of the set in exchange for teaching her workers how to read the elevation drawings and how to construct the set.

Since most women in patriarchy experience some form of abandonment or betrayal from our mothers, we have a powerful subconscious pull to return to the scene of the crime. Relationships that replicate mother-daughter dynamics can be intoxicating with their promise of redeeming the past. They never do. When the "daughter" proves less than adoring, we often take our frustration out on her the way our own mothers did on us. When the "mother" falls short of the impossible standard of unconditional love, we are tempted to reject her in ways that we have been unable to reject our real mothers. Mother-daughter mentoring relationships are fraught with the potential for this kind of abuse. Keep your business relationships businesslike. This doesn't mean you can't love your co-workers or socialize with them. It just means watch your boundaries and know your bottom line.

Boundaries are highly personal. Some women can work well with lovers. Other women cannot. Some women have no trouble socializing with the women with whom they work. For others, this is confusing. Know yourself, and don't put all your eggs in one basket. It's always a good idea to have alternate support systems for backup. The theatre company that tries to be a family stands to inherit the dysfunctional family patterns of every member.

Setting boundaries with staff and cast members is also highly personal. Some directors are formal and impersonal in all their interactions. Other directors are informal and emotionally nurturing. Most are somewhere in the middle. But no matter what your style, a director's decisions will cause pain, starting right with auditions. If you can't stand the thought of hurting anyone, don't take the job. It's part of the heat in the kitchen.

Chapter 33

After the Third Week

The period following the third week is an interesting time. It's usually midpoint in the rehearsal process. It's the time when the initial blocking has all been set. It's the time when the actors begin going off book. And it's the time when the magic starts to take.

After the third week, everyone begins to move into the heart of the play. A different range of skills are required of the director at this point. As the traffic patterns begin to set, the deeper layers of the play begin to reveal themselves.

As the actor eases into the part, her role begins to take possession of her. Initially, she may be moving certain ways because the director told her to, or because she imagines that the character she's playing would move this way. But after about the third week, the actor begins to move a certain way because she *is* the character. The art takes over, and the actors begin to realize that acting is more than just fun and games.

Every play has a moral core, even if it's a dopey play about women who all have sex with one another. The moral core can be a message, like "alcoholism destroys relationships," or it can be an engagement with issues that are not so clear cut. A play about a historical figure, for example, might show that valorous public activism has its roots in personal dysfunction—a disturbing theme for most of us who want to worship our heroines.

The moral core of a play is usually a theme broad enough to be considered universal. In other words, it is an issue for everyone, including the actors. I think of an analogy of fire walking for this stage of rehearsal: The actors must cross the bed of hot coals, barefoot (the actors who keep their psychic shoes on are always boring to watch!), in order to reach the audience. The hot coals are the moral core of the play, and the better the play, the hotter the core. How can the actor get through the material without becoming toast in the process? The same way women can walk the fire. It takes a certain concentration and, paradoxically, a certain detachment. The burn comes in the interface between hot coals and human flesh, between the character in the play and the human on the stage. This is where the actor must be very, very clear in her thinking. And this is where the director can play a critical role.

After the third week, the actor starts to "bring in the character." This is like pouring a volatile chemical into a crucible. That crucible needs to be absolutely pure, or the new chemical may begin its own reactions with whatever residues are still in the crucible. And this may ruin the point of the experiment.

Is this making any sense? Let's take a play about a woman who is violent, and let's say that violence is one of the issues in the play. What if the actor is someone whose life has been touched by violence, and she is subject to violent behaviors herself, or she has internalized unhealthy responses to violence in her environment (placating behaviors, numbing out, denial)? The actor will be trying to commit to honest portrayal of a kind of character who is deeply threatening to her on a subconscious level. There is residue from her childhood left in the crucible. What will she do? Well, if she is in denial about the fact that violence has affected her, she may do a very artificial caricature of the role. Or she may be so terrified of the roots of violence within herself that she is unable to replicate the behaviors of a violent woman, even though she is a proficient actor in other areas and even if she is violent in her personal life! She may be completely unable to access the emotional truth of a woman who becomes violent for fear that it might trigger the unthinkable in herself or reveal a family secret. What I am describing here are deep survival needs from childhood, and these will preempt the lesser needs of the actor for a good performance. Your actor may become bafflingly incompetent.

And now it's time for a digression about acting: The actor must *always* like the character she's playing, even if it's a character who murders all her children. This is because the character must be acting out of what she perceives to be her best or only option. It is not the actor's job to critique the perspective of the character. It is her job to portray the role honestly. If an actor has to take a role such as an abusive mother, she might want to work with the idea that the woman does not relate to her children as people, but as little screaming demons from hell sent to torture her with their incessant demands for attention, depriving her of the right to meet her own needs, which have become increasingly desperate. If the actor is thinking, "These are my innocent daughters, and I'm about to become abusive toward them," she will not be convincing in the part. If she plays a villain, what she is doing is melodrama, not theatre, and the audience will sense the actor's alienation from the role. In order to do her job, the actor must find a way for the woman's actions to make sense to her, or even seem like positive choices under the stress of circumstances.

This blurring of the line between the actor and her character begins to occur around the fourth week, but it may occur sooner, and it may occur later. Frequently, this dynamic will be present into Tech Week. Because of the rush of new stimuli (crew and theatre space, tech, etc.), often the worst of the personal struggles with the material are over before then, but not always. This is one of the reasons why no one should be allowed to observe rehearsals without the entire cast's permission—and not just in the earlier weeks! It's a good idea for the director to bring in a mentor or adviser, a trusted third eye, especially at the beginning of the week before Tech Week, but the actors have a right to know who the person is and why she has been invited. The director should use her discretion about bringing in these "strangers," especially if the actors are at a volatile point with the material. The director needs to understand the process so that she is able to take responsibility for her role in helping her actors when they start cutting their teeth on the core of the play.

The director who approaches acting as a purely mechanical activity will be annoyed at these "behaviors" and probably leave the actor to struggle alone. This is a serious mistake and one that stems from denying the spiritual, magical nature of the transformation that takes place in theatre. It has been my experience that the better the actor, frequently the more severe the crisis. This is because the better actor is taking the deep truth of the play as far into herself as she can. And the deeper she takes her performance, the more possibility of running into those residues I talked about, the ones that will cause the unexpected chemical reactions.

The director cannot help the actor if the director is in denial about aspects of herself regarding the core of the play.

I think of some of the plays I have directed and how they have tried me on in one way or another. I remember *Zoo Story*, where I had to examine the potential for violence and for indifference to the suffering of others inside myself. I think of *The Second Coming of Joan of Arc*, where I had to look at the fact that it was often easier to fight men than to love women. I remember the agony of directing a play about Louisa May Alcott and wrestling with the deep impulse in women to impose on younger women the violations (foot binding, genital mutilations) and restrictions that were imposed on us. Putting up a play is about accelerated evolution. Things that have been tucked away quietly in various corners of our psyches are suddenly brought to light, are suddenly major obstacles to the achievements of our goals. The compression and intensity of theatre demands high-performance equipment. Every part must be in top condition, running clean.

Theatre is a paradoxical world, because many women are drawn to it in order to escape reality—to assume another, supposedly safer identity. Ha. Theatre is superreality. Whatever aspect the actor is running away from in herself, she's likely to be called upon to put it up onstage, front and center. The "unreality" of theatre is a very particular place. Real life requires far less truth from us. Real life is full of ambiguities and inconsistencies where we can weasel out of confronting our shortcomings. Live theatre gives no quarter for cowardice and demands that our truth be in full view.

Theatre, especially Lesbian theatre, is for warrior women, for Lesbians serious about recovery from the effects of patriarchy. Theatre is for Lesbians who can tell the truth, tell the supertruth. Theatre is for Lesbians who are willing to go wherever we have to, in order to bring in the character—even if it means confronting our worst fears and breaking the biggest taboos.

Chapter 34

Time Out!

By the second half of the rehearsal period, the honeymoon is definitely over. The initial euphoria of sisterhood has turned into the reality of individual women, each with her own history and her own agenda; all are struggling with their private demons in a public arena, where their roles are often in conflict with one another.

Some basic grounding in confrontation and conflict resolution skills can be invaluable during this time. It's funny how we all understand the importance of rehearsing scenes for the stage, but most of us take for granted that real life will just take care of itself. The sad truth is that real life is usually just a revival of the family-of-birth drama we were compelled to witness as children. Living well requires as much conscious effort as performing in a play. And sometimes we need to rehearse.

The majority of women seem to have grown up in dysfunctional families where the language we learned was "abuse." I am one of these women, and I have had to learn "respect as a second language." It has not been easy, but it does improve with practice.

When a woman has grown up hearing and speaking abuse, she is often unaware that this second language exists. She may also have difficulty understanding why others react as they do to what she sees as normal speech. She may go through life wondering why everyone around her is always blowing things out of proportion, misunderstanding her, persecuting her (my favorite), and the like. And although she is not responsible for the language she learned as a child, she will be held accountable for using it as an adult. Unfair, yes, but also a fact of life.

Take a little bit of time with your actors to practice speaking a little respect. It may save your company in the long run.

Confrontation

I will now present a model for confronting behaviors. Most women go from "No, that's okay, I don't mind," to "I quit" (or a variation of that theme: "You're fired"). Learning to confront what is bothering us is important for damage control. The authoritarian director who enjoys the fact she can intimidate people is living in a fool's paradise. Just because she doesn't hear about it doesn't mean there isn't trouble. She trades a brief period of discomfort for distorted feedback, factionalizing, mutinies, passive aggression, and possible walkouts.

So, confronting behaviors:

1. Start with the facts. What *exactly* was the action you didn't like? What *exactly* were the words? This is not the place for emotional language. Here are two examples:

    Actor to director: "When you stopped the rehearsal to ask me why I was late . . ."

    Director to actor: "When you refused to try the new blocking in rehearsal yesterday . . ."

    Notice, the actor does not say, "When you pulled your usual power trip today . . ." The director does not say, "When you acted like a prima donna in rehearsal . . ." Just the facts, ma'am.

2. Now, how do you feel about it? And stick to just the feelings, like "I felt afraid," not "I felt bullied" which makes a judgment about the intention of the other person.

    Actor to director: "When you stopped the rehearsal to ask me why I was late, I felt ashamed and then I felt angry . . ."

    Director to actor: "When you refused to try the new blocking in rehearsal yesterday, I felt angry and frustrated . . ."

3. Why? What was the *effect* on you? And don't make threats!

    Actor to director: "When you stopped the rehearsal to ask me why I was late, I felt ashamed and then I felt angry, because the whole company was watching. It reminded me of being a child called down in front of the class. I wanted to turn around and walk out of rehearsal. I was so angry, I couldn't focus on my work for the rest of the rehearsal."

    Director to actor: "When you refused to try the new blocking in rehearsal yesterday, I felt angry and frustrated, because it is my job as director to block the scenes, and you agreed to that as part of your contract with me as an actor. We were unable to rehearse the scene yesterday, and I am angry about that, because it has a lot of problems, and I need to see if changing the blocking will fix it."

Teaching actors to confront behaviors that are bothering them is time well spent. Few of us understand the art of confronting respectfully but firmly. We usually wait until our anger is so great it boils over, and by then we're not very careful with what we say.

The language of abuse is filled with judgments, sweeping generalizations, labels, references to other people who feel the same way (almost always unspecified), hyperbole and colorful analogies, obscenities, and threats. The purpose is to attack, to show force, to make the other back down.

The passive aggressive takes another tack. She may come up to the director after she has perceived herself abused in some way and begin to ask for reassurances about her performance. She tries to manipulate the director into fixing a hurt the director may not even know she has inflicted. And, of course, because this approach is not direct, it is also not satisfying. The passive aggressive's wounds just fester, and each time she tries to meet her needs indirectly, her dissatisfaction grows. She becomes more and more dangerous to herself and to the company.

There is never a guarantee that a respectful confrontation will result in a respectful response. Then a second confrontation about the unacceptable response will be in order, and the actor or director may have to take actions that will allow her to detach from the abusive situation. Firing the actor is one such action, but it should be a last resort. Another possibility is that the confrontation may bring to light a genuine conflict of interests, and this will require a new set of skills.

Conflict Resolution

In patriarchy, the model for conflict resolution is "might makes right," or "my way or the highway." It is a model of dominance, wherein the one with the most power wins and the one with the least power loses.

A better model is win-win. In this model, both parties work together to find a solution that will meet both of their needs, or at least some of them. There are many books on conflict resolution, and many different techniques for achieving that resolution. Here is one model:

1. Find a mutually acceptable definition of the problem. (If the director feels the actor is a prima donna, and the actor feels the director is a control freak, obviously they will experience problems in resolving the conflict! Time to go back to the steps in confronting, and also to practice the skills of "active listening." Active listening is a process of telling the person, in your own words, what you heard them say to you. For example, the director may say to the actor, "I hear you telling me you think you have a right to walk in late for rehearsal." This is *not* what the actor said, and the actor has an opportunity to correct the director's distorted notion of what is going on.)
2. Brainstorm possible solutions. (At this stage, all ideas are valid.)
3. Evaluate the solutions.
4. Decide on one.
5. Implement it.
6. Evaluate it to see how well it is working.

This may seem simple enough in theory, but if you have grown up in a system where the dominance model was used for conflict resolution, you may have trouble switching to a win-win model.

I recommend that you take some rehearsal time to role-play confrontations and conflict resolution. It's not enough to tell the actors that you want them to come to you with their problems. That's what bosses always say, and how often do they really mean it?

If you practice these skills with your company, it will do several things: First, it will show them that you mean business, that you really want to hear about what's bothering them. Second, it provides them with a blueprint for how to confront the director and one another in an acceptable way. Third, it increases the actors' awareness of themselves. It's difficult to experience those things we can't express, and most of us have learned to ignore or repress experiences we feel we can't change. Having a tool for confrontation, we are more likely to notice our discomfort sooner. Fourth, these models help Lesbians meet our needs in a healthy way, and we learn that our needs are not necessarily mutually exclusive. Success is empowerment, and that translates to higher self-esteem. A company of actors with self-esteem is a joy to work with.

And this brings us to the final push, Tech Week.

Chapter 35

Tech Week and Dress Rehearsal

Tech Week

Tech Week may be the longest week in the world.

I always schedule at least three days off before Tech Week, and I tell the actors that this is a period of "deep rehearsal." They are on their honor not to pick up a script or run the blocking at all—even in their heads. Actors are often tempted, especially if they have a large role, to run lines and rehearse blocking obsessively. The more nervous they are, the greater the temptation to work the script; but the process is actually counterproductive. Getting away from the script is an essential part of the rehearsal schedule. I'm not sure how it works, but I know that there are areas of the brain that work overtime behind the scenes—but only after the conscious mind has gone home for the day. I call this process "composting."

One of the things I have noticed about this three-day period is that ground is covered. After the three-day break, I have watched the scenes that never worked before come to life, the actor with the missing motivation become convincing. Problems we have all harassed ourselves over are suddenly no longer an issue. There is nothing like a shift in perspective to unleash our creative potential.

But perspective aside, Tech Week is grueling, and the actors who go into Tech Week anything less than relaxed and refreshed will burn out somewhere midweek and be running on empty for the opening. As a director, you have the responsibility to set a schedule that will prevent this.

So, take a break, and then go into Tech Week. Tech Week often begins on the Friday before the show opens the following Friday. In an ideal situation, the tech crew and stage manager have gone in during the day and hung lights, loaded in the set, and so forth. This is ideal, and often not possible. Sometimes, because of work schedules or rental arrangements, the tech crew shows up at the same time as the actors.

This makes rehearsal more challenging, but either way, expect the first day in the performance space to be chaotic. After five weeks or more of rehearsing in a room with tape on the floor, no costumes, and only rehearsal props, you will all have gotten used to focusing on blocking, intention, and all the finer points of acting. Suddenly, there are real doors, real steps, real furniture, real props, and real costumes. It would be a miracle if these were what you had all been envisioning. And they don't work the same way. The actor carrying the tea table up a flight of stairs suddenly finds that she has another dimension of space with which to contend, or that the Dresden china cups in their saucers on the silver tray are considerably less stable than the coffee mugs on the upside down box lid she'd been using for six weeks. The costumes may bind, sag, bag, or shed in ways that no one had foreseen. I am reminded of a dress Ginger Rogers wore in one of her movies. It was covered with feathers, and as she danced, the feathers began to dislodge themselves until she and Fred Astaire were twirling in a blizzard of feathers.

As a director, your job is not to become overwhelmed. Keep saying to yourself, "It's supposed to be like this," as you add item after item to your list of things that aren't working the way they were planned. Actors may feel that their work is being sabotaged by inappropriate props, costumes that violate their character, awkward furniture, and lighting or sound that detracts from their performance. Designers may be at loose ends with the way the crew is executing their vision. The tech crew may be baffled by the short fuses, when they just got here—and besides, they're working for free!

All of this will be challenging, but the greatest challenge will be to watch the first run-through of the show in the new space. Be prepared for actors who revert to blocking that was changed weeks ago, for actors who suddenly can't remember lines after being off book for two weeks, for mechanical movements and complete loss of any believable motivation. This first rehearsal may make you wonder what it was you'd been doing all those weeks, because it looks like the actors just read the script for the first time the night before. Well, this is to be expected. The actors are very, very distracted by the new surroundings. Don't worry. It goes away quickly.

Tell everyone they did a great job. Restrict your notes to concrete things like, "Don't light her cigarette until she starts to get up." First rehearsal of Tech Week is a poor time to give a note on a character's deep motivation. "Tomorrow, tomorrow, I love ya, tomorrow . . ."

Plan to run the show every night of Tech Week, with one exception: Sacrifice one whole rehearsal for the sake of teching. This means that for one of your seven evenings in the theatre, plan to start and stop and start over and stop again for an entire rehearsal. (If you are using interpreters on the actual set of the play, this would also be the rehearsal for the interpreters to practice working with the actors.) Sometimes this stop-and-start rehearsal is the first one in the new space, but I have found that it is more productive to do this a few days into Tech Week, after the lighting technicians have had an opportunity to hang and focus and play around with the gels. They have also had an opportunity to get used to the show.

Some directors stop and start all through Tech Week. I find this is usually not necessary. If you are scheduling three or four hours of rehearsal a night, you should have time to run the show with the intermission breaks and also have time left over for a cue-to-cue run (where the actors go from one tech cue to the next, skipping all the dialogue, etc., in the middle). You should also have time left over to reblock a scene or try different lighting. Why am I going into this? Because when I was an actor, I worked with too many directors who were "tech happy." During Tech Week, they treated the lighting as if it were the star, and often we actors were unable to run the entire show without stopping until just before dress rehearsal—and sometimes not even then! I call this the "trauma-drama" school of theatre, and what it does to the actor's process is terrible. The actor needs to be taking control of her role. She can't do this unless she has been free to run the show without interruption. Believe me, the lighting won't matter at all if the acting stinks.

Actually, I begin running the show during the rehearsal week that precedes Tech Week. I like to feel that, if I absolutely had to, I could open a week early. That's how I like to go into Tech Week. And if you want your cast to be well rehearsed, that's a goal toward which to aim. Some amateur theatres consider it business as usual that the first time the acting, tech, costumes, etcetera, all come together is opening night. Everyone holds their breath, prays for a miracle (no one has ever seen the whole show yet), and then when the actors actually all say the lines on cue, make their entrances, and use the right props on opening night, then everyone slaps one another on the back and congratulates themselves for "pulling it off."

A good show is a subtle show. That means it's a show where the blocking and lines and tech and everything else have become a reflex, freeing up the actors to focus on the finer points of their performance and to engage in psychic interplay with the audience. If there is still a hold-your-breath-and-keep-your-fingers-crossed atmosphere, the actors will not have the freedom to ascend to the higher vibrational planes of great acting.

What about the actor whose character is not "coming in"? Have compassion for that actor. Take responsibility for the fact you cast her. Her performance is now the problem of both of you, not just the actor. And she may be a late bloomer like Laurette Taylor. I have worked with an actor who didn't really bring in the role until the second performance. Way late from my point of view, but, better late than never.

When you have an actor who is taking her time bringing in the character, I think of it as a kind of connect-the-dot exercise. The actor is still tracing the pattern by going from the seventh dot to the eighth dot to the ninth dot; in other words, she's just running the blocking. But the cumulative effect of these straight lines is to create the illusion of a curve. And the closer together the dots, the more it will look like a curve from a distance. When the actor is slow getting with the part, put your blocking dots very close together. It will pass for performance, and it's just possible that someday the actor may be able to dispense with the dots and draw a freehand curve all by herself. She will be able to make the part her own. That was the case with the actor who finally brought the show in on the second performance. It was like a miracle. But her performance before that had been technically very polished, and I doubt that the average audience member could tell the difference between the dots and the freehand. Maybe the director was the only one who noticed.

But we were talking about the first tech rehearsal:

1. Introduce the cast and crew to one another.
2. Review the chain of accountability: All technical notes go to the director. All notes about the direction go to the director. That means if the actor doesn't like the lighting for a scene, she tells the director, not the lighting technician. If a technician has an idea about the blocking, she tells the director, not the actor. And if actors are having problems with actors, they tell the director.
3. If a crew person screws up in a way that affects an actor or actors in a scene, she needs to go to the actor or actors and take responsibility. This means that if the lightboard operator falls asleep at the wheel and forgets to take the lights out during a scene change, or if the sound technician forgets the telephone bell, these crew members need to hunt up the actors who were left in the lurch and apologize.

   Even if the problem was not the technician's fault (the tape broke, etc.), the technician still needs to acknowledge the actor's inconvenience (putting it mildly), and she needs to take responsibility for seeing that it doesn't happen again. Actors are putting themselves on the line in a show, and they are very dependent on the crew (props, sound cues, furniture changes, etc.). They need to know that the crew takes these lapses as seriously as they do, because the actors are not in a position to do anything about them. (This is not license for an actor to abuse the crew. If an actor is angry, she should take her complaints to the director.)
4. Warn everyone that the first tech rehearsal might look awful. Tell them it's supposed to.
5. Inform the actors that the stage manager is going to be assuming responsibility for rehearsals and that you, the director, will be turning the show over to her during this period. In other words, they will have a new boss. The stage manager will not be giving them notes on performance—no one but the director will ever have the right to do that—but she will have the right to supervise what goes on backstage and in the house.

   And be sure that you give the stage manager this power during Tech Week. Don't try to turn over the show on opening night. Like the actors, she has a need to ease into her position of authority. Start letting go at the first tech rehearsal. Be accessible to her, meet with her frequently during this week, find out what she needs, solicit her input.
6. Encourage the actors to speak up if they have any health or safety concerns about the furniture, props, and so forth.
7. Show them the sign-in sheet for Tech Week. The actors and crew members need to initial the square by their names when they come into the theatre, so that the stage manager can tell who's missing. Sometimes there is a sign-out sheet also, which is helpful if the stage manager or director is looking for someone after rehearsal.

And that's it. You're off and running. Eat well during Tech Week. Take 1,000 milligrams of calcium before bed. Avoid junk food and sugar. Keep a lid on the caffeine. Get lots of protein, lots of B vitamins. Meditate or practice self-hypnosis, just so that you can remember there is life outside the production. This is a period of very high stress, and the mental health of the production will rise no higher than the mental health of the director, so take that responsibility seriously. Be a leader. Support your cast and crew. Do not expect them to take care of you. Have some outside support for that. *Never* confuse your theatre company for family, no matter how tempting that may be.

And a note on notes: Notes are the directions the director gives at the end of a scene or a run-through. During Tech Week, the cast usually assembles on the set for the notes. Technical notes all go to the stage manager. When you give notes, let the actors know it's their responsibility to remember them. I suggest that they write down all their notes for the week in one place and read them over in the dressing room before each night's rehearsal. If they choose not to do this, fine. But I warn them that the first time I have to repeat a note, I will ask them to write it down. It wastes everyone's time to repeat notes, but worse, it wastes precious rehearsal time if an actor keeps running the wrong blocking.

Another practice of the trauma-drama school of directing is keeping actors at the theatre until two or three in the morning. During most of my years of acting, I was subjected to this practice, which, of course, ignores the reality of baby-sitters or working people; I came to believe it was nothing more than a function of egotism, sloppy planning, and sometimes outright sadism. Besides, late-night rehearsals are marvels of inefficiency. Because the actors are tired and losing focus (not to mention tempers), scenes must be repeated and repeated. A half hour of work before rehearsal is equal to two hours of work after midnight. And if you have all-day Saturday and Sunday rehearsals, schedule generously for lunch and dinner breaks. It's not just about food.

In the Chapter 25 on programs, I mentioned the practice of getting cast and crew approval of the rough draft for the program before it goes to the printer. This is the week to send around the mock-up for their additions and corrections.

And a final word on being human: If you do bark at the actors or crew, apologize as soon as your sanity returns, and apologize to everyone who witnessed the episode. If you said something unnecessarily brusque to a technician but the cast overheard it, it's only cricket to apologize in full hearing of the cast, also. And make it a real apology: Claim responsibility for the action, acknowledge the inappropriateness, and lastly if there were factors that contributed to your poor judgment, you may mention them, but your excuse is the least important part of a well-delivered apology.

Somewhere in the middle of Tech Week block the curtain call. The curtain call should be as clean as any of the other blocking in the show. Don't count on the actors to take care of it. Block it and rehearse it. Be sure to hustle it through. No matter what the style and pacing of the show, always have a brisk curtain call.

Curtain calls can be touchy, because the order in which actors take their bows and the order of the lineup indicate a certain hierarchy. Traditionally, the actors in the smallest roles take their bows first and move to the side of the stage as the actors in more prominent roles take their bows. The leading actor usually enters last, stands center stage, and leads the company in the company bow.

Generally, I block the curtain call based purely and simply on number of lines. No one can argue with that. And I do feel that the actor with the most stage time/stage lines deserves acknowledgment for her position in the cast. But if curtain call order is a problem for you, or if the show is really and truly a work where everyone's part is the same size, then you can have the actors come out together.

There is one thing I insist on for the curtain call: that the actors allow the audience to have their turn. They have sat and received for two hours. This is their one chance to give back, and they deserve it. Nothing irritates me more than curtain calls where the actors stay in character to milk an extra laugh from the audience, or where actors who have been bold as brass for the entire evening suddenly turn into bashful and awkward little wallflowers, bobbing their heads quickly and retiring to the wings before the audience has had the opportunity to applaud them properly. When the audience is not allowed full expression of their appreciation, they go away feeling incomplete. Give them a full theatre experience; let them thank you.

I actually give bowing lessons. (The curtsy should go the way of the bustle and hoopskirt.) The actor should face the audience *as herself*, ready to receive, and bow from the waist. She should hold the bow long enough to say the word "hippopotamus" slowly, and then rise, smile, and hustle to the side for the next actor to take her bow. The company bow should be slow and gracious, also. After the company bow, either the lead actor or the whole cast should hold out their hands to indicate the interpreters, the musicians, the technicians in the light booth, and the backstage crew. When in doubt, acknowledge!

And don't be shy about a second curtain call. Lesbian audiences are very, very generous with their ovations. Let the stage manager make the decision about the second call. (She will be in control of the curtain and the lighting.) If the audience is still applauding boisterously after the actors have left the stage, by all means, take another call. Lesbian actors can never be appreciated enough.

And some curtain call protocols: If it's opening night, the company should call the director up onstage and give her flowers. Traditionally, the lead actor performs this function. If it's the premiere of a new play, the company should also call the playwright (and composer, if it's a musical) onstage and present flowers.

Dress Rehearsal

Dress rehearsal is the final rehearsal before opening. It should be held the night before, if possible. Sometimes the rehearsal before the dress rehearsal will be called the "tech rehearsal." In the old days, the tech rehearsal was the first rehearsal where all the technical effects were supposed to come together, and the dress rehearsal was the first rehearsal where all the costumes, props, and the like, were finally assembled. I've already said what I think of that as a practice. The *acting* part of the show should be reasonably well set before Tech Week, the costumes and props should be there the first day of Tech Week, and the tech should get itself together as quickly as possible. And you should run the entire show, no stopping, six of the seven nights of Tech Week.

Dress rehearsal should replicate the conditions of an actual performance. There should be a one-hour call. Cast and crew should do everything they're going to do on opening night. And there should be an audience. This is a good time to invite the ushers, house manager, and concessionaires. I try to have an audience of at least ten people for dress rehearsal. Some directors invite more. You need enough audience members so that they will not feel self-conscious laughing or reacting in other ways to the business onstage. The actors need to begin to get some idea of where the laughs are going to be, and the director needs to notice where they aren't.

Sometimes the director addresses the dress rehearsal audience, and sometimes she doesn't. She may thank them for coming, or warn them that since it is still a rehearsal, the show may be stopped. Needless to say, the stage manager should be in complete charge of dress rehearsal.

There is a myth that a bad dress rehearsal means a good opening. A bad dress rehearsal can also mean a bad opening. My own experience is that a show that is sufficiently rehearsed to warrant opening will be very consistent in quality, including dress rehearsal. Some directors make a point of acting disappointed at the dress rehearsal, I guess on the theory that scaring the actors will make them try harder. This seems manipulative to me. A real actor is plenty scared. I've never seen such a thing as an overconfident actor on an opening night. If the show's good, tell them. Why not? It's supposed to be good, isn't it? The one warning I would give the director about dress rehearsal is not to give too many notes. Keep it simple, keep it positive.

And then turn it over.

Part VIII

Opening and Beyond

Chapter 36

Opening

1. Get a massage, go for a long walk, or sleep in.
2. Call up a friend who has a history of being genuinely thrilled by your successes. Go out for dinner. The nicer, the better.
3. Arrive thirty minutes before curtain at the theatre, and drop in backstage—exuding *nothing* but confidence and goodwill. Give everyone cards and good wishes.
4. Take your seat in the theatre, like any other member of the audience, and behave yourself.

Chapter 37

Pickup, Strike, and Postproduction

Pickup Rehearsal

It's traditional to hold a pickup rehearsal midweek after opening. These are usually lots of fun. Unless there is a serious problem in the show that requires reblocking, I make the pickup a speed-through. Without costumes or props, the actors walk (or run) the blocking and say their lines at top speed. Even the bleakest tragedy becomes a farce when it's a speed-through.

In addition to reminding everyone about lines and blocking, this rehearsal also gives the actors a time to discharge a lot of antagonism about the script in a playful and collective way. The pickup is as much for catharsis as anything else. After all, the show's already opened.

Usually, there is only one pickup, even if the play is going to run longer than two weekends. Personally, I suspect that the pickup was invented to ease the actors' and director's pain of withdrawal from rehearsals. We've practically been living together for six weeks, and suddenly we only get together on weekends. There is a certain emptiness after opening, and the pickup is a kind of farewell rehearsal when we can all appreciate it. Dress rehearsal doesn't count, because it's too intense for anyone to get sentimental about.

Strike

Strike, the dismantling of a production, is often held on closing night, immediately after the last performance. This has two advantages: Everyone is already there, and everyone wants to get it over with and go home.

The stage manager runs the strike, which means she assigns jobs to members of the cast and crew. Generally, everyone stays until the SM gives permission for them to go home. Strike can be one of those grueling all-night affairs, but it doesn't have to be. It can be held the next morning, or even on the weekend.

The key to a good strike is organization. The stage manager should have made up a list ahead of time of all the tasks and made sure that appropriate tools, vehicles, dumpsters, and the like would be available. Sometimes, sets are broken down into platforms and flats for storage. Other times, they are completely torn apart and thrown away. Furniture and props get put in vehicles to be taken back to original owners, costumes get sorted for cleaning or storage, and rented lighting equipment and sound equipment are dismantled to be returned. The house is tidied up (programs collected, etc.), and the stage floor is swept and mopped.

The SM has the check-in sheet, and as each actor and crew member finishes her work, she gives them permission to leave and they sign out. Often the wardrobe manager will need to sign them out also, to be sure that they have turned in all of their costumes.

Postproduction Meeting

If you plan to do another production at any time in the future—even if you don't know when—go ahead and have a postproduction (or "postmortem") meeting after the show. Hold it within two weeks of closing—long enough for everyone to recuperate, but not long enough to forget.

The postproduction meeting is not a shame-and-blame session, and it should be structured to avoid that dynamic. I find that it's helpful for each member of the production staff to give her own evaluation of what worked well for her and what she would do differently in the future. Later, if other members of the staff have concerns about areas outside their own, then they can address these. Postproduction is a time to give yourselves a lot of credit. Keep most of the focus on what you were able to achieve, where you learned new skills and grew personally, and the positive feedback from members of the community. Give yourselves every ounce of credit where credit is due. If you produced Lesbian theatre, you made herstory.

Where there is criticism, keep the focus on how you can solve the problem for future productions, not on who did what and why in the past. The postproduction meeting should be oriented toward future productions.

Chapter 38

Touring

Touring. You should have thought of that earlier.

There is a great temptation in the middle of a popular run to start thinking about where else you can take the show. These ideas are always very exciting, but they seldom pan out. Why? Because live theatre takes a great deal of advance planning. First, you need to consider the publicity time line for the touring venue. If the out-of-town producer decides in the last week of your run to bring the show to Podunk for a weekend, she will probably want at least six weeks lead time for her publicity.

Then there is the question of logistics. How many of your cast members will have fallen in/out of love and moved away by the time your touring dates roll around? And even if they are still in town, will they have the same enthusiasm for the show two months down the line? Many of them will be involved in new projects or productions.

This is not to say that a show that is already up and running can't get booked for touring. It's to say that it's more difficult. Touring is something that should have been built into the initial production concept. The set and the tech should have been designed for touring, the blocking should have been designed for flexible staging, the actors should have been notified at auditions what the additional touring commitment would entail. And the out-of-town producers should have been lined up in advance—with contracts signed.

Sometimes the out-of-town producer will be reluctant to commit until she sees the reviews or even the show itself, but often you can get the booking just by sharing the script. Lesbians are starved for live theatre, and it's high time that producers who have no qualms about booking girl-with-guitar took a risk on ensemble-with-entire-play.

Touring contracts vary, and they usually involve a bit of negotiating. Obviously, with a cast of eight actors and a crew of three technicians, you will probably not get more than gas money for everyone. When I was contracting to tour with my theatre company, I would ask for a minimum guarantee—between $30 and $50 per performance per company member—and then a percentage (60 percent or more) of the profits after the producer's expenses had been reimbursed. (Understand, of course, that there might not be any profits at all.) In addition, I would ask for meals and housing.

The minimum guarantee is important, because it

provides your producer with the incentive to hustle an audience. If she is committed to paying out $1,500 to your theatre whether or not anyone buys a ticket, she will be more motivated to get those flyers and press releases out. The producer who balks at a guaranteed minimum is often one who wants to be in on the profits, but who is not willing to take any risks.

In some cases, the producer may have genuine concerns that she will not be able to come up with the money; but producing is a gambler's game, and I personally feel that we are enabling poor boundaries when we don't get the guarantee. When the producer tells you that she's producing because of her love of women's culture and that she's doing you a favor by producing at all, and when she uses these arguments as a rationale for why she is unwilling to risk a guarantee, watch out! These are poor boundaries, and accepting these conditions sets a bad precedent that keeps our culture at an amateur level and our business in the realm of dysfunctional family politics.

Don't leave home without a written contract. These are some of the issues that should be spelled out in a touring contract: date, time, and exact location for performances; ticket price information (if the performer is being paid a percentage of the gross); exact wording of the billing; whether or not any other outside performances will be included in the evening; *specific* arrangements for publicity (what the materials will be, where they will be sent, how much in advance, who has rights of approval, how many press kits the theatre will provide); accessibility information, including sign-language interpreting; whether or not alcohol will be sold; who will be liable in case of accidents; provisions for food backstage for the actors; housing arrangements (including accessibility concerns); and reimbursement for meals and transportation. And, of course, the contract needs to spell out all of the details about the performance fee, which can include whether or not there is a non-refundable deposit, whether the theatre will be paid with cash, money order, or cashier's check (*don't* take a personal check), and when the payment will be made. If the theatre is being paid a percentage of the producer's net profits after her expenses are met, the contract should specify the documentation and figures the producer will need to provide at the time of payment.

When your company tours, especially when the members will be housed in private homes, be sure that everyone understands that they represent the theatre. Touring accommodations are often full of surprises (fleas, uncomfortable beds, strange pets and/or roommates, etc.), and it's best for everyone to be ready to rough it. No matter how bad it is, remember, it'll make a great story later.

If your production is a one- or two-woman show, there is a potential for the actors to actually make some decent money—especially if the actors are willing to travel for several months, or even years. In a case like this, I would advise the performers to join the Association for Women's Music and Culture (AWMAC) and to attend their annual conference (which is filled with producers looking to book acts), as well as workshops on how to get bookings. And I would advise the performers to attend Lesbian festivals.

Touring can be a headache, but if your company begins to produce shows on a regular basis, you may be able to develop a regular touring circuit to towns a few hours away. As your reputation builds, the producers of the tours will have an easier and easier job; and as you send more shows out on tour, the logistics become more familiar and more streamlined.

The first time one of my shows toured to another city, we arrived on a night when another women's event was scheduled, no one knew who we were, and unfortunately, the publicity for our event had played up the social issues angle more than the entertainment angle. In short, fewer than forty women attended, and our producer lost money. But the word of mouth was great. We came back nine months later with another show, and this time more than 350 women attended, the producer made a pile of money, and we had the best performance experience in the history of our theatre.

Chapter 39

For Women Only

No discussion of Lesbian theatre would be complete without including the issue of "women-only space." In the world of theatre, this means deciding whether or not men—or male children (what age?) or transsexuals or transgendered males—will be allowed to attend your performances. It is a divisive, even explosive, issue, but an important one.

Before I talk about the philosophical aspects of the question, let me just cover some of the legal ramifications. A women-only performance is no longer public. Even if only one night of your eight-week run is designated "women-only," it is still not a public run. This may affect who will carry your ads, your notices, or your press releases—or even where you post your flyers, or how long they stay up. It may also affect where you can perform, because buildings that are subsidized by government money (schools or 501[c]3 art or civic or religious organizations) may not be allowed to rent to you. And they may not want to.

Women-only space arouses amazing responses from people who fail to notice the many signifiers of "men-only space" in the institutions around them. If a women's theatre company with eight members and $200 wants to put up a play that has been rejected by every other theatre in the city and if this theatre company has never had men attend its performances before, all it has to do is start putting up notices of "women-only" and, trust me, suddenly it will be besieged by men insisting, demanding, threatening litigation in order to gain entrance. These men will move heaven and earth to make sure they can have access to the event, even if they choose not to exercise that prerogative after they have won it. These are men who insist they are feminist, and they are willing to resort to force in order to prove it.

They are on a zealot's crusade to teach us women the pain of discrimination. I have a real problem with this when the target is a women-only gym they are suing, where women who are fat or old or anorexic or stunningly beautiful by patriarchal standards are seeking shelter from the male gaze that has ridiculed and degraded them all their lives. I feel rage when the target is the executive board of a coalition against domestic violence. And I feel a special kind of rage when the target is a theatre that exists on the margins of society, specifically because no other theatres would hire us "out" Lesbians, because no other theatres would dream of producing our antipatriarchal scripts, because all of us have been so battered and so brainwashed from the system that we desperately need our privacy to recover our memories, to create the new language to tell the taboo stories, to go through the painful process of rehabilitating our atrophied capacities for intimacy among ourselves. How dare a man claim his right to invade this sacred space, this last outpost for our culture? And those who will lobby most vigorously against a women-only policy have never in their lives confronted a mainstream theatre on their lack of inclusivity for lesbians, their racism, their discrimination against women playwrights, or the subordinate and degrading roles for women in the majority of mainstream plays.

If you are producing a women-only play, check out your contract for your performance space, check out any organizations that might be affiliated with your production, check out the situation with publicity and mailing lists. And understand that along the way you may lose the support of many women who are uncomfortable with the policy, who will throw charges of "male bashing" and "reverse discrimination" at you, who will tell you that they would like to support you, but they have a brother (landlord, husband, son, next-door neighbor) who is completely wonderful and "not like other men," and for his sake, they can never set foot through your doors. These women will probably write letters to the editor of the local paper, or they may be the ones to call up the manager of your theatre space. We are living in a particularly transitional time in the liberation struggle, so be prepared. Nothing is as cutting edge or as controversial as the idea that women could have a right to control our bodies, our definition of family, our health care, our forms of social organization, our expressions of sexuality—and that these choices might not include men. Privacy can be dangerous in a society in which the social order depends on men's ongoing access to women's resources.

Finally, even if a man is a militant activist in the antirape or antipornography fight, the members of the audience will not know that. He will be a strange man sitting next to women in a dark theatre. Possibly his thigh will be touching one of theirs. Or maybe the women will be conscious that he is sitting just behind them. Together they will listen to a play about what men do to women's bodies, or a play that tells the truth about the caste system based on gender. Together they will hear things that will expose women's vulnerabilities or point up men's privilege. To believe that his presence will not affect the women's experience of the play is at best naive, and at worst, a deliberate erasure of the political and social conditions of women—and especially of Lesbians—in the world today. If you are the artistic director of a Lesbian theatre, practicing this kind of denial is hypocritical and irresponsible.

Women in a mixed audience may themselves stay in performance mode, playing their roles as patriarchal females, putting on the act that so many women have had to adopt in the presence of men. Obviously, if your audience is busy performing in their own play, they will be inattentive to yours. The women in your audience may need to reassure the man in the theatre, even if they don't know him, that they are grateful for his liberalism, for his unbelievable open-mindedness in being able to attend a women's theatre. This is the syndrome Gloria Steinem refers to as "terminal gratitude."

Or the women in the audience may fear that he might be taking the play "the wrong way," that he might assume that all women are as angry or as deviant as the ones onstage. Some of the women may become obsessed with telegraphing to him that it's only a play. Some may feel a need to approach him on behalf of the women who really enjoy men's company. Women may feel compelled to take sides when men are present, whereas in a women-only house, they might not experience such immediate pressure to accept or reject the material in the play. Women might be more free to experience without judgment, to take our time processing and assimilating when we are allowed the privacy of women-only space.

Men do apply a double standard when they judge women's plays. Mainstream theatre, which is dominated by the work of male playwrights, has never been overly concerned about themes of male bonding and violence against women. There is no such expression as "female bashing." When the male lead demonstrates more of an affinity for his male colleagues than he does for his girlfriend, there is no accusation from producers that this represents a homosexual theme that might not be acceptable to mainstream audiences. In patriarchy, it is considered normal for men to act out violently against women and to bond with one another. In fact, violence toward us is frequently depicted as a male bonding ritual.

But there is a double standard for women playwrights. We are not allowed the same degree of allegiance to our gender. Our plays are neurotically scrutinized by male and male-identified producers for the slightest evidence that we might prefer our own company to the company of men, or that we bear any grudge against the gender that has historically prevented us from voting, from testifying in court or serving on juries, from gaining an education, from earning or keeping a living wage, from exercising the right to control our own bodies, from owning our children, from defending ourselves against violence or sexual aggression, from accessing health care, and from participating in the culture. That we might actually recommend alliances among women as a political expedient is taken by mainstream culture as an indication that we are not to be taken seriously as writers, or as women.

When a feminist writes a non-Lesbian play that is concerned with intimacy among women, she must expend considerable energy reassuring her audience of these women's heterosexual credentials. Stories in which women confront men are either trivial in theme, or the women must play out the Hedda Gabler syndrome and self-destruct at the end. Thelma and Louise did nothing radical. Ibsen's heroines have been driving themselves over the edge for a hundred years and for the same reason, defying patriarchy. Now . . . what if Thelma and Louise had realized they loved each other? What if they had realized they could meet their needs without depending on men? What if their kiss had been prelude not finale? They would never have found a producer, that's what. The supposedly heterosexual culture that imposes such strictures on the story lines for female companions does not exercise the same censorship regarding male buddies. They are allowed—encouraged, even—to dump the girl and ride off into the sunset.

What other liberation movement in history has had the responsibility of reassuring those in power that their movement is not really a threat? And when this reassurance is mandatory for the expression of our culture, can women really speak for our own interests? When women playwrights must attend to the concerns of men, what can we say for ourselves? Does our work constitute a culture with its own identity, or does it just become a colonized version of the established male culture?

Women's theatre should take a page from the history of men's theatre. We need to start with all-women companies, where the women cross-dress the male roles. We should take our plots all the way to tension, where we can write the passionate love among women and the murderous rage toward men—which is in no way analogous to women loving men (ambiguous at best, when men are so obviously our predators) or women killing women (which, as a displaced action, lacks resolution).

In Lesbian theatre, women are not afraid to love one another. We are not afraid to tell the whole truth. In Lesbian theatre, we don't lobby our oppressors to include us in their culture. Lesbian theatre *is* women's culture. Lesbian theatre does not just offer a strategy; it *is* that strategy.

Chapter 40

The Future

This chapter is for you to write. I can't wait to read it.

Appendixes

Appendix 1

Sample Director's Contract

Directing Agreement

Agreement dated this __25__ day of __November__ 19 __97__, (the "Effective Date") between __Jane Smith__ (herein called Director), whose address is: __21 Collette Court, Petaluma, CA__ and __Wild Sisters Productions__ (herein called Producer), an organization in the State of __CA__ whose address is __345 W. Didriksen St., Petaluma, CA__ concerning directing __The Anastasia Trials__ (herein called Play).

Fees

The Director shall receive $1,000 for directing the play. This amount is due within 7 days after the closing of the last performance of the Play.

Auditions

The Producer shall provide space for the auditions on January 29 and January 30, from 6:00 to 9:00 P.M. The Producer shall provide 15 scripts for the production. These shall be available to the Director prior to auditions. The Director shall provide the Producer with a master copy of the script. The Producer shall be responsible for publicizing the auditions.

Rehearsal Space

The Producer shall provide rehearsal space five days per week for five weeks (February 7–March 11), for periods not less than three hours each. The rehearsal times shall be evenings or weekends. The Producer shall provide rehearsal space for seven consecutive days, March 12–March 18, in the performance space, Theatre Femina, located at 312 N. Ninth Street, Petaluma, CA. Performance dates will be the evenings of March 19, 20, 26, 27, and April 2, 3.

Lighting

The Producer shall provide lighting for the production. The lights shall be available on March 12. The Producer shall provide sound, if required.

Staff

The Producer shall be responsible for providing the following staff: Assistant Director, Stage Manager, Lighting Designer/Operator, Sound Designer/Operator, Set Designer/Tech Director, Costumer, Prop Manager, House Manager, and House Staff (box office, concessions, ushers, etc.).

Budget

In addition to the rental of the theatre and publicity costs, the Producer shall provide a budget of $1,000 for costumes, props, and set. This money shall be made available to the Director at the time of auditions.

Artistic Decisions

Casting and artistic decisions shall be the sole responsibility of the Director, provided they fall within the agreed upon budget.

Director's Responsibilities

The Director shall rehearse no fewer than five times a week for six weeks and shall attend all Tech Week rehearsals. The Director shall attend opening night. The Director shall be responsible for supervising the production staff, and she shall be responsible for the physical production of the play.

Publicity

The Producer shall provide publicity for the auditions and for the play. Director shall have approval of all materials used to publicize the play, as well as approval of the program. The Producer shall be responsible for box office and for programs.

Comp Tickets

Director, cast members, and crew shall receive two comp tickets each.

Producers Who Are Cast as Actors

Members of Wild Sisters who are cast in the Play shall be exempted from all duties as Producers for the duration of the time that the Play is in production or performance. These actors shall be exempted from attending meetings of the producing body, from participating in decisions regarding the production, and from all activities as Producers related to the Play. This provision assures equity among the cast members, it protects actors from conflict-of-interest and split focus regarding the very different activities of producing and performing, and it protects the Director from the boundary conflicts inherent in the situation.

Production Meetings

The Producer (or the Producer's Representative, if the Producer is an organization) and the Director shall meet every two weeks during the period of production at a time and location mutually convenient to both of them. The Producer or Producer's Representative and the Director shall meet at least once prior to auditions. The Producer or Producer's Representative and the Director shall return each other's phone calls within 24 hours of receiving a call. If the Producer is an organization, the Producer's Representative shall be the member who most serves as the clearinghouse for information, whose phone number is the central contact number for organization, and/or who sets the agenda and chairs the meetings. If the Producer is an organization, the Producer's Representative shall be the liaison to the Director, except for exceptional circumstances where this is not possible.

Miscellaneous

This Agreement shall be governed by, and construed in accordance with, the laws of the State of ___California___ applicable to all contracts made and entirely performed within.

All notices to either party shall be in writing. Notices by mail shall be addressed to such party's address as given above, or to such other address as such party may hereafter specify by notice duly given.

This is the entire Agreement between the parties. This Agreement shall not be amended or modified except by a written agreement signed by the parties.

This Agreement shall be binding on the parties hereto and on their executors, administrators, personal representatives, successors, and assigns.

The parties agree that any claim, dispute, or controversy arising between Director and Producer under or in connection with this Agreement shall be submitted to arbitration in the State of ___California___ in accordance with the then obtaining rules of the American Arbitration Association. Judgment upon the award rendered may by entered in the highest Court of the forum, state or federal, having jurisdiction.

The paragraph headings in this Agreement are for convenience only and do not constitute a part of this Agreement.

IN WITNESS WHEREOF each of the parties hereto has signed this Agreement as of the day and year first written above.

By: _____   By: _____

Appendix 2

Resources For Dismantling Racism, Homophobia/Heterosexualism, Anti-Semitism, Classism, Ableism, Ageism, Sizeism

Dismantling racism:

Anzaldua, Gloria, ed. 1990. *Making Face, Making Soul: Hacienda Caras: Creative and Cultural Perspectives by Feminists of Color*. San Francisco: Aunt Lute Foundation Books.

Brah, Avtar. 1997. *Cartographies of Diaspora*. NY: Routledge.

Brandt, Joseph. 1991. *Dismantling Racism: The Continuing Challenge to White America*. Minneapolis: Augsburg Books.

Bulkin, Elly, Minnie Bruce Pratt, and Barbara Smith, eds. 1988. *Yours in Struggle: Three Feminist Perspectives on Anti-Semitism and Racism*. Ithaca, NY: Firebrand Books.

Collins, Patricia Hill. 1990. *Black Feminist Thought*. Boston: Unwin Hyman.

de Ishtar, Zohl. 1994. *Daughters of the Pacific*. North Melbourne, Australia: Spinifex Press.

Frankenber, Ruth. 1993. *White Women, Race Matters: The Social Construction of Whiteness*. Minneapolis: University of Minnesota Press.

Hongo, Garrett, ed. 1994. *Under Western Eyes: Personal Essays from Asian America*. NY: Anchor Books.

hooks, bell. 1981. *Ain't I A Woman: Black Women and Feminism*. Boston: South End Press.

———. 1992. *Black Looks: Race and Representation*. Boston: South End Press.

———. 1984. *Feminist Theory from Margin to Center*. Boston: South End Press.

———. 1995. *Killing Rage: Ending Racism*. NY: Henry Holt and Company.

———. 1993. *Sisters of the Yam: Black Women and Self-Recovery*. Boston: South End Press.

———. 1987. *Talking Back: Thinking Feminist, Thinking Black*. Boston: South End Press.

———. 1990. *Yearning: Race, Gender and Cultural Politics*. Boston: South End Press.

Kivel, Paul. 1995. *Uprooting Racism: How White People Can Work for Racial Justice*. Philadelphia: New Society Publishers.

Lester, Joan Steinau. 1994. *The Future of White Men and Other Diversity Dilemmas*. Berkeley, CA: Conari Press.

Lewis, Reina. 1995. *Gendering Orientalism: Race, Femininity and Representation*. New York: Routledge.

Mankiller, Wilma. 1993. *Mankiller: A Chief and Her People*. NY: St. Martin's Press.

Moraga, Cherrie, and Gloria Anzaldua, eds. 1981. *This Bridge Called My Back: Writings by Radical Women of Color*. Watertown, MA: Persephone Press.

Said, Edward W. 1978. *Orientalism*. NY: Pantheon Books.

sapphire. 1996. *american dreams*. NY: Vintage Books.

Segrest, Mab. 1994. *Memoir of a Race Traitor*. Boston: South End Press.

Shohat, Ella, and Robert Stam. 1994. *Unthinking Eurocentrism*. NY: Routledge.

Smith, Barbara, ed. 1983. *Home Girls: A Black Feminist Anthology*. NY: Kitchen Table—Women of Color Press.

Three Rivers, Amoja. 1991. *Cultural Etiquette: A*

Guide for the Well-Intentioned. Available from Market Wimmin, Box 28, Indian Valley, VA 24105. $6.00.

Trask, Haunani-Kay. 1993. *From a Native Daughter: Colonialism and Sovereignty in Hawaii*. Monroe, ME: Common Courage Press.

West, Cornel. 1993. *Race Matters*. Boston: Beacon Press.

Young, Lola. 1996. *Fear of the Dark: 'Race,' Gender and Sexuality in the Cinema*. New York: Routledge.

Dismantling heterosexualism:

Epstein, Debbie, ed. 1994. *Challenging Lesbian and Gay Inequalities in Education*. Philadelphia: Open University Press.

Plummer, Ken. 1995. *Telling Sexual Stories: Power, Change and Social Worlds*. New York: Routledge.

Steinberg, Deborah Lynn, Debbie Epstein, and Richard Johnson, eds. 1997. *Border Patrols: Policing the Boundaries of Heterosexuality*. London: Cassell.

Dismantling Lesbian oppression:

Daly, Mary. 1978. *Gyn/ecology: The Metaethics of Radical Feminism*. Boston: Beacon Press.

———. 1984. *Pure Lust: Elemental Feminist Philosophy*. Boston: Beacon Press.

Dworkin, Andrea. 1974. *Woman Hating*. NY: Dutton.

Frye, Marilyn. 1983. *The Politics of Reality: Essays in Feminist Theory*. Trumansburg, NY: The Crossing Press.

———. 1992. *Willful Virgin: Essays in Feminism, 1976–1992*. Freedom, CA: The Crossing Press.

Hoagland, Sarah Lucia, and Julia Penelope, eds. 1988. *For Lesbians Only: A Separatist Anthology*. London: Onlywomen Press, Ltd.

Hoagland, Sarah Lucia. 1989. *Lesbian Ethics*. Palo Alto, CA: Institute of Lesbian Studies.

Jeffreys, Sheila. 1993. *The Lesbian Heresy*. North Melbourne, Australia: Spinifex Press.

Kitzinger, Celia and Rachel Perkins. 1993. *Changing Our Minds: Lesbian Feminism and Psychology*. New York: New York University Press.

Penelope, Julia. 1992. *Call Me Lesbian: Lesbian Lives, Lesbian Theory*. Freedom, CA: The Crossing Press.

Pharr, Suzanne. 1988. *Homophobia: A Weapon of Sexism*. Inverness, CA: Chardon Press.

Strega, Linda, and Bev Jo. 1990. *Dykes-Loving-Dykes: Dyke Separatists Politics for Lesbians Only*. Oakland, CA: Battleaxe.

Dismantling anti-Semitism:

Balka, Christie, and Andy Rose, eds. 1989. *Twice Blessed: On Being Lesbian, Gay and Jewish*. Boston: Beacon Press.

Beck, Evelyn Torton, ed. 1982. *Nice Jewish Girls: A Lesbian Anthology*. Watertown, MA: Persephone Press.

Bulkin, Elly, Minnie Bruce Pratt, and Barbara Smith, eds. 1988. *Yours in Struggle: Three Feminist Perspectives on Anti-Semitism and Racism*. Ithaca, NY: Firebrand Books.

Kaye/Kantrowitz, Melanie and Irene Klepfisz, eds. 1989. *The Tribe of Dina: A Jewish Women's Anthology*. Boston: Beacon Press.

Moore, Tracy, ed. 1995. *Lesbiot: Israeli Lesbians Talk About Sexuality, Feminism, Judaism, and Their Lives*.

Dismantling class elitism:

Albelda, Randy, et al. 1988. *Mink Coats Don't Trickle Down: The Economic Attack on Women and People of Color*. Boston: South End Press.

Penelope, Julia, ed. 1994. *Out of the Class Closet: Lesbians Speak*. Freedom, CA: Crossing Press.

Dismantling ableism:

Browne, Susan, Debra Connors, and Nanci Stern, eds. 1985. *With the Power of Each Breath: A Disabled Women's Anthology*. San Francisco: Cleis Press.

Saxton, Marsha, and Florence Howe. 1987. *With Wings: An Anthology of Literature by and about Women with Disabilities*. NY: The Feminist Press.

Sinister Wisdom, vol. 39, Winter 1989–1990. Berkeley, CA.

Tremain, Shelley, ed. 1996. *Pushing the Limits: Disabled Dykes Produce Culture*. Toronto, Canada: Women's Press.

Von Beltz, Heidi. 1996. *My Soul Purpose: Living, Loving, and Learning*. NY: Random House.

Dismantling ageism:

Copper, Baba. 1984. *Over the Hill: Reflections on Ageism between Women*. Freedom, CA: The Crossing Press.

MacDonald, Barbara with Cynthia Rich. 1983. *Look Me in the Eye: Old Women, Ageing, and Ageism*. San Francisco: Spinsters Ink.

Dismantling fat oppression:

Bennett, William, and Joel Gurin. 1982. *The Dieter's Dilemma*. NY: Basic Books.

Schoenfielder, Lisa, and Barb Wieser, eds. 1983. *Shadow on a Tightrope: Writings by Women on Fat Oppression*. Iowa City, IA: Aunt Lute Book Co.

Stinson, Susan. 1994. *Fat Girl Dances with Rocks*. Minneapolis, MN: Spinsters Ink.

About survivors of sexual abuse:

Davis, Laura. 1991. *Allies in Healing: When the Person You Love Was Sexually Abused as a Child*. NY: HarperPerennial.

Herman, Judith. 1992. *Trauma and Recovery*. NY: Basic Books.

Appendix 3

Selected Bibliography of Lesbian and Gay/Lesbian Play Anthologies

Allen, Claudia. 1993. *She's Always Liked the Girls Best*. Chicaco: Third Side Press.
Barnes, Noreen C., and Nichola Deutsch, eds. 1992. *Tough Acts to Follow: One-Act Plays on the Gay/Lesbian Experience*. San Francisco: Alamo Square Press.
Butler, Audrey. 1990. *Radical Perversions: Two Dyke Plays*. Toronto: Women's Press.
Curb, Rosemary, ed. 1996. *Amazon All Stars: Thirteen Lesbian Plays*. New York: Applause Books.
Davis, Jill, ed. 1987. *Lesbian Plays*. London: Methuen.
———. 1989. *Lesbian Plays II*. London: Methuen.
Dreher, Sarah. 1988. *Lesbian Stages*. Norwich, VT: New Victoria Publications.
Furtado, Ken, and Nancy Hellner. 1993. *Gay and Lesbian American Plays: An Annotated Bibliography*. Lanham, MD: Scarecrow Press.
Gage, Carolyn. 1996. *Scenes and Monologues for Lesbian Actors*. Santa Rosa, CA: Gage Press.
———. 1994. *The Second Coming of Joan of Arc and Other Plays*. Santa Cruz, CA: HerBooks, Inc.
Helbing, Terry, ed. 1993. *Gay and Lesbian Plays Today*. Portsmouth, NH: Heinemann Educational Books.
Lane, Eric, and Nina Shengold, eds. 1995. *The Actor's Book of Gay and Lesbian Plays*. New York: Penguin Books.
McDermott, Kate, ed. 1985. *Places, Please! The First Anthology of Lesbian Plays*. Iowa City, IA: Aunt Lute Book Company.

Appendix 4

Accessibility Survey

This survey serves two purposes. First, it is an educational instrument which serves to let individuals and organizations in our community become more knowledgeable about accessibility issues and concerns. Second, it is a tool to gather needed data for community members who are working to create better access. Some items may seem frivolous, but they are vital to some people. Having this information may make it possible for more people to attend local events/use your services. If you are not accessible in all these ways—and you won't be—please consider making appropriate changes. This survey is in no way meant to be complete. It is a beginning.

1. Deaf and Hearing Impaired:
   A. ASL Interpretation
   B. Hearing Loop
   C. TDD/TTY (If so, what is the phone #? ___)
   D. Deaf-Blind ASL Interpretation
   E. Closed Captioning (for film, video, etc.)

2. Blind and Partially Sighted
   A. Braille
      a. Printed Media
      b. Elevators, Room Numbers
      c. Maps and Guides
   B. Audio Cassette
   C. Large Print (18 point type or larger)
   D. Audio Indicators (as in elevators)

3. Seating:
   A. Armless Chairs (for people transferring from wheelchairs and big people)
   B. Level Floor Space (for wheelchair users)
   C. Folding Chairs (for friends of people in wheelchairs)
   D. Couches (for seating comfort and big people)
   E. Reserved, Unobstructed, Close-up Seating (for a range of accessible needs)
   F. Wide Aisles (36″ or more and unobstructed path of travel)
   G. Non-smoking Area
   H. Smoking Area

4. Alternate Media and Materials Format: Formats include: (1) large print (2) audio cassette (3) braille (4) floppy disk (5) modem transfer (6) e-mail (7) other:
   specify _____
   Specify format: (by number)
   A. Newspapers _____
   B. Newsletters _____
   C. Program Guides _____
   D. Flyers _____
   E. Pamphlets _____
   F. Displays _____
   G. Menus _____
   H. Directories _____
   I. Other _____

5. Wheelchair Access: Entrances and Doors:
   A. Ramped Entrance (ramp needs to be 12″ in length for every 1″ gain in elevation, non-skid, 48″ wide, free of debris, ice, and snow, railings on both sides, level, unobstructed platform with 48″ turning radius)
   B. Entranceway (level space 60″ on both inside and outside of door, free from debris, door frames 34–36″ wide)
   C. Doors 34–36″ wide
      a. Powered, Automatic
      b. Levered
      c. Handles in Bathrooms

D. Stalls
   a. State Certified (60″ deep, 36″ wide)
   b. Preferred/ADA (60″ unobstructed turning radius)
   c. Inaccessible
E. Grab Bars (2 or 3 bars, both sides and behind toilet, non-slip surface, 1¼″ outside diameter, 1½″ clearance from wall, 30″ above and parallel to floor)
F. Sinks
   a. Faucets Levered and Manual Shutoff
   b. Wall Mounted (no legs or pedestal, recessed and insulated pipes)

6. Financial/Funding:
   A. Sliding Fee Scale
   B. Childcare
   C. Scholarships
   D. Work Exchange
   E. No Charge for Personal Assistance Attendants

7. Parking:
   A. Marked, Accessible Places for vans and autos (level, 12 feet wide, ice and snow free, debris free, within 200 feet of accessible entrance including curb cut)
   B. Number of accessible parking places _____

8. Elevators:
   A. One Story Building—Don't Need
   B. Elevators (54″ wide × 54″ deep)
   C. Elevator not accessible
   D. Control Panel
      a. lowered
      b. braille
   E. Hallway Buttons
      a. lowered
      b. braille
   F. Audible Floor Indicator
   G. Door Jamb Markings in braille
   H. Hand Rails
   I. Emergency Phone
   J. Porch Lift (for people in wheelchairs)

9. Environmental Access:
   A. No Resident Animals
   B. No Carpeting
   C. Date Last Painted _____
   D. Perfumes, Colognes, Other Scented Products Discouraged
   E. Air Ionizers/Purifiers
   F. Fireplace that is used? (smoke and ash)
   G. Sell or Regularly Use Incense, Candles or Scented Products
   H. Non-smoking Environment
      a. Non-smoking Meeting Rooms
      b. Non-smoking Bathrooms
      c. No Smoking in Hallways
      d. No Smoking Anywhere on Premises
   I. Unscented Soaps in Bathrooms
   J. Unscented Cleaning Products Used
   K. Unscented Toilet Paper

10. Food
    A. Food Well-Labeled with All Ingredients
    B. Range of Foods Offered Includes:
       a. Dairy-free
       b. Vegetarian
       c. Wheat-free
       d. Vegan (no meat, dairy, or eggs)
       e. Meat Products
       f. Sugar-free (includes sugar, honey, syrups, maltose, dextrose, sucrose, lactose, fructose)

11. Drinks
    A. Water Available at All Times
    B. Alcohol-free Events/Space
    C. Drinks Available Include:
       a. Sugar-free
       b. Fruit Juices
       c. Caffeine-free
       d. Caffeinated Drinks

12. Breaks/Intermissions:
    A. Meals, Rest Breaks and Intermissions Appropriate to the Circumstances
    B. Location for Someone to Lie Down?

13. Promotional Clothing:
    A. 100% Cotton
    B. Size Ranges to 10X
    C. Size Ranges to 4X
    D. Size Ranges to 1X

Source: This survey was developed by Catherine Odette, Sara Karon, Kathy Younger, and Melinda Burns. It originally appeared in *Dykes, Disability & Stuff Quarterly* (P.O. Box 8773, Madison, WI 53708-8773) volume 4, number 1, issue 13. This survey has been updated and modified since its development in 1992 and has been in use by The United, one of Madison's Lesbian and gay core organizations. For more detailed information on creating access, including specific or detailed ADA (Americans with Disabilities Act) codes, or for development of accessible media for your community, write *DD&S* at the above address.

Appendix 5

Sample Production Budget

EXPENSES:

Royalties
    (if a percentage of gross, estimate) $400.00
Director's Fee 500.00
Scripts
    (actors, designers, and crew) 100.00
Rental of Audition Space 50.00
Rental of Theatre Space 2000.00
Rental of Rehearsal Space 500.00
Costumes 200.00
Props 50.00
Rental of Lights 100.00
Sound Equipment Rental 0
Sound 10.00
Tickets 30.00
Programs (including graphics) 50.00
Flyers/ Posters (including graphics) 150.00
Bulk Mailing 200.00
Interpreter 100.00
Advertising 0
Concessions 50.00
Miscellaneous 200.00
TOTAL 4690.00

INCOME:

Box Office 6000.00
Program Ads 200.00
Concessions 150.00
Donations 100.00
TOTAL 6450.00

PROJECTED NET PROFIT: $1760.00

Appendix 6

Sample Three-Month Production and Publicity Calendar

January

SUNDAY	MONDAY	TUESDAY	WEDNESDAY	THURSDAY	FRIDAY	SATURDAY
	1 Select a play and get playwright's permission to produce.	2 Draw up a budget and make plans to raise funds.	3 Reserve or rent performance, audition, and rehearsal space.	4 Set schedule, recruit staff, get scripts to designers.	5	6
7	8 Typeset audition flyer and make copies.	9 Draft press releases and calendar spots for auditions.	10 Mail audition notices to monthly and weekly papers.	11	12	13 Production Meeting
14	15 Mail audition notices to daily papers and post audition flyers around town.	16	17	18	19	20
21	22 Meet with designers this week and schedule photograper.	23	24	25	26	27 Production Meeting
28 This week: Contact organizations for selling block tickets.	29 Meet with graphic artist about flyer/ poster design.	30 Contact sign-language interpreter if show will be signed.	31 Contact women's/ Lesbian papers about special article.			

February

Sunday	Monday	Tuesday	Wednesday	Thursday	Friday	Saturday
				1	2	3 Auditions
4 Auditions (Callbacks?)	5 Cast the show.	6 Photo call with actors. Rush order contact sheet.	7 Order prints from contact sheet.	8	9 Pick up and proofread graphics for posters and flyers.	10 Production Meeting
11 Draft press releases and calendar spots.	12 First Rehearsal (read-through) Pick up photos.	13 Mail PR to weeklies and monthlies with photo. Place ads. (optional)	14 Script to sign language interpreter. Print posters/flyers and tickets.	15	16 Pick up posters/flyers and tickets from printer.	17
18	19 Line up lighting and sound equipment. Ask for bios.	20 Begin selling program ads.	21	22	23 Production meeting.	24
25 Mailing party	26 Deliver tickets to outlets.	27	28	29		

March

Sunday	Monday	Tuesday	Wednesday	Thursday	Friday	Saturday
31					1 Collect and edit cast bios.	2 Flyers to actors.
3	4 Take program copy to graphic designer. Actors off book.	5 Mail PR, spots, photos to dailies and radio stations. Post flyers around town	6	7	8 Production Meeting	9
10	11 Actors off prompt. Begin running the show.	12	13 Rough draft of program to director.	14	15	16 Production Meeting. Schedule rehearsal with interpreter.
17 Tech Week. Cast and crew edit and approve program.	18 Amended program to typesetter.	19 Program to printer.	20 Production Meeting.	21 Pick up programs. Dress rehearsal.	22 Opening Night	23 Performance
24	25	26	27 Pickup Rehearsal	28 Performance	29 Performance	30

Appendix 7

Sample Ticket Seller's Contract

AGREEMENT BETWEEN (*Producer*) _____ and (*Seller*) _____ for the sale of tickets to a performance by (*theatre*) _____ on (*dates*) _____ at (*times*) _____ at (*location*) _____. Child care and ASL interpretation provided. Wheelchair accessible.

1. Ticket price is $_____.

2. People aged 16 and under, 60 and over, or persons with disabilities may buy tickets for $_____. Such tickets shall be marked by Producer. Seller shall sell only those tickets so marked as $_____ tickets.

3. Seller may charge a service fee to customer of _____ percent of ticket price (or $_____ per ticket) in cash for the service of selling tickets.

4. Seller will be responsible for the number of tickets given to sell. In the event of a discrepancy between the amount of money collected by Seller and the amount due Producer for the number of tickets sold, Seller will be responsible for the difference.

5. In the event Seller runs money through her or his books, Producer will be responsible for bad checks, provided that Seller obtained proper identification from ticket buyer (including name, address, phone number, driver's license number). Seller will receive no service fee on bad checks.

6. In the event Seller does not run ticket money through her or his books, Seller will have ticket buyers make checks payable to _____. Seller will get proper identification.

7. *No tickets will be sold after (time)* _____ *on (date)* _____: Approximately four hours before the show on (*date*) _____ (or the preceding day if Seller is not open on (*date*) _____. Producer will call Seller and get final count of tickets sold and tickets remaining.

8. Seller shall provide Producer with all unsold tickets upon completion of the performances.

I have received ____ **tickets, numbers** _____ **date** _____ **initials** _____

_____   _____
Producer   Ticket Seller

_____   _____
Address/Phone   Contact Person

                                        _____
                                        Address/Phone

Total tickets sold _____ at $_____ = $_____.

Total received by Producer $_____.

Total fee received by Seller $_____.

Source: Note by Note: A Guide to Concert Production (Takoma Park, MD: Community Music, Inc., 1996).

Appendix 8

Sample Ticket

67

RIVER MOON PRODUCTIONS
-presents-
**THE LAST READING
OF CHARLOTTE CUSHMAN**
Written and Directed by Carolyn Gage
Starring Debra Wright

FRIDAY, AUGUST 25TH
8:00 P.M.

ACTORS' THEATRE,
SANTA CRUZ $10.00 GENERAL ADMISSION

Appendix 9

Sample Costume Plot

Costumes: *The Amazon All-Stars* Act I				
	Scene 1	Scene 2	Scene 3	Scene 4
Ursula	sweats		Butchette costume	punk rock costume
Slide	sweats	leather jacket		
Gloria	sweats		Butchette costume	Bossy Femme costume
Leona	sweats	slacks/ nice shirt	Butchette costume	Women's Studies professor costume
Hitch	sweats	slacks/ nice shirt		
Ruth	sweats			
K.C.	sweats			
Jan	sweats	red shirt/ black pants		oversize T-shirt
Kelly	sweats	pink shirt/ brown pants		nightgown
First Extra	reporter costume	black shirt/ black pants	weight-lifter costume	sweats
Second Extra	photographer costume	sleazy teddy	weight-lifter costume	
Third Extra		men's suit w/ tie		
Leather Woman	leather jacket and pants	red silk shirt and leather vest		dog collar, chains, etc.

Appendix 10

Sample Lighting Plot

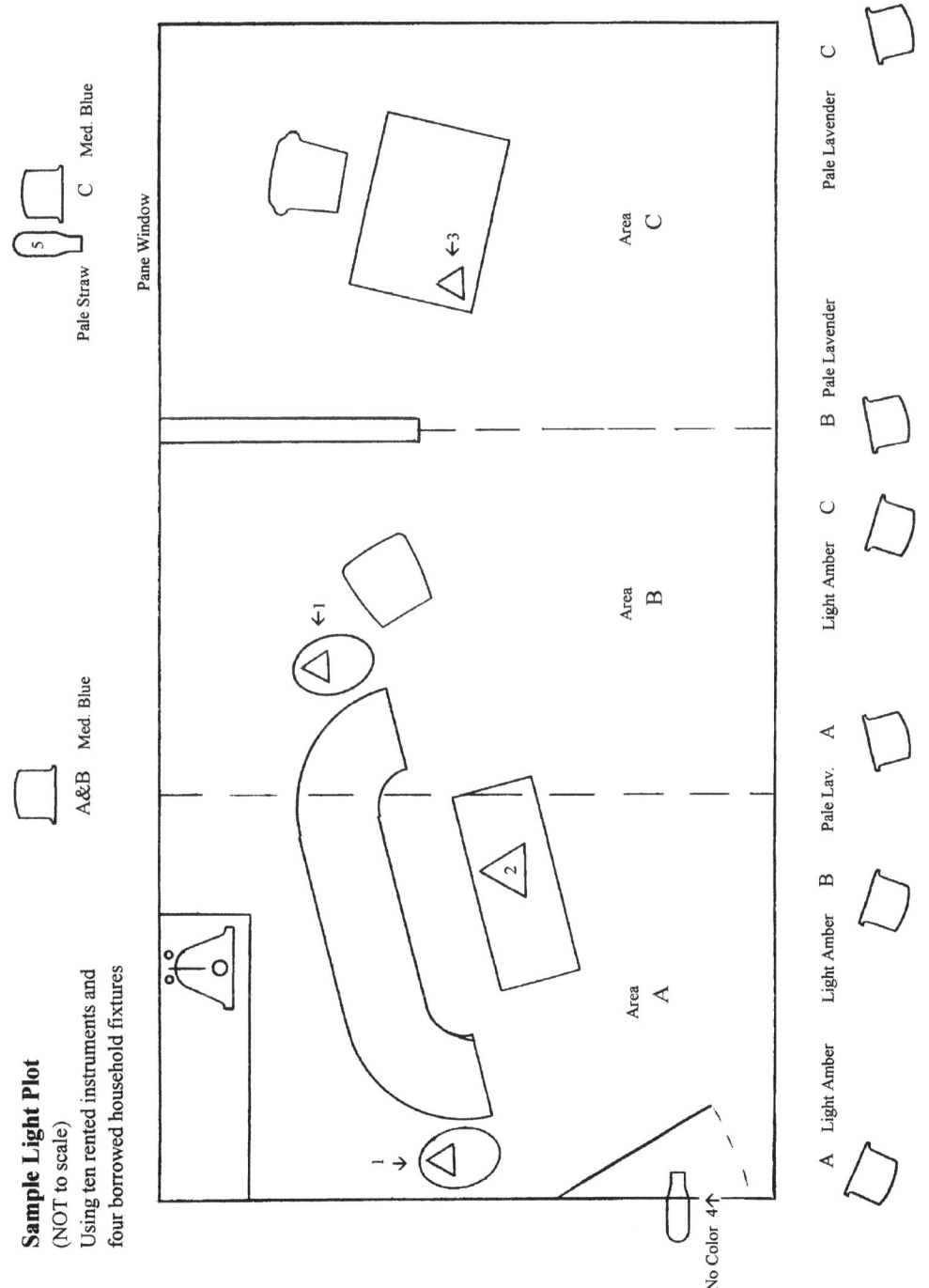

Key for Sample Light Plot

General Notes
Letter in front of instrument indicates area of focus.
Color is to the side of the instrument.
Number inside or beside instrument is a focus or color note specific to that instrument.

Practicals—Functional onstage lights/scenic elements
1. Small table lamps, matching, pale pink shade, low wattage lamps to avoid harshness or shadows.
2. Suspended chandelier, not gaudy.
3. Banker's lamp, green shade.

Small ellipsoidals—3 1/2-inch size
4. Shuttered to simulate door opening, no color, sharp focus.
5. Shuttered and patterned to simulate pane window, gel to simulate sunlight, sharp focus.

Fresnels—6-inch
Areas A and B can be combined and front-lit with two fresnels, but with a loss of coverage and separation control.
Key color fom left, light amber.
Fill with pale lavender.
Backlight with medium blue.

Appendix 11

Suggested Accountability Flowchart

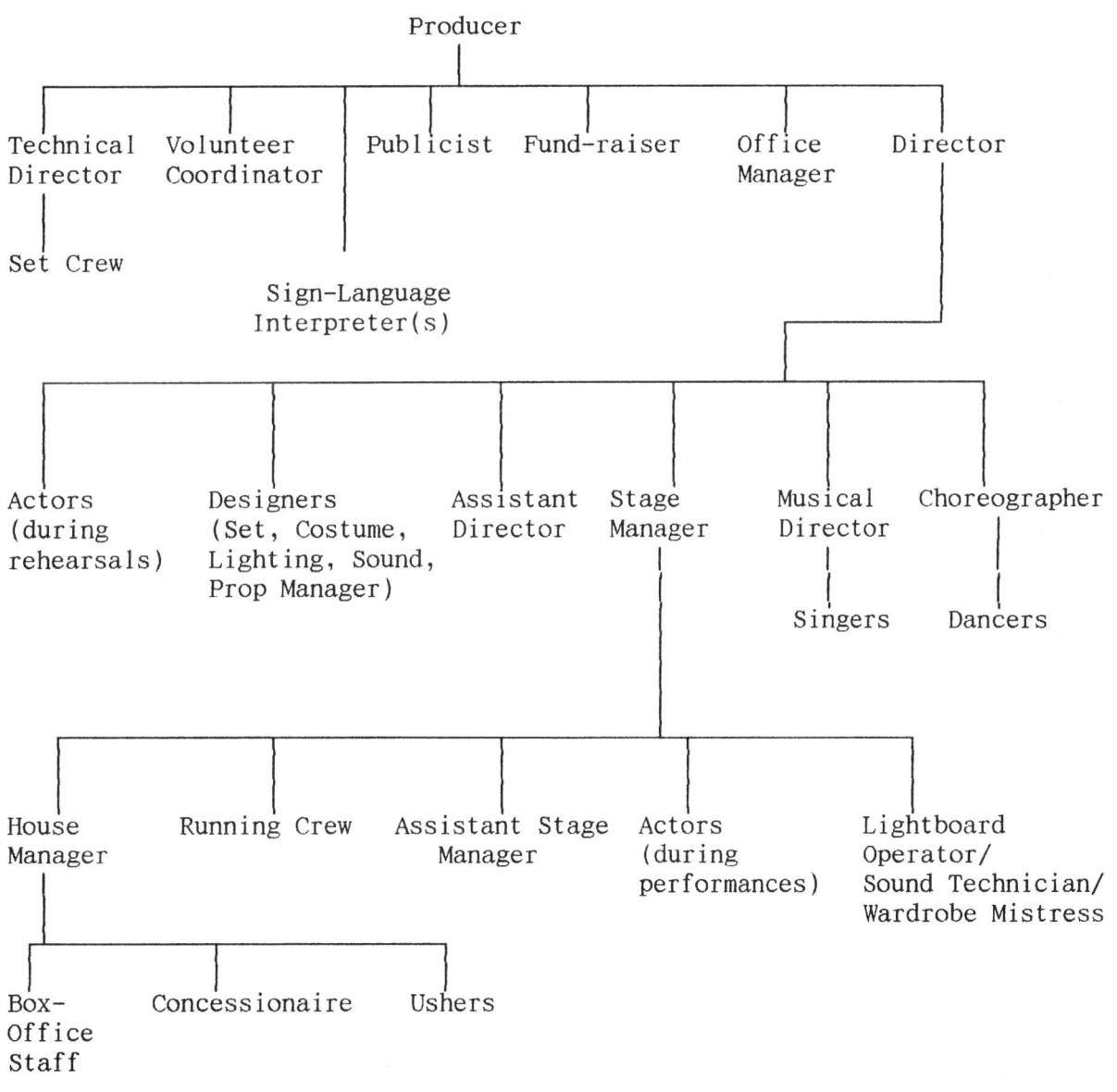

Appendix 12

Accessibility Symbols

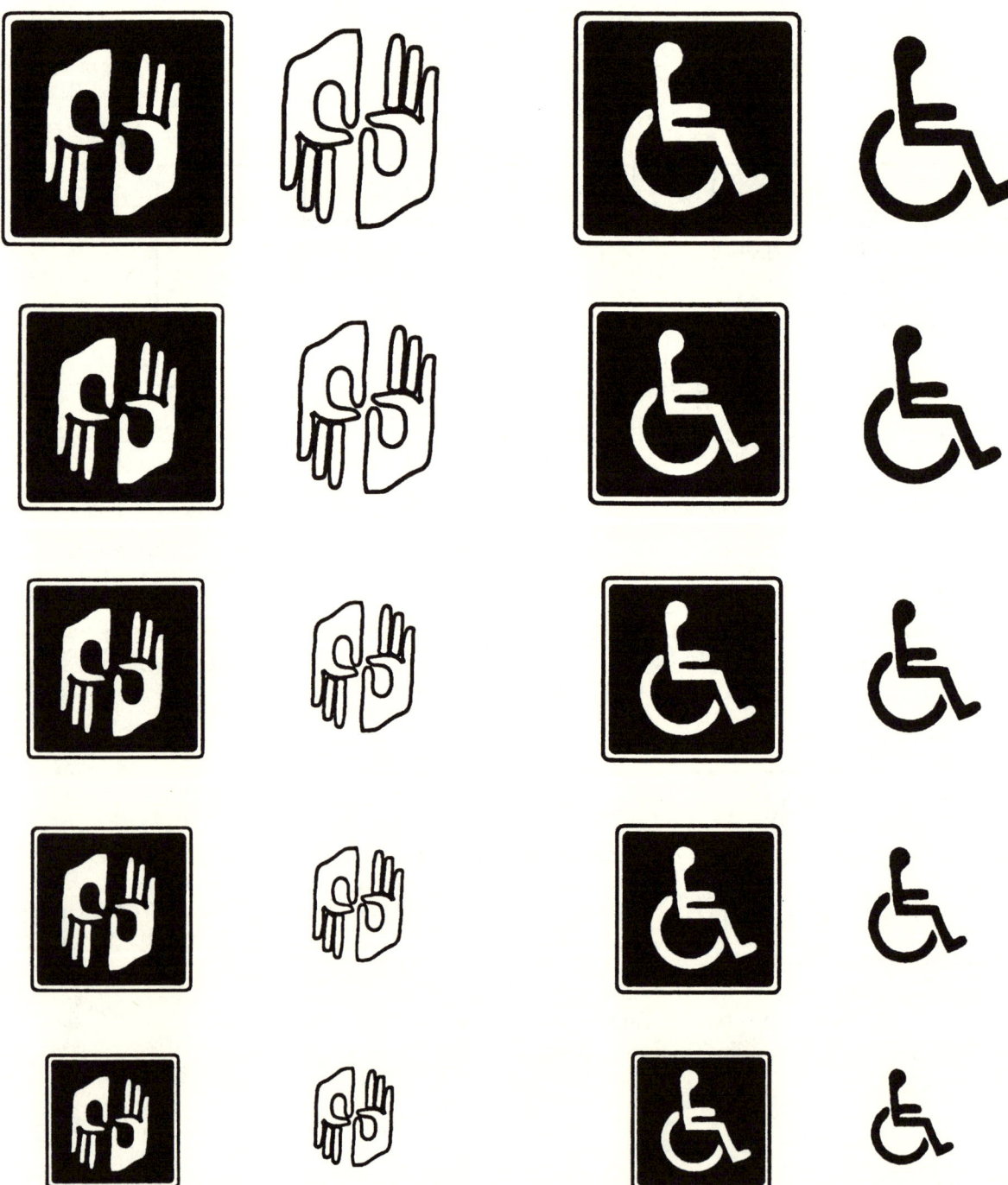

Appendix 13

Sample Press Release

NTM Productions
P.O. Box 718
Ashland, OR 97520
(541) 428-2201

Contact: Carolyn Gage 428-2201
End Date: September 10

Lesbian Musical Comedy Premieres in Ashland

The hottest Lesbian musical on the West Coast is premiering this month in Ashland. *THE AMAZON ALL-STARS*, a new musical comedy about the romantic adventures of a rowdy women's softball team, opens November 2, at 8:00 P.M., at Positively Fourth Street, and plays November 2 & 4, 9–11, and 16–18. There will be an Actors' Benefit on Saturday, November 17.

The book and lyrics are written by award-winning playwright Carolyn Gage, who will be directing the show for NTM Productions. The score is by Susan Carney, a member of the Ashland-based Irish band Criona and a musician with the Oregon Shakespeare Festival Green Show. The show is choreographed by Robin Collen, a dancer with the Oregon Shakespeare Festival.

Akia Woods emcees the show as Leather Woman, singing the fifties takeoff "Ballad of the Butch," the torch song "Cruisin," and admonishing the team to play ball the way they make love in a heavy metal number, "Under the Glove." Cil Stengel plays Jan, new girl on the team, replacing the team maverick Ruth (Michaelia Morgan) as shortstop. The action picks up at the Rubyfruit Bar and Grill, where Jan makes her pitch to leftfielder Kelly (Yolanda Rygiel), who is really "out in left field," preferring her fantasy life to reality.

Tickets are $10 at the door. For reservations, call (541)

Appendix 14

Model Release Form

For valuable consideration, I hereby irrevocably consent to and authorize the use and reproduction by _____ (hereafter called the Photographer), or anyone authorized by the Photographer, of any and all photographs which the Photographer has this day taken of me, negative or positive or proofs, for any purpose whatsoever, without futher compensation to me. All negatives and positives together with the prints shall constitute the Photographer's property, solely and completely.

Model _____
Address _____
Phone _____
Signature of Parent or Guardian if Minors _____
Witnessed by _____
Date _____

Appendix 15

Sample Calendar Announcement

NTM Productions
P.O. Box 718
Ashland, OR 97520
(541) 428-2201

Contact: Carolyn Gage, 428-2201
End Date: November 19, 1990

Calendar Announcement

EVENT: *THE AMAZON ALL-STARS*, a new musical comedy by Carolyn Gage and Susan Carney. Directed by Carolyn Gage and Produced by NTM Productions.

WHEN: November 2 & 4, 9–11, 16–18 at 8:00 P.M. (Actors' Benefit November 17)

WHERE: Positively Fourth Street, 265 Fourth Street, Ashland

TICKETS: $10 at the door. Call (541) 535-5267 for reservations.

The hottest Lesbian musical on the West Coast is premiering this month in Ashland. *THE AMAZON ALL-STARS*, a new musical comedy about the romantic adventures of a rowdy women's softball team, opens November 2 at 8:00 P.M. at Positively Fourth Street, and plays November 2 & 4, 9–11, and 16–18. There will be an Actors' Benefit on Saturday, November 17. Tickets are $10 and will be on sale at the door. Call (541) 535-5267 for reservations.

ONE FOOL

or

How I Learned to Stop Worrying & Love the Dutch

or

The Astonishing & Terrifying Adventures of a Yankee Dyke in the Land of Dikes and Tulips

or

How She Found Love & Lost Love & Found Love & Lost Love, Etc.

Written & Performed
by
TERRY BAUM

"Baum is a lesbian Woody Allen."
San Francisco Chronicle

"She made me weep with delight."
Boston Phoenix

"Hilarious, insightful and raunchy."
San Francisco Bay Guardian

**Thursday - Sunday, Oct 25 - Nov 18
8:00 PM • $8.00**

**Josies Cabaret & Juice Joint
3583 Sixteenth Street at Market, SF
Reservations: 861-7933**

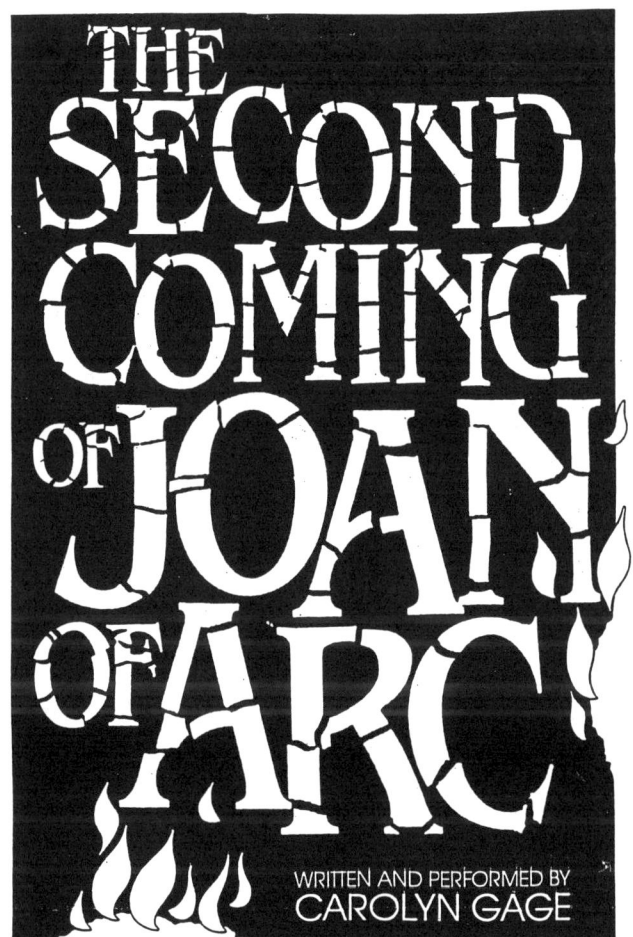

The League of Lesbian Actors (LOLA)
presents
An award-winning one-woman play
about one of the most famous women leaders in history

Saturday, October 31 at 8 p.m.
Sunday, November 1 at 7 p.m.
At the Luther Burbank Center for the Arts Concert Chamber

Tickets are available at: the LBC box office, Clairelight Bookstore and North Light Books in Santa Rosa; and at Storyteller Books in Guerneville, $10 to $12 sliding scale

For more information call 545-7720
The League of Lesbian Actors is affiliated with the Women's Support Network

Appendix 17

Sample Audition Flyer

Auditions

for a new Lesbian play

BUTCH O' MY DREAMS

By Sandra de Helen
Directed by Jan Marks

Six singing roles: Five for butches and one for a femme who can pass for butch.
Casting open to all ages, races, & levels of experience.
Auditions involve a prepared Elvis song and reading from the script.

Sunday, June 13, 1993
4:00 - 7:00 pm

call for directions
Jan - 795-6537

Appendix 18

Sample Audition Calendar Announcement

NTM Productions
P.O. Box 718
Ashland, OR 97520
(541) 428-2201

Contact: Carolyn Gage, 428-2201
End Date: September 10

Calendar Announcement

EVENT: Auditions for *The Amazon All-Stars*, a new Lesbian musical by Carolyn Gage and Sue Carney

WHEN: Sunday, September 9, 1:00 P.M.
Monday, September 10, 7:30 P.M.

WHERE: Positively Fourth Street, 265 Fourth Street, Ashland

WHO: Women of all ages, abilities, races, ethnicities.
Singers—bring two contrasting songs with sheet music.
Actors—readings from the script
Musicians—call for appointment.

FOR INFORMATION CALL (541) 535-5267

Come out for the team! NTM Productions in Ashland is holding auditions for a new Lesbian musical about a women's softball team, *The Amazon All-Stars*, by Carolyn Gage and Sue Carney.

Auditions for this world premiere will be held Sunday, September 9, at 1:00 P.M., and Monday, September 10, at 7:30 P.M. at Positively Fourth Street, 265 Fourth Street in Ashland. Actors will read from the scripts. Singers are asked to bring two contrasting songs. Musicians, please call for an appointment: (541) 535-5267. Performance dates will be the first three weekends in November.

In *The Amazon All-Stars*, Kelly, the left fielder, is truly "out in left field," preferring her fantasies to reality. This makes for some great Lesbian-style Walter Mitty scenes. When Jan, the new shortstop decides to test Kelly's resistance, she finds herself unable to get to first base. Team spirit prevails amid numbers like "Come Out for the Team," "When Women Do It to Each Other," and "Under the Glove."

Appendix 19

Sample Audition Press Release

NTM Productions
P.O. Box 718
Ashland, OR 97520
(541) 428-2201

Contact: Carolyn Gage, 428-2201
End Date: September 10

Lesbian Theatre Holds Auditions for Zany Musical!

Come out for the team! NTM Productions in Ashland is holding auditions for a new Lesbian musical about a women's softball team, *The Amazon All-Stars*, by Carolyn Gage and Sue Carney.

Auditions for this world premiere will be held Sunday, September 9, at 1:00 P.M., and Monday, September 10, at 7:30 P.M., at Positively Fourth Street, 265 Fourth Street in Ashland. Actors will read from the scripts. Singers are asked to bring two contrasting songs. Musicians, please call for an appointment: (541) 535-5365. Performance dates will be the first three weekends in November.

In *The Amazon All-Stars*, Kelly, the left fielder, is truly "out in left field," preferring her fantasies to reality. This makes for some great Lesbian-style Walter Mitty scenes. When Jan, the new shortstop, decides to test her sexual prowess with Kelly, she finds that she can't get to first base. Team spirit prevails amid numbers like "Come Out for the Team," "When Women Do It to Each Other," and "Under the Glove."

Appendix 20

Sample Publicity Budget

		Subtotals:
Design (logo for theatre, ads, posters/flyers)	$75.00	
		$75.00
Ads:		
We the People (Lesbian-and-gay monthly)	104.00	
(ad ran for two months)		
Women's Voices (women's monthly)	90.00	
(ad ran for two months)		
Entertainment Guide (monthly calendar)	50.00	
Women's Comedy Night Program	50.00	
		294.00
Copying costs (400 postcard mailers, 100 posters, 300 flyers)	234.00	
		234.00
Photography (for press releases and poster cover)	108.00	
		108.00
Postage (mailing postcards)	75.00	
		75.00
Program		
Typesetting and design	50.00	
Copying	172.00	
		222.00
	TOTAL	$1008.00

Appendix 21

Sample program

Act I

Intermission (15 minutes)

Act II

Charlotte Cushman .... Debra Wright

Playwright's Notes

CHARLOTTE CUSHMAN was the greatest American actress of the 19th century. Her career spanned four decades, and she was the toast of two continents. Much of her fame derived from her success in playing "breeches parts," roles written for male actors. Cushman was at the center of a community of women sculptors in Rome, and it was largely her matronage which enabled this lesbian art colony to survive. Cushman was a powerful role model for women and Charlotte Cushman fan clubs were still in existence as late as the 1950s, seventy-five years after her death. And yet, few lesbians today know about this remarkable woman. The reason? She was large, butch, and very public about her marriages to women. She had risen to the top of a field dominated by men, where women were - and still are - relegated to a form of statutory prostitution, and she rose to the top, not "in spite of," but because of her lesbianism. For this reason, her example continues to pose a threat to heterosexist mainstream culture.

Playwright's Biography

CAROLYN GAGE is a lesbian-feminist playwright. Her recent collection, entitled *The Second Coming of Joan of Arc and Other Plays*, was named a national finalist for the 1995 Lambda Book Awards. She has toured nationally as a solo performer, and has founded three theatre companies, including a radical lesbian company in Southern Oregon, which produced 19 plays in two years. Gage has been a feminist theatre activist for ten years - organizing protests, lobbying art commissions and foundations, and filing lawsuits to end homophobic and sexist discrimination against lesbian actors, composers, and playwrights. Her essays, reviews, and short stories have been widely published in national and international women's publications, and she has written the first manual on lesbian theatre production: *Take Stage!* She currently teaches lesbian acting at the Harvey Milk Institute in San Francisco.

Actor's Biography

DEBRA WRIGHT is the lesbian performer most associated with Carolyn Gage's work, having performed lead roles in *"Calamity Jane Sends a Message to her Daughter," "Artemisia and Hildegarde,"* and *"All Passion Unspent."* For seven years, from 1983 to 1991, she worked with a grassroots gay and lesbian theater company, the Blue Slide Players of Garberville, developing and performing original material. Since moving to Santa Rosa, she has been featured in several plays by Tribad Productions, including Debby Klein's lesbian comedy *"Coming Soon"* and Victoria Rue's touring show *"Cancer Bodies"* (now titled *"Ruffled Irises"*). Wright has a passionate commitment to lesbian theater and the challenging work it offers to women outside the traditional stereotypes of mainstream theater.

Appendix 22

Sample Audition and Volunteer Forms

Auditioner Information Sheet

Name _____ Phone _____

Address _____

Recent Acting Experience:

SCHEDULE CONFLICTS: Please mark an *X* through all the times you *cannot* rehearse.

	Mon.	Tues.	Wed.	Thurs.	Fri.	Sat.	Sun.
9:00 -- 10:00 A.M.							
10:00 -- 11:00 A.M.							
11:00 -- 12:00							
12:00 -- 1:00 P.M.							
1:00 -- 2:00 P.M.							
2:00 -- 3:00 P.M.							
3:00 -- 4:00 P.M.							
4:00 -- 5:00 P.M.							
5:00 -- 6:00 P.M.							
6:00 -- 7:00 P.M.							
7:00 -- 10:00 P.M.							

Will you accept any role assigned?

List any particular role for which you wish to be considered:

Please list any dates from February 12 to March 31 that you will not be available at all:

Volunteer Information Sheet

NAME _____

ADDRESS _____

_____

HOME PHONE _____ BUSINESS PHONE _____

FAX _____ EMAIL _____

Previous experience in theatre, if any:

Previous work experience related to theatre job: (e.g.: carpentry, sewing)

Please check position or positions that interest you:

_____ Stage Manager (run the show the week before opening and during performances)

_____ Assistant Director (take down script notes at rehearsals)

_____ Set Designer

_____ Technical Director (supervise construction of set)

_____ Costume Coordinator (rent, buy, borrow, sew costumes)

_____ Wardrobe Person (care of costumes before and after shows)

_____ Prop Person (rent, buy, borrow, make props)

_____ Lighting Designer

_____ Lightboard Operator (run lights at performances)

_____ Sound Designer (put together a tape of show music and/or sound effects)

_____ Sound Operator (run the sound at performances)

_____ Set Crew (build, paint, set up, dismantle sets)

_____ House Manager (supervise ushers and ticket sellers, handle problems "out front" during performances)

_____ Ushers/ Ticket Sellers

_____ Publicity (design, contract, run, distribute posters/flyers)

If you would like to volunteer for "spot labor" (painting, sewing, taking down the set, hanging lights, etc.), please indicate the kind of work you prefer and the amount of time you could give:

If you have signed on for a job requiring attendance at performances, please be sure you are available for the performance dates. These are:

>March 23, 24, 30, 31   7:00–10:00 P.M.

Appendix 23

Sample Audition Grid

	Mar-mee	Jo	Laurie	Amy	Meg	Brooke	Mr. Law-rence	Hanna	Beth
Audition Grid for *Little Women*									
Mar-mee	6	53	87 top				37 -38 90		
Jo		12 52	49 83	76 - 77	61				104 -- 105
Laurie			45	76 - 77					
Amy								37 89	
Meg					51	64			
Brooke									
Mr. Law-rence									57
Hanna									
Beth									

Appendix 24

Sample of Beat/Unit Division of Script

LOUISA
You're a tomboy. You just need to grow up.

JO
Look again, Louisa. You need to grow up. | I'm a lesbian.

UNIT 5: "I'M A LESBIAN AND SO ARE YOU!"

LOUISA
No! No, you're not!

JO
Yes, I am. Remember what you had me tell Laurie - "It's impossible for people to make themselves love other people if they don't..." Remember? We told him, "I don't believe it's the right sort of love, and I'd rather not try it." You know why I said that.

Beat 1: Jo batters Louisa with the truth. Louisa resists with vigorous denial.

LOUISA
Laurie was a friend, but I never intended those remarks to refer to all men.

JO
Louisa, you know I love women. You know that. You know because you created me out of your own need to love women.

LOUISA
I don't want to love them like that.

JO
Oh yes, you do, Louisa May Alcott. And you want them to love you like that.

LOUISA
No!

Beat 2: Jo seduces Louisa. Louisa encourages her by not moving away.

JO crosses to LOUISA. She takes her hand, the writing hand, and caresses it. LOUISA closes her eyes. JO takes her hand and brings it to her lips. She begins to kiss and caress her fingers.

JO
Louisa, you are so beautiful. You take care of everybody. Who takes care of you? Nobody sees you like I do. I see who you are - I see how beautiful you are. Let me love you, Louisa.
(She kisses her lips. LOUISA, after the kiss, turns away in confusion.)

LOUISA
I was in love with David.

JO

Louisa...

LOUISA

I was. I would have married him.

[handwritten: Beat 3: Louisa rejects Jo's kiss, protesting her heterosexuality. Jo attacks her credentials]

JO

Henry David Thoreau despised women, and you know it. He liked little boys.

LOUISA

I loved him.

JO

You loved him, because you knew you'd never have to do anything about it.

LOUISA

And I loved Ladislas.

JO

That boy you met three years ago in Switzerland?

LOUISA

I was in love with him.

JO

You were infatuated. He was eighteen. You were thirty-three. You were attracted to him, because he was the closest thing to a woman you could find.

LOUISA
(Turning to look at JO)
No! You're twisting things.

[handwritten: Beat 4: Louisa attacks Jo. Jo ridicules Louisa.]

JO

Louisa, you're the one twisting things. Look at who you pick to fall in love with - homosexual men and adolescent boys!

LOUISA
(Rising)
No!

JO

Yes! The reason you have never married, is because you're a lesbian. Like me.
(She puts her arms around LOUISA.)

Appendix 25

Sample Page from Prompt Book

MEI LI

I was a mail order bride.

ALDONZA

XDC

You see? You show me the women who don't have to suck dick to live, and then I will be ashamed to be a prostitute.

MARIA

Lesbians.

ALDONZA

What about lesbians? — *turning quickly*

MARIA

↑ The women who don't have to sell themselves to men.

ALDONZA

XDL to Maria

Don't tell me that! Half of the prostitutas are lesbians.

MARIA

XDC

My lover and I, we don't work for men. We don't live with them, we don't go out with them, we don't talk to them. We don't have anything to do with them.

ALDONZA

So where does your money come from?

She executes a karate punch.

MARIA

We have a karate school for women, and we publish a magazine for Latina lesbians.

ALDONZA

And with this you make big money. — *plays with her bracelets*

MARIA

Not big money. But we can live. *crossing UR to UL in wide semicircle as she speaks to the other women*

ALDONZA

XDC

To live! Women want more than just to live! We want our cars. We want our houses. We want some good clothes for the children. We want to eat well. Maybe even go to a restaurant every now and then. Buy a few flowers. To live! To live with nothing is sucking on the dick!

MARIA

No, it's not!

Appendix 26

Sample Three-Month Rehearsal Schedule

September

SUNDAY	MONDAY	TUESDAY	WEDNESDAY	THURSDAY	FRIDAY	SATURDAY
1 All rehearsals at Postively Fourth Street, until Tech Week.	**2**	**3**	**4**	**5**	**6**	**7**
8 Auditions 4:00 -- 7:00 P.M.	**9** Callbacks 7:00 -- 10:00 P.M.	**10** Cast the show	**11**	**12**	**13**	**14**
15 Read-through 6:30 -- 9:30 P.M. Full cast.	**16** 6:00 -- 9:00 P.M. Jan/Slide/Kelly Act I	**17** 6:00 -- 9:00 P.M. Kelly/Reporter/ Leather Woman Act I	**18** 6:00 -- 9:00 P.M. Jan/Slide/Kelly Act I	**19**	**20** 6:00 -- 9:00 P.M. Full Cast. Photo Shoot. Act I	**21** 9:00 -- 11:00 A.M. Hitch/Ruth 11:00 -- 1:00 Hitch/Leona
22 5:00 -- 9:00 P.M. Full Cast. RUN ACT I BLOCKING	**23** 6:00 -- 9:00 P.M. Full Cast minus Leather Woman Act II	**24** 6:00 -- 9:00 P.M. Leather Woman/ Butchettes Act II	**25** 6:00 -- 9:00 P.M. Full Cast minus Leather Woman Act II	**26** 6:00 -- 9:00 P.M. Full Cat minus Ruth/ K.C. Act II	**27**	**28** 9:00 -- 11:00 A.M. Jan/Ruth/Kelly Act II
29	**30** 6:00 -- 9:00 P.M. Full Cast. RUN ACT II BLOCKING					

October

Sunday	Monday	Tuesday	Wednesday	Thursday	Friday	Saturday
		1 6:00 -- 9:00 P.M. Leather Woman/ Butchettes Acts I & II	**2** 6:00 -- 9:00 P.M. Full Cast. RUN ACT I.	**3** 6:00 -- 9:00 P.M. Full Cast. RUN ACTS I & II.	**4** 6:00 -- 9:00 P.M. Jan/ Kelly Acts I & II	**5**
6 11:00 A.M. -- 1:30 P.M. Leather Woman Acts I & II	**7** 6:00 -- 9:00 P.M. Full Cast Acts I & II OFF BOOK	**8** 6:00 -- 9:00 P.M. Full Cast minus Ruth Acts I & II	**9** 6:00 -- 9:00 P.M. Run-Through	**10** 6:00 -- 9:00 P.M. Butchettes Acts I & II	**11** 6:00 -- 9:00 P.M. Jan/ Kelly Acts I & II	**12**
13 3:00 -- 4:00 P.M. Leather Woman 5:00 -- 7:00 Run-Through	**14** 6:00 -- 9:00 P.M. Full Cast Acts I & II OFF PROMPT	**15** 6:00 -- 9:00 P.M. Full Cast minus Leather Woman Acts I & II	**16** 6:00 -- 9:00 P.M. Slide/Jan/Hitch/ K.C./ Butchettes Acts I & II	**17** 6:00 -- 9:00 P.M. Jan/Kelly Acts I & II	**18** 6:00 -- 8:00 P.M. Slide/K.C. Acts I & II	**19**
20 7:00 -- 10:00 P.M. Full Cast Run-Through	**21** 6:00 -- 9:00 P.M. Full Cast minus Ruth/ L.Woman Acts I & II	**22** 6:00 -- 9:00 P.M. Full Cast Acts I & II	**23** 6:00 -- 9:00 P.M. Full Cast Acts I & II	**24**	**25**	**26**
27 9:00 A.M -- 9:00 P.M. TECH WEEK Full Cast/ Crew IN THEATRE	**28** 7:00 -- 10:00 P.M. Full Cast/Crew Run-Through	**29** 7:00 -- 10:00 P.M. Full Cast/Crew Run-Through	**30** 6:00 -- 9:00 P.M. Full Cast/Crew Run-Through	**31** 7:00 P.M. Call 8:00 P.M. Curtain DRESS REHEARSAL		

November

Sunday	Monday	Tuesday	Wednesday	Thursday	Friday	Saturday
					1 7:00 P.M. Call 8:00 P.M. Curtain OPENING	2 7:00 P.M. Call 8:00 P.M. Curtain SHOW
3 1:00 P.M. Call 2:00 P.M. Curtain MATINEE	4	5	6 6:00 -- 9:00 P.M. Pickup Rehearsal at Positively Fourth Street	7	8 7:00 P.M. Call 8:00 P.M. Curtain SHOW	9 7:00 P.M. Call 8:00 P.M. Curtain SHOW
10 1:00 P.M. Call 2:00 P.M. Curtain MATINEE	11	12	13 7:30 -- 10:30 P.M. VIDEOTAPING	14	15 7:00 P.M. Call 8:00 P.M. Curtain SHOW	16 7:00 P.M. Call 8:00 P.M. Curtain ACTORS' BENEFIT
17 1:00 P.M. Call 2:00 P.M. Curtain CLOSING/ 4:00 STRIKE	18	19	20	21	22	23
24	25	26	27	28	29	30

Appendix 27

Resources for Locating Lesbian Plays

Dialogus Play Service, PO Box 815761, Dallas, TX 75381, 214-693-4337.

The Dramatists Guild Newsletter, 1501 Broadway, Ste. 701, New York City, NY 10036, 212-398-9366.

The Lesbian Exchange of New Drama (LEND) Newsletter, c/o Anne Harris, 559 Third Street, Brooklyn, NY 11215.

The Purple Circuit Newsletter, c/o Bill Kaiser, 2025 Griffith Park Boulevard #4, Los Angeles, CA 90039. <purplecir@aol.com>

Index

ableism. *See* multiculturalism

actors: director-actor contract, 112–14. *See also* acting; auditions; rehearsal; Tech Week

accessibility: and anti-ableism, 33; codes for, 40; and food, 71; of performance space, 40; and publicity, 40, 79; survey of, 162–64; symbols of, 176; and ushers, 70. *See also* sign-language interpretation

accountability: achieving of, 12; director-actor contract, 112–14; and hidden agendas, 13; and inaccessibility, 12, 18–19; vs. myths of sisterhood, 11; organizations vs. people, 12; and producing, 11–13; and publicity, 92–93; suggested flowchart for, 175; testing for, 12. *See also* job descriptions

acting, 123–26; representational vs. presentational, 123–24; and sex, 124–25; and violence, 124–25

AD. *See* assistant director

adultism. *See* multiculturalism

advertising: paid, 83; and program, 94. *See also* publicity

affirmative action, 32, 38

ageism. *See* multiculturalism

agendas, 21, 111

agents, 38

Al-Anon, 26

All About Eve, 25

anonymity. *See* closets

anti-classism. *See* multiculturalism

anti-discrimination. *See* multiculturalism

anti-racism. *See* multiculturalism

anti-Semitism. *See* multiculturalism

ASL. *See* sign-language interpretation

ASM. *See* assistant stage manager

assistant director, 60–61; and prompt book, 119; role of at auditions, 108–9

assistant stage manager (ASM), 61

Association for Women's Music and Culture, 147

audiences, 39

auditions, 103–7; actors at, 107–8; assistant director's role at, 108–9; calendar spot for (sample), 183–84; callbacks for, 108; closed, 104–5; cold readings at, 105; flyer for (sample), 182; forms for auditioners at, 46, 105; grids for, 106; for musicals, 86, 105; notifying actors after, 109; and physical appearance, 32–33; and precasting, 106–7; press release for (sample), 185; publicity for, 84–86; sample form for, 191–93; sample grid for, 192; schedule for, 45–46, 115; space rental, 104

AWMAC. *See* Association for Women's Music and Culture

backers' audition, 44

bank accounts, 44

Barber, Jill, 25

beats, 117; sample analysis of, 193–94

Bernstein, Albert J., 22
betrayal, 24–27, 127–28
block ticket sales, 50; publicizing of, 89
blocking, 116–19
boards of directors: and bottom lines, 9; conflicts with, 10; working with, 9
bookkeeping, 44
bottom line, 3; and accountability, 11; and boards of directors, 9; and boundaries, 28–30; and brainwashing, 3; and collective theatres, 10; determining, 3–4; and discrimination, 34; and fundraising, 43–44; and leadership, 22; and script selection, 36–37; significance of, 3; and volunteers, 28–30
boundaries, 13; and burnout, 28–29; in rehearsal, 127–28; and volunteers, 28–29
box office staff, 70
brainwashing: and bottom lines, 3; and unrealistic business models, 21. See also conditioning of women
budget. See production budget
bulk mailing. See mailings
burnout, 28–29

calendar announcement, 82; audition calendar announcement (sample), 183–84; calendar announcement (sample), 179
callbacks, 108
casting: open, 31–32; and physical appearance, 32; as sacred art, 100. See also multiculturalism
Channing, Margo, 25
Charge of the Goddess, 101
child care, 69
classism: and accountability, 12. See also multiculturalism
closets: and programs, 96. See also photos
collaboration, 56
collective theatres, 9–10; and bottom lines, 10; and healthy process, 10; liabilities of, 10; members as actors, 18; membership in, 10; vs. non-profit theatres, 9–10; process of, 20
communication skills, 22–23, 132–34
complimentary tickets, 50
compulsory heterosexuality, 21
concessionaire, 71
conditioning of women: and accountability, 11; and bottom lines, 3; and co-dependency, 29; and deference to men, 8; for dominance and submission, 22; and fear of incompetency, 12; and gratitude, 7; and horizontal hostility, 24–27; and jealousy, 12–13; and lack of management skills, 21; lies and secrets and silences, 27; manipulation vs. leadership, 20–23; as opposed to that of men and boys, 11; and overcommitment, 28–29; and skills in subversion, 21; and territorialism, 25; and victimization, 24. See also boundaries; denial; dissociative disorders
conflict resolution, 133–34
confronting, 132–33
contracts: director-actor, 112–14; sample for director's, 15–57; sample for ticket seller's, 169–70. See also accountability; job descriptions
co-producing: with another Lesbian organization, 5–6; with non-Lesbians, 7–8. See also gay-and-Lesbian theatres, 8
costume designer, 56–57; at first rehearsal, 112; and prop manager, 66
costume plot, 56; sample of, 172
costumes. See costume designer; wardrobe manager
critics. See reviews
curtain call, 138–39

DBA. See Doing Business As
deadlines. See press calendar; production schedule
denial: of lesbian shortcomings, 22; of victimization, 22. See also myths
detachment, 26
Dialogus Play Service, 36, 199
Dinosaur Brains: Dealing with All Those Impossible People at Work, 22
directing. See auditions; blocking; director; rehearsal
director, 127–28; and assistant director, 60–61; contract for (sample), 155–57; contract guarantees for, 18; and director-actor contract, 112–14; emotional well-being of, 100; firing of, 18; liaisons with producers, 18–19; at opening, 143; as priestess, 99–102; vs. producer, 17–19; and production schedule, 45; and program, 95; and sign-language interpretation, 73; and stage manager, 61–63. See also rehearsal; script; suggested accountability flowchart, 175
discrimination, 125–26; resources for dismantling of, 158–60. See also Lesbophobia; multiculturalism; women-only performances
dissociative disorders, 25–26; and Lesbian theatre, 26; third week of rehearsal, 129–31; triggers for, 26
Doing Business As (DBA), 5, 44
double standards, 149–50
Dramatists Guild, 38; newsletter for, 36, 199

dress rehearsal, 139
dresser, 67

Fantasia, 99
first rehearsal, 112–15; director-actor contract, 112–14; read-through, 115; schedule at, 115
501[c]3. *See* non-profit theatres
flyers, 82–83; audition flyer (sample), 182; posting of, 89; production flyer (sample), 180, 181
fundraising, 43–44; professional fund raiser, 74

Gage, Carolyn, ix, 200
gay-and-Lesbian theatres, 8
goddess. *See* theatre as sacred art
Gordon, Thomas, 22
gossip, 113–14, 127

Harrington, Eve, 25
hidden agendas, 13
hierarchy, 74–75; and curtain calls, 138; and programs, 96
Hoagland, Sarah, 22
homophobia. *See* Lesbophobia
house manager, 69–70
house staff, 69–71

inaccessibility, 12, 18–19. *See also* accessibility
internet: web page on, 83. *See also* script selection
interpreting. *See* sign-language interpretation
interviews, 90

jealousy, 12–13
job descriptions, 74

leadership, 20–23; and communication skills, 22; vs. dictatorship, 22; as problem-solving, 22
Leadership Effectiveness Training, 22
leasing agreement, 40–41
LEND. *See Lesbian Exchange of New Drama Newsletter*
Lesbian Ethics, 22
Lesbian Exchange of New Drama Newsletter, 36, 199
Lesbian theatre, xi; creation of, xi; diversity of, ix; myths about, 6. *See also* producing Lesbian theatre
Lesbophobia, 103–4; in gay-and-Lesbian theatres, 8; and publicity, 93. *See also* closets
licensing agreements, 38
lies, 27
lightboard operator, 65
lighting designer, 57–58

lighting plot, 57; sample of, 173–74
logo, 79–80
looksism. *See* multiculturalism

magic. *See* theatre as sacred art
mailings, 88–89
male bashing, 149
media. *See* publicity
meetings: agendas, 21; between directors and producers, 17–19; responsibilities of attendees, 21
mentoring, 127–28; and betrayal, 25
misogyny, 93–94. *See also* multiculturalism
mission statement, 9, 21
model release form, 178
money, 42–44. *See also* production budget
multiculturalism, 31–34; resources for, 158–60
Multiple Personality Disorder, 25
musicals. *See* auditions
myths: about business, 21; about collectives, 18, 20; cutting through, 4; about Lesbian theatres, 6; of sisterhood, 11, 20. *See also* denial

National Endowment for the Arts, 48
NEA. *See* National Endowment for the Arts
The Need to Thrive, 22
negotiations: demanding accountability at, 18; and deference, 8; with gay-and-Lesbian theatres, 8; and gratitude, 7; with mainstream theatres, 7; need for, 6; with pride, 7; and tag teams, 18
non-profit theatres, 9–10; bulk mailings by, 88–89; and women-only performances, 148–49
Note by Note: A Guide to Concert Production, 40, 51

office manager, 74
open casting, 31–32
oppression: of ambitious women, 25; and horizontal hostility, 24–27; process of internalizing, 24. *See also* multiculturalism
organizing: need for books about Lesbian organizing, 22; and leadership, 22. *See also* producing Lesbian theatre

patriarchy, 24, 25
performance space, 39–41; accessibility of, 40, 162–64; image of, 41; leasing of, 39, 40–41; lighting in, 57–58
photo call, 47
photos, 80–81. *See also* model release form; photo call
pickup rehearsal, 144

plays: bibliography of gay/lesbian anthologies, 161. *See also* script selection
political correctness, 33
posters, 82–83
postmortem. *See* postproduction meeting
postproduction meeting, 145
power: and accountability, 11; director's, 127–28; taking of, 8
press kit. *See* publicity
press release, 80; audition press release (sample), 185; press release (sample), 177
privilege, 12. *See also* multiculturalism
producer: checks and balances of, 18; contract with director, 18–19; job description, 17–19; liaisons with director, 18–19; vs. the director, 17–19. *See also* producing Lesbian theatre
producing Lesbian theatre: and accountability, 11–13; with another Lesbian organization, 5–6; and bottom lines, 3; independently, 9–10; with non-Lesbians, 7–8; reasons for, 3. *See also* Doing Business As; producer
production budget: costume designer's, 56; lighting designer's, 57; and playwright's royalties, 38; and program, 94; prop manager's, 66; sample of, 165; sample publicity budget, 186; scene designer's, 56; technical director and, 65. *See also* money
production meeting, 110–11
production schedule, 45–47; sample of, 166–68; and stage manager, 61; *See also* pickup rehearsal; publicity calendar; Tech Week
program, 94–95; sample of, 187–88
prompt book, 119; sample page from, 195
prop manager, 66
props. *See* prop manager
PSA. *See* public service announcement
public domain, 38
public service announcement, 82
publicist, 72. *See also* auditions; program; publicity
publicity: audition calendar announcement (sample), 183–84; audition flyer (sample), 182; audition press release (sample), 185; budget for (sample), 186; calendar announcement (sample), 179; press kit, 79–83; press release (sample), 177; production flyer (sample), 180, 181; publicity calendar (sample), 87, 90, 166–68; publicizing auditions, 84–86; publicizing show, 87–91. *See also* program
Purple Circuit Newsletter, 36, 199

racism. *See* multiculturalism
read-through. *See* first rehearsal

rehearsal: as ritual, 101; sample schedule for, 196–98; schedule, 45–47; third week of, 129–31. *See also* dress rehearsal; first rehearsal; pickup rehearsal; Tech Week
Remington, Judy, 22
reservations, 51, 70
reviews, 87; getting reviewed, 90–91
ritual. *See* theatre as sacred art
royalty fees, 38
Rozen, Sydney Craft, 22
running crew, 67–68

scapegoating: of directors, 18. *See also* jealousy
scene designer, 55–56; acting areas, 118; and technical director, 64–65
schedule: sample for rehearsal, 198. *See also* production schedule; publicity calendar
script: analysis of, 105–6, 117; as guided visualization, 101. *See also* script selection
script selection, 36–38; and acting pool, 37; bibliography of gay/Lesbian plays, 161; bottom line, 36–38; criteria for, 36; for in-house scripting, 37–38; and the internet, 36; and play readings, 37; producer vs. director, 17; and royalties, 38; and technical considerations, 37
secrets, 27
Sedna, 100–101
self-esteem: at auditions, 104; and gratitude, 7; and jealousy, 12–13; and money, 43; and performance space, 41; and press release, 80; and publicizing auditions, 84. *See also* communication skills
set crew, 67
sexism: in gay-and-Lesbian theatres, 8; in gay male culture, 8; and the production schedule, 46. *See also* multiculturalism
sexual harassment, 114–15
sign-language interpretation, 33, 72–73; and space requirements, 40; symbols for, 176
sign master, 73. *See also* sign-language interpretation
signing. *See* sign-language interpretation
silences, 27
Sisterhood Betrayed, 25
sizeism. *See* multiculturalism
sliding scale, 49
SM. *See* stage manager
sound designer, 58–59
sound technician, 65–66
stage manager (SM), 61–63; and house manager, 69. *See also* strike; Tech Week

strike, 144–45; and stage manager, 62
structure: overt vs. covert, 5; working with another Lesbian organization, 5–6; working with mainstream theatres, 7–8

tag teams, 18
Tech Week, 135–39; and costumes, 57; and program, 95; schedule for, 46; and sign-language interpretation, 73. *See also* stage manager
technical director, 64–65; and scene designer, 56
theatre nights, 50; publicizing, 89
theatre as sacred art, 99–102
theatres. *See* performance space
ticket sellers. *See* box office staff
tickets, 48–52; complimentary, 50; discounting of, 49; information printed on, 52; outlets for, 52 52–52; reservations for, 51; samples of, 171; sample ticket seller's contract, 169–70; setting prices for, 48–49; sliding scale, 49; work-exchange, 49. *See also* block ticket sales; theatre nights
tokenism, 7–8
touring, 146–47; contracts for, 146–47; performance spaces for, 39
trashing, 12

Uniform Resource Location (URL), 83
units. *See* beats
URL. *See* Uniform Resource Location
ushers, 70

victimization, 24–27
videotaping, 38, 69–70
volunteer coordinator, 73–74
volunteers, 28–30; and auditions, 86

wardrobe manager, 66–67
Watson, Rita E., 25
wheelchairs. *See* accessibility
woman-hating. *See* misogyny
women-only performances, 148–50

About the Author

CAROLYN GAGE is a Lesbian-feminist playwright, activist, and director.

In 1996, she was named national winner of the Nancy Dean Distinguished Playwriting Award, given annually at the Sisters on Stage Lesbian Theatre Conference in New York. Gage's collection of plays *The Second Coming of Joan of Arc and Other Plays* (Santa Cruz, CA: Her Books, Inc., 1994) was named National Finalist for the Lambda Literary Award in drama. From 1988 to 1993, she toured nationally in the title work, a one-woman show about a Lesbian Joan of Arc.

Gage has founded and directed three theatre companies, the last of which was a radical Lesbian theatre in Ashland, Oregon. Between 1989 and 1991, this theatre produced nineteen different plays, including ten one-acts, two musicals, and a one-woman show—all written by Gage. Her Lesbian musical *The Amazon All-Stars* generated an ACLU national priority lawsuit when the composer was fired from the public school system for collaborating with Gage on the show. In 1996, the show was published as the title work in an anthology of Lesbian plays by Applause Books. Gage has also written *Scenes and Monologues for Lesbian Actors*, the world's first scene study book for lesbians.

A longtime activist for women's theatre and Lesbian theatre, she has written a collection of essays, *Live Like There's No Tomorrow: Meditations for Women Leaving Patriarchy*, published in 1997 by Common Courage Press. Her play *Harriet Tubman Visits a Therapist* was a national winner of the 1996 Perishable Theatre Women's Playwriting Festival.

In 1995, Gage's one-woman show about the nineteenth-century butch actress Charlotte Cushman won the Arch and Bruce Brown Foundation Grant. She has also won the Oregon Playwrights Award from the Oregon Institute of Literary Arts, the Walden Writer's Fellowship from Lewis and Clark College, the Oregon Institute of Literary Arts Writer's Grant, and the Oregon Arts Commission Individual Artist Grant. Gage has also been published in the Lesbian journals *Trivia*, *Sinister Wisdom*, and *Lesbian Ethics*. She has taught Lesbian acting through the Harvey Milk Institute in San Francisco.